Get the eBook FREE!

(PDF, ePub, Kindle, and liveBook all included)

We believe that once you buy a book from us, you should be able to read it in any format we have available. To get electronic versions of this book at no additional cost to you, purchase and then register this book at the Manning website.

Go to https://www.manning.com/freebook and follow the instructions to complete your pBook registration.

That's it!
Thanks from Manning!

CORS in Action

Creating and consuming
cross-origin APIs

MONSUR HOSSAIN

MANNING

SHELTER ISLAND

For online information and ordering of this and other Manning books, please visit
www.manning.com. The publisher offers discounts on this book when ordered in quantity.
For more information, please contact

> Special Sales Department
> Manning Publications Co.
> 20 Baldwin Road
> PO Box 761
> Shelter Island, NY 11964
> Email: orders@manning.com

Manning Publications Co.	Development editors: Cynthia Kane, Monique Bos
20 Baldwin Road	Technical development editor Deepak Vohra
PO Box 761	Copyeditor: Jodie Allen
Shelter Island, NY 11964	Proofreader: Elizabeth Martin
	Technical proofreader: Konstantin Yakushev
	Typesetter: Dennis Dalinnik
	Cover designer: Marija Tudor

ISBN: 9781617291821
Printed in the United States of America

For Haroun and Annisa

brief contents

PART 1 INTRODUCING CORS..1

     1 ■ The Core of CORS   3

     2 ■ Making CORS requests   12

PART 2 CORS ON THE SERVER...37

     3 ■ Handling CORS requests   39

     4 ■ Handling preflight requests   63

     5 ■ Cookies and response headers   94

     6 ■ Best practices   112

PART 3 DEBUGGING CORS REQUESTS....................................149

     7 ■ Debugging CORS requests   151

contents

foreword   *xv*
preface   *xvii*
acknowledgments   *xix*
about this book   *xxi*
author online   *xxv*
about the author   *xxvi*
about the cover illustration   *xxvii*

PART 1   INTRODUCING CORS 1

1   *The Core of CORS*   *3*

1.1   What is CORS?   4

1.2   CORS by example   5

Setting up the request   7 ▪ Sending the request   7
Processing the response   7

1.3   Benefits of CORS   9

Wider audience   9 ▪ Servers stay in charge   9
Flexibility   10 ▪ Easy for developers   10
Reduced maintenance overhead   10

1.4   Summary   10

2   *Making CORS requests   12*

2.1   What is a cross-origin request?   13

2.2   Browser support for CORS   14

2.3   Using the XMLHttpRequest object   15

Sending an HTTP request   17 ▪ Handling the HTTP response   20 ▪ Including cookies on cross-origin requests   27

2.4   XDomainRequest object in Internet Explorer 8 and 9   28

Differences between XDomainRequest and XMLHttpRequest   30

2.5   Canvas and cross-origin images   32

2.6   CORS requests from jQuery   34

2.7   Summary   36

PART 2   CORS ON THE SERVER 37

3   *Handling CORS requests   39*

3.1   Setting up the sample code   40

Setting up the sample API   40 ▪ Setting up the sample client   42 Running the sample app   44

3.2   Making a CORS request   45

3.3   Anatomy of a CORS request   47

The players in a CORS request   48 ▪ Lifecycle of a CORS request   49

3.4   Making a request with the Origin header   51

Viewing the Origin header   51 ▪ What is an origin?   52 Setting the Origin header   55

3.5   Responding to a CORS request   55

The Access-Control-Allow-Origin header   55 Access-Control-Allow-Origin with a wildcard (*) value   56 Access-Control-Allow-Origin with an origin value   59 Rejecting CORS requests   59

3.6   Summary   62

4   *Handling preflight requests   63*

4.1   What is a preflight request?   64

Lifecycle of a preflight request   64 ▪ Why does the preflight request exist?   64

4.2 Triggering a preflight request 67

When is a preflight request sent? 71

4.3 Identifying a preflight request 72

Origin header 72 ▪ *HTTP OPTIONS method 73*
Access-Control-Request-Method header 74 ▪ *Putting it
all together 75*

4.4 Responding to a preflight request 75

Supporting HTTP methods with Access-Control-Allow-Methods 76
Supporting request headers with Access-Control-Allow-Headers 78
Sending the actual request 83 ▪ *Rejecting a preflight request 83*

4.5 Recapping preflights 85

4.6 Preflight result cache 90

4.7 Summary 93

5 **Cookies and response headers 94**

5.1 Supporting cookies in CORS requests 95

Setting cookies with a login page 95 ▪ *Reading the cookie on
the server 97* ▪ *Including cookies in CORS requests 99*
*How withCredentials and Access-Control-Allow-Credentials
interact 102* ▪ *Caveats to cookie support 104*

5.2 Exposing response headers to the client 107

Reading a response header 108 ▪ *Adding response
header support 108*

5.3 Summary 111

6 **Best practices 112**

6.1 Refactoring the sample code 113

6.2 Before you begin 114

6.3 Setting the Access-Control-Allow-Origin header 114

Allowing cross-origin access for everyone 115 ▪ *Limiting CORS
requests to a set of origins 116* ▪ *CORS and proxy servers 121*
Null origin 123 ▪ *Origin header on same-origin requests 124*

6.4 Security 126

Including cookies on requests 128 ▪ *Authorizing requests
using OAuth2 132*

6.5 Handling preflight requests 135

Whitelisting request methods and headers 135

6.6 Reducing preflight requests   139

  Maximizing the preflight cache   139 ▪ Changing your site to
  reduce preflight requests   141

6.7 Exposing response headers   142

6.8 CORS and redirects   144

6.9 Summary   147

PART 3 DEBUGGING CORS REQUESTS 149

7 *Debugging CORS requests   151*

7.1 Solving CORS errors   152

7.2 Using the browser's developer tools   153

  Using the console   155 ▪ Using the Network tab   155

7.3 Monitoring network traffic   158

  Using Wireshark   159 ▪ Using Fiddler   161

7.4 Using curl to simulate CORS requests   165

  Making CORS requests using curl   165 ▪ Making preflight
  requests using curl   167 ▪ Why use curl?   168

7.5 Sending requests using test-cors.org   169

  Sending requests to a remote server   169 ▪ Sending requests to
  the local server   171 ▪ Understanding how the client works   173

7.6 Tips for mobile debugging   174

  Log requests on the server   175 ▪ Use test-cors.org   175
  Use remote debugging tools   175 ▪ Use a mobile simulator   175

7.7 Getting help   176

7.8 Summary   177

APPENDIXES 178

A *CORS reference   178*

A.1 HTTP headers   178

  Request headers   178 ▪ Response headers   178

A.2 Other terms used in CORS   180

  Simple method   180 ▪ Simple header   180
  Simple response header   181

B Configuring your environment 182

B.1 Setting up for the sample application 182

Node.js and NPM 182 ▪ Express 186

B.2 Debugging tools 187

Wireshark 187 ▪ Fiddler 189 ▪ Curl 189

B.3 Resources 190

C What is CSRF? 191

C.1 What is CSRF? 191

C.2 Implementing CSRF protection for same-origin requests 195

D Other cross-origin techniques 199

D.1 JSONP 199

D.2 Flash 201

D.3 postMessage and easyXDM 203

D.4 Server-side request 204

index 206

foreword

No one can argue that AJAX was an important advancement in the evolution of the web. In a few short years, a single technology (`XMLHttpRequest`) revolutionized how users interacted with our content. Instead of loading entire pages, portions of the page could refresh with minimal distraction to the user. In a time when broadband wasn't the norm, this change was amazingly powerful.

The web grew up during that time. The birth of AJAX catalyzed the transformation of "web pages" into "web apps," but it also paved the way for modern client-side development. Today's JavaScript frameworks, which launched single page apps (SPAs), were a result of this early paradigm shift. But as more code moved off the server and into the client, it was clear `XMLHttpRequest` wasn't keeping up. JavaScript's single-origin policy suffocated our creative potential. Web developers like you and I developed clever techniques (JSONP and proxy servers) to wiggle around the restrictions, but ultimately, all our cleverness was just a bandage. Gone were the days of the mashup. Web services were becoming a ubiquitous "back end" for web applications. True dependencies in our applications are critical to making web services tick. However, for services to be accessible from JavaScript meant a better tool was needed for dealing with remote resources. Enter cross-origin resource sharing, better known as CORs.

CORs is a powerful addition in the evolution of `XMLHttpRequest` and the advancement of web apps. By definition, CORs creates a standard way for JavaScript to securely communicate with cross-domain resources. Practically speaking, it opens up a whole new world for front-end developers. CORs brings back flexibility to JavaScript developers and allows them to access APIs and services from anywhere on web. For example, organizations can publish read/write JSON APIs or make their entire data sets accessible to the world of JavaScript.

Monsur Hossain is fellow Googler and expert in cross-domain JavaScript communication. He and I first crossed paths working on Google's XML-based Data APIs and later as engineers on Google's JavaScript client library. Over the years, Monsur lead many facets of the client library, including its OAuth authentication flow and adding CORS support for APIs like YouTube and Google Drive.

CORs in Action is a well-rounded resource for developers wanting to learn the entire spectrum of CORs. Monsur does an excellent job of covering the basics. He highlights important sections with figures and provides excellent code snippets to teach by example.

I particularly like how often Monsur references the browser DevTools. It's a critical tool for gaining insight into the browser's network stack. His use of real-world APIs like Google Calendar and Flickr also give readers practical hands-on experience. I have no doubt you'll walk away learning a great deal from *CORs in Action*.

ERIC BIDELMAN
STAFF DEVELOPER RELATIONS ENGINEER
GOOGLE

I first encountered cross-origin requests around 2006, when I joined Google and became the owner of the GData JavaScript Client. The GData JavaScript Client was a library that gave developers access to various Google APIs from JavaScript. The library itself was written in JavaScript, and the code was pretty straightforward...except for this little corner of code that made cross-origin requests to Google's servers. This was before CORS existed, so this little corner jumped though crazy hoops to load data from Google's APIs. From the developer's perspective, the code simply worked. But between the request and the response was a dark and convoluted maze of code that was difficult to understand and debug.

So you can imagine my happiness when I discovered CORS. Here was a clean, simple, and standard way for making cross-origin requests. Instead of code that's difficult to understand, I could have simple HTTP response headers. Instead of code that's difficult to debug, I could have a single standard that worked across all browsers. I quickly set out to add support for CORS to Google's APIs.

And that's when the real fun started. While CORS uses HTTP headers to enable cross-origin requests, there are many subtle ways in which these headers can interact. It's not as simple as adding an HTTP header to your server and calling it a day. And because CORS was such a new feature, there weren't a lot of resources to guide me. Armed with the CORS spec, Wireshark, and a lot of patience, I spent the next few weeks building a flexible and configurable CORS library that could work for various types of requests. Based on that experience, I started contributing CORS knowledge to the community by participating in Stack Overflow and writing an article about CORS for HTML5Rocks.com.

That was almost three years ago, and in the years since, CORS has grown from a specification to a feature supported by most major APIs. You can find CORS support in APIs from Amazon, Dropbox, Facebook, Flickr, Google, and GitHub (to name just a few). This book distills those three years of experience into an easy and illuminating resource for learning CORS. My hope is that this book helps make CORS a little less daunting, and encourages you to add CORS support to your own systems. Open access to information is a cornerstone of the web, and CORS is one of the ways to enable this. The more developers become comfortable with CORS, the more it will become a part of the everyday vocabulary of the web.

acknowledgments

This book would have never come together were it not for the generous support from many individuals. I'd like to take a moment to acknowledge them here.

Thank you to all the Googlers who helped guide my own understanding of CORS, including Eric Bidelman, Jad Boutros, Antonio Fuentes, Joe Gregorio, Jason Hall (whose prompting led me to investigate CORS in the first place), Yaniv Inbar, Sven Mawson, Eduardo Vela Nava, Jeffrey Posnick, Louis Ryan, Benjamin Carl Wiley Sittler, and Mark Stahl. And special thanks to Eric for contributing the foreword to the book.

Thank you to Anne van Kesteren for authoring the CORS spec that made this book possible, to Evan Hahn and Will Stranathan for their insights on particularly thorny areas of this book, and to Nicholas Zakas, whose blog post was my first introduction to CORS. Michael Hausenblas, thank you for starting enable-cors.org, and passing the torch to me.

Thank you to everyone at Manning for their support and guidance during the crafting of this book. To my editors Cynthia Kane and Monique Bos, thank you for the readings and rereadings that elevated the chapters to the next level. To Konstantin Yakushev, thank you for your in-depth technical review across multiple platforms. Thank you also to Michael Stephens, Kevin Sullivan, Jodie Allen, Deepak Vohra, Elizabeth Martin, and Chuck Larson.

Thank you to the reviewers who took time to read the manuscript at various stages of its development and who provided invaluable feedback: Christopher Haupt, Cristian Antonioli, Jeroen Benckhuijsen, Joshua Frederic, Margriet Bruggeman, Nickie Buckner, Nikander Bruggeman, Roger Keizer, Roger Le, and Tom Rutka.

Thank you to Amma, Abba, Mom, Dad, Irene, Marvin, Seema Apa, and Jav Bhai for your enthusiasm and support. And finally, thank you to my wife, Suraiya, whose patience, advice, understanding, and love were necessary ingredients for writing this book.

about this book

The idea behind CORS is simple: allow one site to make a request to another. It's a fairly trivial thing to do from most programming languages. So why does there need to be a book about it?

Hidden behind this simple idea are a lot of complex concepts. While other programming languages have no restrictions on HTTP requests, things are different in a browser, where the browser's same-origin policy prevents requests from different sites. CORS must balance the need to enable cross-origin requests while preserving the same-origin policy for sites that don't use CORS.

Also, CORS has both a client- and a server-side component. For a cross-origin request to succeed, the client and the server must be in agreement. This is different from other web technologies. For example, CSS lives solely in the client-side code; there is no server-side component.

This book serves as an introduction to CORS and attempts to demystify the issues that make CORS complicated.

What this book will give you

Here is an overview of the topics this book will cover:

- *CORS from the client*—This book starts by looking at how to make CORS requests from JavaScript code. It introduces the XMLHttpRequest object, which can be used to make CORS requests. While the XMLHttpRequest object may be familiar to JavaScript developers, the book focuses on what is unique about CORS. The book also covers alternative mechanisms for making CORS requests, such as images in canvas elements, media uploads, and using JQuery.

- *CORS from the server*—The server uses HTTP headers to control CORS behavior. HTTP headers can be used to indicate things like which HTTP methods are allowed, whether cookies can be included on requests, and whether cross-origin requests are allowed at all. This book takes an in-depth look at what these headers are and how they're used.
- *Debugging CORS requests*—Because CORS has client and server components, it can sometimes be difficult to debug CORS issues when things go wrong. This book ends with a look at how to debug issues with CORS requests. It introduces such tools as the browser's debugging tools, Wireshark, and Fiddler.

What this book won't give you

This book isn't an introduction to JavaScript or the web. This doesn't mean you need to be a JavaScript expert. It assumes that you have a basic understanding of how the web, HTTP requests, and JavaScript work.

Although this book uses Node.js and Express for the sample code, you won't find fully programmed CORS solutions for your specific language or platform (unless, of course, you happen to be using Node.js and Express). The core concepts of CORS are the same regardless of what web platform or programming language you use. The goal of this book is to give you the foundation for understanding CORS, so that you can then go off and implement it on your own platform.

How to read this book

Because this book is an overview of CORS, you can approach it from different perspectives:

- *API owners*—Whether you maintain an existing API or are building a new API from scratch, CORS is a great way to extend your API's reach.
- *API consumers*—Building dynamic sites on top of APIs can sometimes be difficult. CORS can make this easier by giving developers a pure JavaScript mechanism for making API requests.
- *JavaScript developers*—Even if you aren't making CORS requests, JavaScript developers can benefit from understanding the basics of how XMLHttpRequest and CORS work. Most modern web pages are built on top of asynchronous HTTP requests (AJAX), and it's useful to have CORS as another tool in your toolbox.

Roadmap

This book is divided into three parts. The first part looks at how to make CORS requests from the browser. The second part looks at how to add CORS support to a server. The third part looks at how to debug CORS requests.

PART 1: INTRODUCTION TO CORS

Chapter 1 begins by giving an overview of what CORS requests are and how they work. It then dives into CORS with an example that makes cross-origin requests to the Flickr API.

Chapter 2 introduces the XMLHttpRequest object, which can be used to make cross-origin requests. Next, it covers the XDomainRequest object, which is used to make CORS requests from Internet Explorer 8 and 9. Then it covers other places where CORS shows up, such as canvas images. Finally, it looks at how to make CORS requests using JQuery.

PART 2: IMPLEMENTING CORS

Chapter 3 switches gears to see how a server can be configured to support CORS. It takes a closer look at the role that the client code, the browser, and the server play in the lifecycle of a cross-origin request. It introduces the Access-Control-Allow-Origin header, which is how a server indicates that it allows cross-origin requests.

Chapter 4 introduces the concept of a *preflight request*, which is a small request that asks the server for permission to make the actual CORS request. It covers how the preflight request fits into the CORS lifecycle, and introduces a new set of HTTP headers for controlling the response.

Chapter 5 looks at how to include user credentials such as cookies on the request. It also shows how the server can grant permission to the client to read certain response headers.

The preceding chapters set the foundation for using CORS from the server. Chapter 6 expands on these ideas by providing a set of best practices for implementing CORS on your own server.

PART 3: CORS IN PRACTICE

Chapter 7 looks at how to debug CORS requests when something goes wrong. It introduces tools like the browser's debugging tools, Wireshark, and Fiddler, which can be used to monitor and diagnose CORS issues.

APPENDIXES

Appendix A provides a reference for all the CORS-related headers. Appendix B looks at how to set up Node.js and Express, which are used throughout the book for the sample code. Appendix C takes a closer look at CSRF issues, and how they relate to CORS. Appendix D looks at other cross-origin request techniques.

Online resources

This book provides a general introduction to CORS. If you'd like more information, here are a few resources you can turn to:

- The sample code for this book is hosted at GitHub (https://github.com/monsur/CORSinAction). You can either follow along with the book and type the code out, or download and run the code from here.

- enable-cors.org is a site I maintain that has pointers to various server-side CORS implementations. If you're looking to add CORS support to a particular programming framework (for example, Java Tomcat), here's where you should turn.
- The CORS spec (www.w3.org/TR/cors/) defines exactly how CORS works.
- Stack Overflow (http://stackoverflow.com/) is a great resource for getting help on CORS-related questions. I hang out there as well, and often answer questions tagged with #cors.

Code conventions and downloads

All source code in the book is in a `fixed-width font like this`, which sets it off from the surrounding text. In many listings, the code is annotated to point out the key concepts, and numbered bullets are sometimes used in the text to provide additional information about the code. We have tried to format the code so that it fits within the available page space in the book by adding line breaks and using indentation carefully.

Code examples appear throughout this book. Longer listings appear under clear listing headers, whereas shorter listings appear between lines of text.

Source code for all the working examples is available from www.manning.com/CORS in Action or www.manning.com/hossain. Sample code is also available at https://github.com/monsur/CORSinAction.

author online

Purchase of *CORS in Action* includes free access to a private web forum run by Manning Publications where you can make comments about the book, ask technical questions, and receive help from the authors and from other users. To access the forum and subscribe to it, point your web browser to www.manning.com/CORSinAction. This page provides information on how to get on the forum once you are registered, what kind of help is available, and the rules of conduct on the forum. It also provides links to the source code for the examples in the book, errata, and other downloads.

Manning's commitment to our readers is to provide a venue where a meaningful dialog between individual readers and between readers and the author can take place. It is not a commitment to any specific amount of participation on the part of the author, whose contribution to the Author Online forum remains voluntary (and unpaid). We suggest you try asking the author challenging questions lest his interest stray!

The Author Online forum and the archives of previous discussions will be accessible from the publisher's website as long as the book is in print.

about the author

Monsur Hossain is a software engineer at Google, where he has worked on various API related projects, including the Google APIs JavaScript Client and the Google APIs Discovery Service. He is also responsible for adding CORS support to Google APIs. He maintains the site enable-cors.org. Monsur lives in Chicago with his wife and two children.

about the cover illustration

The figure on the cover of *CORS in Action* is captioned "A Rabbit-skin Seller." The illustration is taken from a nineteenth-century edition of Sylvain Maréchal's four-volume compendium of regional dress customs published in France. Each illustration is finely drawn and colored by hand. The rich variety of Maréchal's collection reminds us vividly of how culturally apart the world's towns and regions were just a little over 200 years ago. Isolated from each other, people spoke different dialects and languages; in the streets or in the countryside, it was easy to identify where they lived and what their trade or station in life was just by their dress.

Dress codes have changed since then and the diversity by region, so rich at the time, has faded away. It is now hard to tell apart the inhabitants of different continents, let alone different towns or regions. Perhaps we have traded cultural diversity for a more varied personal life—certainly for a more varied and fast-paced technological life.

At a time when it is hard to tell one computer book from another, Manning celebrates the inventiveness and initiative of the computer business with book covers based on the rich diversity of regional life of two centuries ago, brought back to life by Maréchal's pictures.

Part 1

Introducing CORS

Cross-Origin Resource Sharing (CORS) enables web clients to make HTTP requests to servers hosted on different origins. CORS is a unique web technology in that it has both a server-side and a client-side component. The server-side component configures which types of cross-origin requests are allowed, while the client-side component controls how cross-origin requests are made.

Part 1 focuses on the client-side component of CORS. Chapter 1 is an introduction to CORS, how it works, and its benefits. It also gives a taste of what CORS looks like by introducing a sample application that makes CORS requests to the Flickr API.

Chapter 2 dives deeper into this sample application to show how the client-side component of CORS works. It starts by looking at how the browser's `XMLHttpRequest` object (which is already familiar to any developer making same-origin requests) can be used to make cross-origin requests. Then, it turns to Internet Explorer 8 and Internet Explorer 9, which support a subset of CORS via the `XDomainRequest` object. Next, it looks at other places where CORS requests turn up, such as the `canvas` element. The chapter concludes by looking at how CORS requests can be made from jQuery.

The Core of CORS

This chapter covers

- Which issues CORS solves
- How a CORS request works
- The benefits of CORS

Suppose you're building a web mashup to load photos from the New York Public Library's (NYPL) Flickr page and display them on your own page. What would the code look like? You could start with an HTML page to display the photos, add JavaScript code to load the photos from the Flickr page, and display them on the page. Pretty straightforward, right?

But if you were to run this code in the browser, it wouldn't work because the browser's same-origin policy limits client code from making HTTP requests to different origins. This means that a web page running from your desktop or web server can't make an HTTP request to Flickr.com.

Cross-Origin Resource Sharing, or CORS, was built to help solve this issue. Before CORS, developers would need to go to great lengths to access APIs from JavaScript clients in the browser. CORS enables cross-origin requests in a safe, standard manner. From a client's perspective, CORS is awesome because it opens up a new world of APIs that previously wasn't available to browser JavaScript. From a server's perspective, CORS is awesome because it allows the server to open up its APIs to a new world of users.

This chapter gives an overview of what CORS is and how it's used. It begins by reviewing CORS's features and benefits. It then walks through the code to make a CORS request.

1.1   What is CORS?

CORS is simply a way of making HTTP requests from one place to another. This is a trivial thing in other programming languages. But it's difficult to do in client-side JavaScript, because for years the browser's same-origin policy has explicitly prevented these types of requests.

This may make CORS sound like a contradiction. How can CORS allow cross-origin requests if the same-origin policy explicitly forbids them? The key is that CORS puts servers firmly in charge of who can make requests, and what type of requests are allowed. A server has the choice to open up its API to all clients, open it up to a small number of clients, or prevent access to all clients.

So if browsers enforce a same-origin policy, how does CORS work? The secret lies in the request and response headers. The browser and the server use HTTP headers to communicate how cross-origin requests behave. Using the response headers, the server can indicate which clients can access the API, which HTTP methods or HTTP headers are allowed, and whether cookies are allowed in the request.

Figure 1.1 shows what an end-to-end CORS request to the Flickr API looks like.

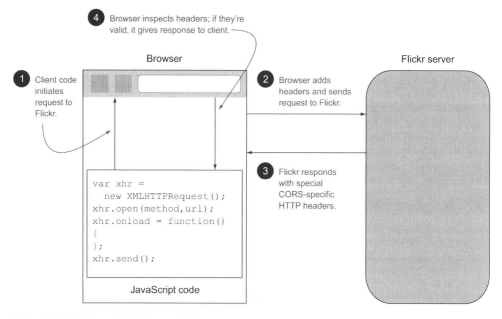

Figure 1.1   End-to-end CORS request flow

Here is a simplified look at the steps to making a CORS request (there are a few more nuances to some CORS requests, which we'll cover in later chapters):

1 The CORS request is initiated by the JavaScript client code.

2 The browser includes additional HTTP headers on the request before sending the request to the server.

3 The server includes HTTP headers in the response that indicate whether the request is allowed.

4 If the request is allowed, the browser sends the response to the client code.

If the headers returned by the server don't exist, or aren't what the browser expects, the response is rejected and the client can't view the response. In this way, browsers can still enforce the same-origin policy on servers that don't allow cross-origin requests. Now that you have a sense of what CORS is, let's turn our attention to making a CORS request.

1.2 CORS by example

Let's demonstrate how CORS works by building a Flickr sample app. Figure 1.2 shows the app, which loads photos from the NYPL's Flickr site and displays them on the page.

The following listing shows the code behind this sample.

Listing 1.1 Making a CORS request

```
<!DOCTYPE html>
<html>
<body onload="loadPhotos();">
<div id="photos">Loading photos...</div>
<script>
function loadPhotos() {
  var api_key = '<YOUR API KEY HERE>';
  var method = 'GET';
  var url = 'https://api.flickr.com/services/rest/?' +        ⟵ Request to Flickr API
      'method=flickr.people.getPublicPhotos&' +
      'user_id=32951986%40N05&' +
      'extras=url_q&format=json&nojsoncallback=1&' +
      'api_key=' + api_key;

  var xhr = new XMLHttpRequest();                              ⟵ Makes sure browser supports CORS
  if (!('withCredentials' in xhr)) {
    alert('Browser does not support CORS.');
    return;
  }
  xhr.open(method, url);

  xhr.onerror = function() {
    alert('There was an error.');
  };

  xhr.onload = function() {
    var data = JSON.parse(xhr.responseText);
    if (data.stat == 'ok') {
      var photosDiv = document.getElementById('photos');
      photosDiv.innerHTML = '';
```

```
          var photos = data.photos.photo;
          for (var i = 0; i < photos.length; i++) {
            var img = document.createElement('img');
            img.src = photos[i].url_q;
            photosDiv.appendChild(img);                      ◁──┐  Displays photos
          }                                                     │  on page
        } else {
          alert(data.message);
        }
      };

    xhr.send();
  }
</script>
</body>
</html>
```

NOTE   If you'd like to run this sample in your browser, you'll need to obtain an API key from Flickr and substitute it for the <YOUR API KEY HERE> string in the code. You can obtain an API key at www.flickr.com/services/apps/create/.

Figure 1.2 Loading photos from Flickr using CORS

If you save this code to an HTML file (and set the API key as mentioned in the preceding note) and then open that file in your browser, you should see a bunch of photos. The key thing to note about this example is that although the web page is running from your local filesystem, it's making a request to the server at api.flickr.com. Let's walk through the code to get a better understanding of what each section is doing.

1.2.1 Setting up the request

The code starts by creating a new XMLHttpRequest object:

```
var xhr = new XMLHttpRequest();
if (!('withCredentials' in xhr)) {
  alert('Browser does not support CORS.');
  return;
}
xhr.open(method, url);
```

The first and last lines are the same for same-origin and cross-origin requests. The first line creates the XMLHttpRequest object, the last sets the HTTP method and URL.

The three middle lines highlight the difference between a same-origin-capable browser and a cross-origin-capable browser. If the browser fully supports CORS, the XMLHttpRequest object will contain a withCredentials property. You can use this property to check if the browser supports CORS. The preceding code alerts you if the browser doesn't support CORS.

1.2.2 Sending the request

Once the request is set up, you send the request to the server using the send method:

```
xhr.send();
```

This method initiates the HTTP request to the server. Chrome's Network tab gives you a better understanding of what the request looks like, as shown in figure 1.3. The figure shows the fact that even though the request originates from the filesystem ❶, the destination server is in fact flickr.com ❷.

Notice how the response has a header set to Access-Control-Allow-Origin: * ❸. The Access-Control-Allow-Origin header is the magic behind CORS. The server uses this header to indicate that cross-origin requests are allowed. The Access-Control-Allow-Origin header must always be present on a CORS response, but it's just one of many headers that can be used to configure CORS behavior. Part 2 of this book will cover these headers in greater detail.

1.2.3 Processing the response

Once the browser receives the response, it checks the response headers to verify that the cross-origin request is valid. If the request isn't valid, the browser will log an error

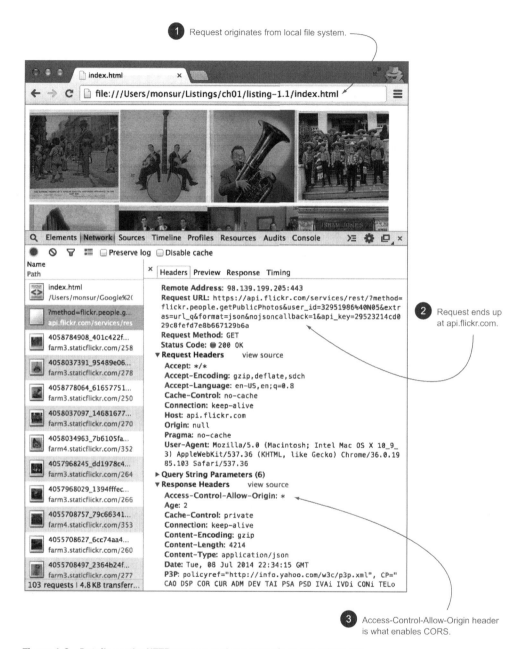

Figure 1.3   Details on the HTTP request and response from the Flickr API

to the console, then fire the XMLHttpRequest's onerror event. But because the response here is valid, the browser fires the XMLHttpRequest's onload event:

```
xhr.onload = function() {
  var data = JSON.parse(xhr.responseText);
```

```
    if (data.stat == 'ok') {
      var photosDiv = document.getElementById('photos');
      photosDiv.innerHTML = '';
      var photos = data.photos.photo;
      for (var i = 0; i < photos.length; i++) {
        var img = document.createElement('img');
        img.src = photos[i].url_q;
        photosDiv.appendChild(img);
      }
    } else {
      alert(data.message);
    }
  };
```

This code parses the response text into a JavaScript Serialized Object Notation (JSON) object, grabs the images from the object, and displays them on the page. In addition to the response text, the `XMLHttpRequest` object also has properties for the HTTP status, HTTP status text, and methods that retrieve response headers.

1.3   Benefits of CORS

The example from the previous section gave you a sense of power of CORS. Now let's turn our attention to some of the benefits CORS provides.

1.3.1   Wider audience

If you're building a public API, you want to open up access to as wide an audience as possible. Developers in other languages can easily use native libraries to make API requests. For example, a Python developer can use the httplib2 library to make HTTP requests to any server, regardless of where the request originates. The following snippet shows what a Python request to Flickr looks like. The httplib2 library doesn't care whether the server is CORS-enabled; it indiscriminately makes the request and processes the response, as this sample code shows:

```
import httplib2
h = httplib2.Http(".cache")
resp, content = h.request("http://www.flickr.com/photos/nypl/", "GET")
```

JavaScript developers don't have that advantage because the browser's same-origin policy limits HTTP requests to a single domain. CORS enables JavaScript developers to use an API the same way a developer in another language could.

1.3.2   Servers stay in charge

Safety is an important factor when making cross-domain requests. Any cross-domain mechanism needs to be careful not to break the browser's same-origin policy and inadvertently send requests to an unsuspecting server.

CORS achieves this safety by allowing servers to opt-in to CORS. For the request to succeed, the server must use response headers to explicitly acknowledge that the request is allowed. That way, if a CORS request is made to a server that doesn't support CORS or doesn't have the right CORS headers, the request fails.

1.3.3 *Flexibility*

CORS gives servers the flexibility to configure cross-origin access in a variety of ways. The server can specify various features:

- Which domains are allowed to make requests
- Which HTTP methods are allowed (for example, GET/PUT/POST/DELETE)
- Which headers are allowed on the HTTP request
- Whether or not requests may include cookie data
- Which response headers the client can read

These rich settings put the server firmly in control of how the CORS request works.

1.3.4 *Easy for developers*

Because CORS is a standardized specification, it works in a consistent manner across sites. Developers need only learn about CORS once; then they can use the same techniques across all sites that support CORS.

While CORS requires new configuration on the server side, the client-side developer experience remains largely unchanged. JavaScript's XMLHttpRequest object has been available in browsers for over 10 years. Developers make CORS requests using the same XMLHttpRequest object they are familiar with. There isn't any new code for the developer to learn. From the developer's perspective, same-origin and cross-origin requests look mostly the same. (There are some slight differences, which we'll cover in chapter 2.)

1.3.5 *Reduced maintenance overhead*

There are ways to make cross-origin requests without using CORS (appendix D covers some of these techniques). But these techniques require custom code, custom servers, or additional documentation. This leads to an additional maintenance burden for the server developer.

Conversely, CORS only requires a few additional response headers. This reduced maintenance means that API owners can focus their attention on other things, rather than worrying about reinventing and maintaining new cross-domain mechanisms. Because CORS is a published specification with broad browser support, site owners can rest assured that their implementation is stable and that details won't change.

1.4 *Summary*

CORS allows client code to make cross-origin requests to remote servers. CORS is necessary because the browser's same-origin policy traditionally disallows cross-origin requests, which makes it difficult to load data from other sites. Here are some benefits of CORS:

- Opens an API to a wider audience
- Puts servers in charge of how CORS behaves
- Allows flexible configuration options
- Makes it easy for client developers to use
- Reduces maintenance overhead for server developers

The next chapter will dive into the details of how to make CORS requests from the browser.

Making CORS requests

2

This chapter covers

- Which browsers support CORS
- How to use the XMLHttpRequest object to make CORS requests
- How to use the XDomainRequest object in Internet Explorer 8 and 9
- How to load cross-origin images in a canvas element
- How to make CORS requests from jQuery

A CORS request consists of two sides: the client making the request, and the server receiving the request. On the client side, the developer writes JavaScript code to send the request to the server. The server responds to the request by setting special CORS-specific headers to indicate that the cross-origin request is allowed. Without both the client's and the server's participation, the CORS request will fail.

This chapter focuses on how to make CORS requests from JavaScript. It assumes you have an existing CORS-enabled API (such as the Flickr API, the GitHub API, or your own API) to make requests to (if you don't have an existing CORS-enabled API, don't worry. Part 2 looks at how to set one up). The chapter starts by defining what a cross-origin request is and which browsers support it. It then covers the main ways to make

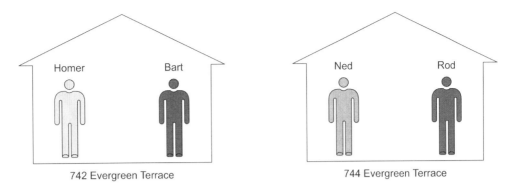

Figure 2.1 Two houses with two people in each. Each house represents a website, and the people in the house are web pages.

CORS requests, including the `XMLHttpRequest` and `XDomainRequest` objects. Next it looks at how the HTML5 `<canvas>` element uses CORS to load images. It ends with a look at jQuery support for CORS. The server-side details of CORS will be covered in chapter 3.

2.1 *What is a cross-origin request?*

Before learning how to make a cross-origin request, let's define what a cross-origin request is. Think of a website as a house, and each page on the website as an inhabitant of that house. Suppose there are houses located at 742 Evergreen Terrace and 744 Evergreen Terrace, and each house has two residents: Homer and Bart at 742 Evergreen Terrace, and Ned and Rod at 744 Evergreen Terrace (as shown in figure 2.1).

An HTTP request is a conversation between two people. When Homer talks to Bart, the conversation takes place solely within the confines of the house. This is called a *same-origin request.* If Homer calls Ned, the conversation crosses the boundaries of the house. This is called a *cross-origin request.* Figure 2.2 shows the distinction between a same-origin and a cross-origin request.

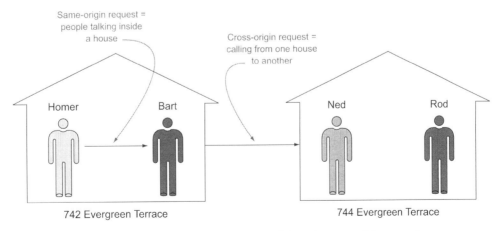

Figure 2.2 Illustrating the difference between a same-origin and a cross-origin request

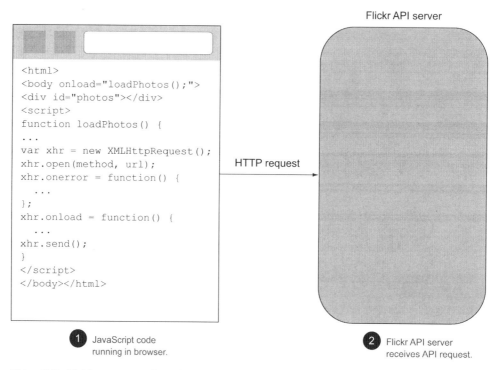

Figure 2.3   **Making a request from the browser to the Flickr API**

Now let's apply this analogy to the Flickr example from chapter 1. In that example, there is JavaScript code running in the browser, which initiates a request to the Flickr API, as shown in figure 2.3. This request is a cross-origin request because the Java-Script code making the request and the API server receiving the request live on two different websites.

There are a lot of different pieces to making a successful cross-origin request. The client and the server must work together to ensure that the request succeeds. This chapter focuses on the first part of this process: how the client initiates a request to the server ❶. Let's start by taking a look at which browsers do and don't support CORS.

2.2   *Browser support for CORS*

Browser support for CORS can be divided into three tiers: full support, partial support, and no support. If you're developing with CORS, it's helpful to know which browsers your users are using, so you know which of these three tiers you need to focus on.

CORS is fully supported in the following desktop browsers:

- Chrome 3+
- Firefox 3.5+
- Safari 4+

- Internet Explorer 10+
- Opera 12+

In addition to desktop browsers, CORS is fully supported in most mobile browsers, including iOS 3.2+ and Android 2.1+. Mobile devices tend to have up-to-date software, so if you're developing for mobile browsers, you can be comfortable knowing your users have CORS support.

Internet Explorer 8 and 9 support a limited version of CORS using something called the XDomainRequest object, which is limited to only certain types of CORS requests. If cross-origin requests in Internet Explorer 8 or Internet Explorer 9 are important to your application, you'll want to learn about the limitations in XDomainRequest.

If the browser's version is older than the ones mentioned here, it probably doesn't support CORS. If you need to support cross-origin requests in an older browser, there are still options. As we'll cover in appendix D, there are other mechanisms available for making cross-origin requests in older browsers. But you won't be able to use the techniques described here.

Table 2.1 breaks down the landscape of CORS support in browsers. As of mid-2014, approximately 83% of the browsers out there have full support for CORS, and another 6% have partial support.

Table 2.1 CORS support in browsers

Tier	CORS support	Browsers
1	Full CORS support	Chrome 3+, Firefox 3.5+, Safari 4+, Internet Explorer 10+, Opera 12+
2	Partial CORS support	Internet Explorer 8, Internet Explorer 9
3	No CORS support	Chrome 2 and below, Firefox 3 and below, Safari 3 and below, Internet Explorer 7 and below, Opera 11 and below

(*Source*: http://caniuse.com/#search=cors.)

The next two sections look at how to work with CORS in tier 1 and tier 2 browsers. Tier 1 browsers use the XMLHttpRequest object to make cross-origin requests, while tier 2 browsers use the XDomainRequest object. Let's start by looking at the XMLHttpRequest object.

2.3 Using the XMLHttpRequest object

JavaScript code can make HTTP requests with the XMLHttpRequest object. Listing 1.1 showed you how the XMLHttpRequest object can be used for a CORS request to the Flickr API. The following listing shows the code from listing 1.1 and highlights the individual pieces of the request.

Listing 2.1 Making a CORS request to the Flickr API

```
<!DOCTYPE html>
<html>
<body onload="loadPhotos();">
```

```
<div id="photos">loading photos...</div>
<script>
function loadPhotos() {
  var api_key = '<YOUR API KEY HERE>';
  var method = 'GET';
  var url = 'https://api.flickr.com/services/rest/?' +
      'method=flickr.people.getPublicPhotos&' +
      'user_id=32951986%40N05&' +
      'extras=url_q&format=json&nojsoncallback=1&' +
      'api_key=' + api_key;

  var xhr = new XMLHttpRequest();
  if (!('withCredentials' in xhr)) {
    alert('Browser does not support CORS.');
    return;
  }
  xhr.open(method, url);

  xhr.onerror = function() {
    alert('There was an error.');
  };

  xhr.onload = function() {
    var data = JSON.parse(xhr.responseText);
    if (data.stat == 'ok') {
      var photosDiv = document.getElementById('photos');
      photosDiv.innerHTML = '';
      var photos = data.photos.photo;
      for (var i = 0; i < photos.length; i++) {
        var img = document.createElement('img');
        img.src = photos[i].url_q;
        photosDiv.appendChild(img);
      }
    } else {
      alert(data.message);
    }
  };

  xhr.send();
}
</script>
</body>
</html>
```

> **Sets up request parameters** ← (`xhr.open(method, url);`)
>
> **Sends request** ← (`xhr.onload = function() {`)
>
> **Processes response** ← (`xhr.send();`)

There are three parts to making an HTTP request:

- Sets up request parameters.
- Sends request.
- Processes response. (The code to process the response is defined before the request is actually sent, which is why `xhr.onload` comes before `xhr.send`.)

The rest of this section will examine how to use the XMLHttpRequest object during these three phases of the HTTP lifecycle. While the XMLHttpRequest object can be used to make either same-origin or cross-origin requests, this section will pay special attention to any CORS-specific behavior. Even if you have worked with the XMLHttpRequest object before, some of this information may still be new, because the XMLHttpRequest object underwent a revision around 2010. The latest version has new properties that help enable CORS. The older version of XMLHttpRequest works in older tier 3 browsers, but because it doesn't support CORS, it isn't covered here.

2.3.1 Sending an HTTP request

The first step in making an HTTP request is setting up a new XMLHttpRequest object. The following listing highlights the code that sets up the request.

Listing 2.2 Setting up an HTTP request to the Flickr API

```
<!DOCTYPE html>
<html>
<body onload="loadPhotos();">
<div id="photos">Loading photos...</div>
<script>
function loadPhotos() {
  var api_key = '<YOUR API KEY HERE>';
  var method = 'GET';
  var url = 'https://api.flickr.com/services/rest/?' +
      'method=flickr.people.getPublicPhotos&' +
      'user_id=32951986%40N05&' +
      'extras=url_q&format=json&nojsoncallback=1&' +
      'api_key=' + api_key;

  var xhr = new XMLHttpRequest();
  if (!('withCredentials' in xhr)) {
    alert('Browser does not support CORS.');
    return;
  }
  xhr.open(method, url);

  xhr.onerror = function() {
    alert('There was an error.');
  };

  xhr.onload = function() {
    var data = JSON.parse(xhr.responseText);
    if (data.stat == 'ok') {
      var photosDiv = document.getElementById('photos');
      photosDiv.innerHTML = '';
      var photos = data.photos.photo;
      for (var i = 0; i < photos.length; i++) {
        var img = document.createElement('img');
        img.src = photos[i].url_q;
        photosDiv.appendChild(img);
      }
    } else {
      alert(data.message);
    }
  };

  xhr.send();
}
```

Annotations:
- Defines HTTP method and URL
- Creates new XMLHttpRequest object
- Assigns HTTP method and URL to XMLHttpRequest object

```
</script>
</body>
</html>
```

It starts by defining the HTTP method and URL to the API. In the case of a cross-origin request, the URL is the full URL to the resource. There is no other special information that needs to be set to delineate a request as cross-origin. The browser does the work of parsing the URL and determining if the request is a same-origin or a cross-origin request.

The code then creates a new XMLHttpRequest object, and verifies that it supports CORS by checking that the XMLHttpRequest object has a withCredentials property. The withCredentials property will be covered in more detail later in this chapter. For now, all you need to know is that if the XMLHttpRequest object has a withCredentials property, then it supports CORS.

The open method is called to set the values of the HTTP method and URL. The open method also does some basic validation to ensure that the HTTP method and URL are valid. For example, if the HTTP method contains a space, calling open will throw a syntax error.

ADDING HTTP HEADERS

The setRequestHeader method lets you add HTTP headers to the request. This method accepts a header key and header value, and includes the header on the request. The following code snippet, which should be included after the open method, shows an example of using the setRequestHeader method to set the X-Requested-With request header:

```
xhr.setRequestHeader('X-Requested-With', 'CORS in Action');
```

There are some headers that are set by the browser that can't be set by the user (see the following sidebar for the complete list). As you'll see in the next chapter, the browser sets an Origin header on cross-origin requests. If you try to override this header in your code, the browser will ignore your value. This is a security measure that helps prevent user code from overriding trusted header values. The server can trust these values because it knows the user hasn't accidentally (or maliciously) tainted the value.

> ### Setting request headers
> Here is the list of headers that cannot be set by the setRequestHeader method: Accept-Charset, Accept-Encoding, Access-Control-Request-Headers, Access-Control-Request-Method, Connection, Content-Length, Cookie, Cookie2, Date, DNT, Expect, Host, Keep-Alive, Origin, Referer, TE, Trailer, Transfer-Encoding, Upgrade, User-Agent, Via, and any headers starting with 'Proxy-' or 'Sec-'.
>
> These headers have special meaning and can only be set by the browser. There is no error if the code tries to set the header. The value is just ignored.

The server has to give its permission for the client to include custom request headers on a cross-origin request. This behavior is unique to cross-origin requests; same-origin requests can include any custom request header. If the server doesn't whitelist the request headers, the request will fail. We'll dive into more details on how a server does this in chapter 4.

MAKING THE REQUEST

Once the request is set up, calling the `send` method will send the HTTP request to the server, as shown in the following listing.

> **Listing 2.3   Calling the `send` method to initiate the HTTP request**

```
<!DOCTYPE html>
<html>
<body onload="loadPhotos();">
<div id="photos">Loading photos...</div>
<script>
function loadPhotos() {
  var api_key = '<YOUR API KEY HERE>';
  var method = 'GET';
  var url = 'https://api.flickr.com/services/rest/?' +
      'method=flickr.people.getPublicPhotos&' +
      'user_id=32951986%40N05&' +
      'extras=url_q&format=json&nojsoncallback=1&' +
      'api_key=' + api_key;

  var xhr = new XMLHttpRequest();
  if (!('withCredentials' in xhr)) {
    alert('Browser does not support CORS.');
    return;
  }
  xhr.open(method, url);

  xhr.onerror = function() {
    alert('There was an error.');
  };

  xhr.onload = function() {
    var data = JSON.parse(xhr.responseText);
    if (data.stat == 'ok') {
      var photosDiv = document.getElementById('photos');
      photosDiv.innerHTML = '';
      var photos = data.photos.photo;
      for (var i = 0; i < photos.length; i++) {
        var img = document.createElement('img');
        img.src = photos[i].url_q;
        photosDiv.appendChild(img);
      }
    } else {
      alert(data.message);
    }
  };

  xhr.send();                          The send method initiates
}                                      the HTTP request.
</script>
</body>
</html>
```

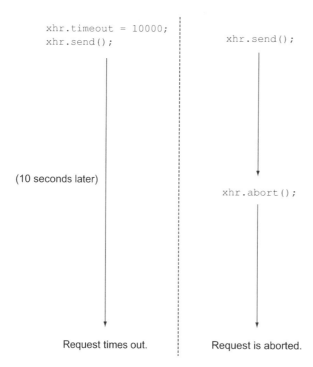

Figure 2.4 Canceling a request that is still in progress using the `timeout` **property and** `abort` **method**

If the HTTP request has a request body, the body can be passed in as a parameter to the send method as follows:

```
xhr.send('request body goes here');
```

Once the send method is called, the HTTP request is sent to the server. Even though the request has been sent, there are still a couple of ways to cancel the request. First, the timeout property can be used to ensure that the request doesn't exceed a certain number of milliseconds. Setting the timeout property to 10000 will kill the request after 10 seconds. The default value for the timeout property is 0, which means there is no timeout, and the request will continue until the server responds. Second, the client can manually kill the request by using the abort method. Calling the abort method will abort the request immediately. Figure 2.4 shows how to use the timeout property and the abort method.

When the server receives a cross-origin request, it determines whether or not the request is allowed, and replies accordingly. Chapter 3 will cover how the server replies to cross-origin requests. But for now, let's assume there is a successful HTTP response, and look at how to handle it.

2.3.2   Handling the HTTP response

The XMLHttpRequest object handles the server's response through a set of events. Events are functions that are invoked at specific moments in the lifecycle of an HTTP request. Events aren't unique to the XMLHttpRequest object; when a user clicks a link on an HTML page, the browser fires a click event.

Asynchronous versus synchronous requests

By default, the XMLHttpRequest object makes asynchronous requests. This means that the send method makes the request in the background, and fires events when the status of the request changes. The XMLHttpRequest object can also make synchronous requests. In a synchronous request, the send method will wait until the response is received (or an error is encountered).

Client code can trigger a synchronous request by setting the third parameter to the open method to false. For example: xhr.open('GET', 'http://', false). Synchronous requests don't fire any events. Instead the code waits until the request is finished. This can cause the entire page to become unresponsive until the request returns. In general, you should avoid synchronous requests and stick with the default asynchronous requests.

The functions that handle these events are called *event handlers*. Table 2.2 gives an overview of all event handlers supported by the XMLHttpRequest object.

Table 2.2   Event handlers exposed by the XMLHttpRequest object

Event handler	Description
onloadstart	Fires when the request starts.
onprogress	Fires when sending and loading data.
onabort	Fires when the request has been aborted by calling the abort method.
onerror	Fires when the request has failed.
onload	Fires when the request has successfully completed.
ontimeout	Fires when the timeout has been exceeded (if the client code specified a timeout value).
onloadend	Fires when the request has completed, regardless of whether there was an error or not.
onreadystatechange	Legacy handler from the previous version of XMLHttpRequest; fires when legacy readyState property changes. It is superseded by other events and is only useful for non-tier 1 browsers.

Figure 2.5 shows when these events are fired during the lifecycle of an HTTP request. Some events, such as onloadstart and onloadend, are always fired once per request. Others may be fired multiple times, such as onreadystatechange and onprogress. Some event handlers may not fire at all, depending on the status of the request; these include onload, onerror, ontimeout, and onabort.

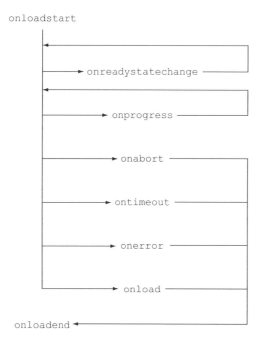

Figure 2.5   Which event handlers fire during the course of an HTTP request

The user can assign a function to each of these event handers to process the particular event. If you need to always run some code at the end of the request (regardless of whether or not there was an error), you'd assign a method to the `onloadend` event handler. The code isn't required to handle each of those events; if an event handler is unassigned, nothing happens when that event is fired. Let's take a closer look at some of the more important event handlers.

HANDLING A SUCCESSFUL RESPONSE WITH THE ONLOAD EVENT HANDLER

The `onload` event handler fires when the request is successful. In the Flickr example, the `onload` handler is responsible for displaying the photos on the page, as shown in the following listing.

> **Listing 2.4   Assigning a function to the `XMLHttpRequest`'s `onload` event handler**

```
<!DOCTYPE html>
<html>
<body onload="loadPhotos();">
<div id="photos">Loading photos...</div>
<script>
function loadPhotos() {
  var api_key = '<YOUR API KEY HERE>';
  var method = 'GET';
  var url = 'https://api.flickr.com/services/rest/?' +
      'method=flickr.people.getPublicPhotos&' +
      'user_id=32951986%40N05&' +
      'extras=url_q&format=json&nojsoncallback=1&' +
      'api_key=' + api_key;
```

```
var xhr = new XMLHttpRequest();
if (!('withCredentials' in xhr)) {
  alert('Browser does not support CORS.');
  return;
}
xhr.open(method, url);

xhr.onerror = function() {
  alert('There was an error.');
};

xhr.onload = function() {
  var data = JSON.parse(xhr.responseText);
  if (data.stat == 'ok') {
    var photosDiv = document.getElementById('photos');
    photosDiv.innerHTML = '';
    var photos = data.photos.photo;
    for (var i = 0; i < photos.length; i++) {
      var img = document.createElement('img');
      img.src = photos[i].url_q;
      photosDiv.appendChild(img);
    }
  } else {
    alert(data.message);
  }
};

xhr.send();
}
</script>
</body>
</html>
```

Assigns a method to onload event handler

When processing the HTTP response, the code has access to various response variables, such as the HTTP status code, the HTTP status text, the response body, and the response HTTP headers. For example, the code in listing 2.4 uses the responseText property to grab the body of the response. Table 2.3 gives an overview of the properties that are available on the response.

Table 2.3   Response properties on the XMLHttpRequest object

Response property	Description
status	The HTTP status code (for example, 200 for a successful request).
statusText	The response string returned by the server (for example, OK for a successful request).
response	The body of the response, in the format defined by responseType. If the client indicated that the response type is json, the response will be a JSON object parsed from the response body.
responseText	The body of the response as a string. Can only be used if responseType was not set or was set as text.
responseXML	The body of the response as a DOM element (XML is here for historical reasons). Can only be used if responseType was not set or was set as document.

The getResponseHeader and getAllResponseHeaders methods can be used to read the HTTP headers on the response. getResponseHeader returns the value of a given response header, while getAllResponseHeaders returns all the response headers as a single string. There is one caveat to reading response headers on a cross-origin request. By default, CORS only allows the client code to read the following response headers:

- Cache-Control
- Content-Language
- Content-Type
- Expires
- Last-Modified
- Pragma

If the server sets any additional response headers that aren't in this list, the client won't be able to see them. But the server can also override this behavior by specifically indicating that these additional response headers should be visible to the client code. The details of how to do this are covered in chapter 5.

To understand when the onload handler fires, it's important to distinguish a successful response from a successful response status code. HTTP responses have an associated status code. A successful response usually has a status code of 200, although any status code in the 200 range signals a success. Status codes in the 300 range signal that the request is being redirected, while status codes of 400 or above signal an error (the 400 range is reserved for client errors while the 500 range is reserved for server errors).

Regardless of the underlying response status code, if the response makes it back to the browser, the onload event handler will fire. So although a request may fail due to a file not found (status code 404) or an internal server error (status code 500), the onload event handler will still fire. Figure 2.6 shows the relationship between the response and the response status code.

If the request fails for some other reason, the onerror event handler will fire. These are errors where the server doesn't send a valid response to the browser, or the server doesn't support CORS. The next section takes a look at how to use the onerror event handler.

HANDLING AN ERROR USING THE ONERROR HANDLER

The onerror event handler will fire if there is an issue with the request. This can happen if, for example, the servers powering the Flickr API are down and not responding. But the onerror event is particularly relevant to CORS because it fires if the server rejects the CORS request. If the Flickr API didn't support CORS, the onerror event handler would fire.

As we'll cover in the next part of this book, the server has many reasons to reject a CORS request. The server may allow cross-origin GET and POST requests, but not PUT or DELETE requests. In this case, if a client attempts a PUT request, the onerror handler will fire instead of the onload handler.

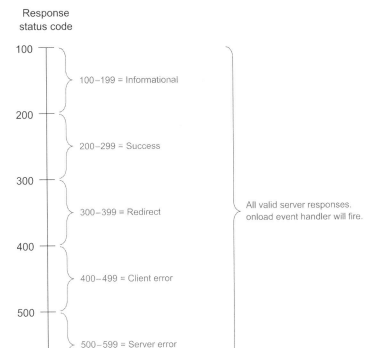

Figure 2.6 **Distinction between the response and response status code. The status code may have an error, but the `onload` event handler will still fire.**

Listing 2.5 shows how to add an `onerror` handler to the sample code. Note that while the `onerror` event signals that something went wrong with the cross-origin request, it doesn't tell you what went wrong. The `statusText` property will be empty, and the `status` will be 0. The code will only know that a request failed, and nothing more.

Listing 2.5 Handling a CORS error using the `onerror` event handler

```html
<!DOCTYPE html>
<html>
<body onload="loadPhotos();">
<div id="photos">Loading photos...</div>
<script>
function loadPhotos() {
  var api_key = '<YOUR API KEY HERE>';
  var method = 'GET';
  var url = 'https://api.flickr.com/services/rest/?' +
      'method=flickr.people.getPublicPhotos&' +
      'user_id=32951986%40N05&' +
      'extras=url_q&format=json&nojsoncallback=1&' +
      'api_key=' + api_key;

  var xhr = new XMLHttpRequest();
  if (!('withCredentials' in xhr)) {
    alert('Browser does not support CORS.');
```

```
      return;
    }
  xhr.open(method, url);

  xhr.onerror = function() {          Assigns a method
    alert('There was an error.');     to onerror event
  };                                  handler

  xhr.onload = function() {
    var data = JSON.parse(xhr.responseText);
    if (data.stat == 'ok') {
      var photosDiv = document.getElementById('photos');
      photosDiv.innerHTML = '';
      var photos = data.photos.photo;
      for (var i = 0; i < photos.length; i++) {
        var img = document.createElement('img');
        img.src = photos[i].url_q;
        photosDiv.appendChild(img);
      }
    } else {
      alert(data.message);
    }
  };

  xhr.send();
}
</script>
</body>
</html>
```

If you're curious to understand why a cross-origin request failed, some browsers (such as Chrome) will display the reason in the console log. This message will give more context to a human who is able to read the message, but there is no way to read this message from JavaScript. Chapter 7 will go into more detail on how to debug and fix a failing CORS request.

OTHER EVENT HANDLERS

Together, the onload and onerror event handlers will handle most of your needs. But the XMLHttpRequest object exposes a few more event handlers that you can hook into, as shown in table 2.4.

Table 2.4   XMLHttpRequest event handlers

Event handler	Function
onloadstart	Fires when the request is successfully initiated asynchronously.
onloadend	Similar to onloadstart, onloadend always fires when the request ends. This event handler is useful if you want to execute some piece of code at the very end of the request, regardless of whether or not the request is successful.
onabort	Fires if the client aborts the request by calling the abort method. If onabort fires, the onload and onerror event handlers will not fire.

Table 2.4 `XMLHttpRequest` **event handlers** *(continued)*

Event handler	Function
`ontimeout`	Fires if the code set a timeout value, and that timeout has been exceeded. If your code sets a timeout of 10,000 milliseconds (10 seconds), this event handler will fire if the response hasn't been received after 10 seconds. If `ontimeout` fires, the `onload` and `onerror` event handlers will not fire.
`onprogress`	Monitors progress of a request or response. It's most helpful in the context of uploading or downloading binary data, such as an image. If you're uploading an image to a website, `onprogress` can be used to create a progress indicator showing how much of the image has been uploaded.
`onreadystatechange`	Fires when the request changes states. The `XMLHttpRequest` spec defines five states a request can be in: unset, opened, headers received, loading, and done. The value of the ready state is stored in the `XMLHttpRequest` object's `readyState` property. For example, when a request goes from loading to done, its `readyState` changes from 3 to 4 (the numeric values for loading and done, respectively), and `onreadystatechange` fires.

When the `XMLHttpRequest` spec was first devised, `onreadystate` was the only event handler available. Now that there are much finer-grained events available, you're better off using them.

2.3.3 *Including cookies on cross-origin requests*

Many websites need a way of identifying the user visiting the page. If you check your email using Gmail, Gmail needs some way of knowing who you are so that it can load your emails.

Websites can identify users through *user credentials*, a general term for any bit of information that can identify a user. The most popular form of user credentials is the cookie. Servers will use cookies to store a unique ID that identifies the user. The browser then includes this cookie on every request to the server.

> **NOTE** Same-origin HTTP requests will always contain the cookie in the request. In contrast, cross-origin requests don't include cookies by default.

Cookies can be included on cross-origin requests by setting the `XMLHttpRequest`'s `withCredentials` property to `true`. Setting the `withCredentials` property to `true` indicates that user credentials such as cookies, basic authentication information, or client-side Secure Sockets Layer (SSL) certificates should be included on cross-origin requests. The following code snippet shows an example of setting the `withCredentials` property to `true`:

```
xhr.withCredentials = true;
```

If you were to run this code in a web browser, it would fail because setting the `with-Credentials` property to `true` isn't enough to complete the request. The server must also indicate that it allows cookies for the request to succeed. Chapter 5 will delve deeper into how the server can enable cookies on requests.

NOTE   The `withCredentials` property doesn't work with synchronous requests.

This section covered the basics of using the `XMLHttpRequest` object in the context of cross-origin requests. You can use the techniques from this section to make cross-origin requests to a CORS-enabled server. If you'd like to learn more about how the `XMLHttpRequest` object works, you can turn to *Ajax in Practice* by Dave Crane et al. (Manning, 2007), or go directly to the `XMLHttpRequest` spec at http://xhr.spec.whatwg.org/.

While the `XMLHttpRequest` object allows you to make cross-origin requests from most browsers, Internet Explorer 8 and Internet Explorer 9 support a limited set of cross-origin requests. These browsers use a different object, called `XDomainRequest`, to make these requests. The next section looks into how the `XDomainRequest` works and how it's different from the `XMLHttpRequest` object.

2.4   *XDomainRequest object in Internet Explorer 8 and 9*

Internet Explorer 8 and Internet Explorer 9 support cross-origin requests, but in a different way. These browsers still have an `XMLHttpRequest` object for making same-origin requests, but they also have a different `XDomainRequest` object specifically for making cross-origin requests. This `XDomainRequest` object is only relevant to Internet Explorer 8 and Internet Explorer 9. Internet Explorer 10 and above support the regular `XMLHttpRequest` object for both same-origin and cross-origin requests. If CORS support for Internet Explorer 8 and Internet Explorer 9 is important to you, you'll want to learn the details of how the `XDomainRequest` object works.

Listing 2.6 changes the Flickr API example to use the `XDomainRequest` object. The `XDomainRequest` object looks a lot like an `XMLHttpRequest` object. If you compare this listing to the original code, there is only a one-line difference when creating a new `XDomain-Request` object ❶. Once you have a new `XDomainRequest` object, you can use it in the same way you use the `XMLHttpRequest` object. You can use the `send` method to send the request, and then use the `onload` and `onerror` event handlers to process the response.

Listing 2.6   Using the `XDomainRequest` object to make a request to the Flickr API

```
<!DOCTYPE html>
<html>
<body onload="loadPhotos();">
<div id="photos">Loading photos...</div>
<script>
function loadPhotos() {
  var method = 'GET';
  var url = 'http://s3.amazonaws.com/corsinaction/flickr.json';
  var xhr = new XDomainRequest();          ⟵─┐
  xhr.open(method, url);                       ❶
```

```
  xhr.onerror = function() {
    alert('There was an error.');
  };

  xhr.onload = function() {
    var data = JSON.parse(xhr.responseText);
    if (data.stat == 'ok') {
      var photosDiv = document.getElementById('photos');
      photosDiv.innerHTML = '';
      var photos = data.photos.photo;
      for (var i = 0; i < photos.length; i++) {
        var img = document.createElement('img');
        img.src = photos[i].url_q;
        photosDiv.appendChild(img);
      }
    } else {
      alert(data.message);
    }
  };

  xhr.send();
}
</script>
</body>
</html>
```

NOTE You may have noticed that the request URL changed from a Flickr URL to an Amazon one. This is because the Flickr API only supports HTTPS, and the XDomainRequest object can't make requests to HTTPS origins from non-HTTPS origins. The URL in listing 2.6 is a copy of the Flickr response that is served from an Amazon S3 server via HTTP. Additionally, since the XDomain-Request object does not support local files, you can find a version of this sample hosted at http://corsinaction.s3.amazonaws.com/flickr.html.

If you're writing client-side JavaScript code to make cross-origin requests, it can be annoying to write two different sets of code for Internet Explorer 8 and Internet Explorer 9 and other browsers. Luckily, the following listing (which is from the blog at www.nczonline.net/blog/2010/05/25/cross-domain-ajax-with-cross-origin-resource-sharing/) provides a simple function for choosing the correct cross-origin request object.

Listing 2.7   Creating the correct CORS request object across browsers

```
function createCORSRequest(method, url){
  var xhr = new XMLHttpRequest();
  if ("withCredentials" in xhr){             ◁─ If browser supports CORS,
    xhr.open(method, url, true);                returns XMLHttpRequest
  } else if (typeof XDomainRequest != "undefined"){   object.
    xhr = new XDomainRequest();        ◁─ If browser has an
    xhr.open(method, url);                XDomainRequest
  } else {                                 object, uses that.
    xhr = null;          ◁─ Otherwise, browser
  }                          doesn't support
  return xhr;                CORS; returns null.
}
```

This code runs in all browsers, and does one of the following:

- If the browser has an XMLHttpRequest object and it supports CORS, it returns a new XMLHttpRequest object.
- If the browser supports XDomainRequest, it returns a new XDomainRequest object.
- If the browser doesn't support either of those objects, it doesn't support CORS. It returns null to indicate that CORS isn't supported.

While the XDomainRequest object looks similar to its XMLHttpRequest object, there are many differences between the two. The next section takes a closer look at these differences.

2.4.1 *Differences between XDomainRequest and XMLHttpRequest*

Although the XDomainRequest and XMLHttpRequest objects let you make cross-origin requests, there are many differences between the two objects. The XDomainRequest object is very limited in the types of cross-origin requests it can make. Table 2.5 compares and contrasts the XMLHttpRequest object to the XDomainRequest object.

Table 2.5   Comparison of XMLHttpRequest and XDomainRequest

Supported feature	XMLHttpRequest	XDomainRequest
HTTP methods	All	GET POST
HTTP schemes	All	HTTP HTTPS
Request content type	All	text/plain
Synchronous requests	Yes	No
Custom request headers	Yes	No
User credentials (such as cookies)	Yes	No
Event handlers	onloadstart onload onerror onabort ontimeout onprogress onreadystatechange onloadend	onload onerror ontimeout onprogress
Response properties	status statusText responseType response responseText responseXML getResponseHeader getAllResponseHeaders	responseText contentType

The reason for this difference is historical. Internet Explorer 8 was released in 2009, when the CORS spec was still young. The Internet Explorer developers wanted to ensure that cross-origin requests were done in a safe manner, so they limited how cross-origin requests could be made. As the CORS spec has evolved, the kinks have been worked out to the point where Internet Explorer 10 and above have support for all CORS functionality. But Internet Explorer 8 and Internet Explorer 9 represent a large proportion of the browsers still in use, so they can't be ignored. Here is a look at how the XDomainRequest object is different from XMLHttpRequest.

GET AND POST ONLY

The XDomainRequest object can only make HTTP requests using GET or POST. Other HTTP methods such as HEAD, PUT, or DELETE aren't allowed.

LIMITED SCHEME SUPPORT

XDomainRequest only supports CORS from the http:// or https:// schemes. This means that opening a file on your computer won't work, because this uses the file:// scheme. Furthermore, HTTP pages can only make CORS requests to other HTTP pages, and HTTPS pages can only make CORS requests to other HTTPS pages.

CONTENT-TYPE TEXT/PLAIN ONLY FOR REQUESTS

The XDomainRequest object can only make requests with the text/plain Content-Type. Content-Type identifies the data type of the HTTP body. It's an HTTP header that can be present on both HTTP requests and HTTP responses. When visiting a web page, for example, the HTML file has a Content-Type of text/html, and a JPEG image has a Content-Type of image/jpeg. The Content-Type serves as a hint to browsers and servers about what data type to expect. If your server expects a different content type on requests, it will have to be modified to also allow the text/plain Content-Type.

ASYNCHRONOUS REQUESTS ONLY

The XDomainRequest object supports only asynchronous requests; there is no way to use it to make synchronous requests. But this is a feature that won't be missed. The blocking nature of synchronous requests can lead to a frustrating user experience, because the user can't interact with the page until the request completes.

NO CUSTOM REQUEST HEADERS

Earlier I showed how the XMLHttpRequest object uses the setRequestHeader method to include custom request headers on the request. The XDomainRequest object doesn't have a setRequestHeader function, and doesn't allow custom request headers on requests.

NO COOKIES OR USER CREDENTIALS

The XDomainRequest object never includes cookies or other user credentials in requests. Furthermore, there is no withCredentials property to override behavior. Cookies are the main mechanism for identifying visitors to a website, which means the XDomainRequest object is best suited for making requests to public data that doesn't serve any user-specific information.

FEWER EVENT HANDLERS

The XDomainRequest object only has four event handlers: onload, onerror, onprogress, and ontimeout. These behave the same as their XMLHttpRequest counterparts. There is no onabort method, because there is no corresponding abort method to abort the request, and there aren't onloadstart and onloadend methods to mark the beginning and end of the request.

HMLHttpRequest's onloadend handler is useful for ensuring a piece of code always executes, regardless of whether the request was a success or a failure. For example, the onloadend handler could be used to hide a status message at the end of the request. If you need to execute a piece of code at the end of a request, be sure to put it in the onload, onerror, and ontimeout methods.

LESS RESPONSE INFORMATION

Once the server sends an HTTP response, the XDomainRequest object only gives the JavaScript code access to the response body and response content type. There is no way to access the HTTP status code or status text, or any of the response headers.

The XMLHttpRequest and XDomainRequest objects allow HTTP requests to be made from JavaScript. But these aren't the only way the browser uses CORS. The next section covers how the HTML5 <canvas> element uses CORS to load images.

2.5   *Canvas and cross-origin images*

HTTP requests from JavaScript are the most common way to use CORS, but they aren't the only way. The HTML <canvas> element also relies on CORS when loading images from different origins. Canvas was introduced in HTML5 as a way to draw shapes and images from JavaScript. The following listing shows how to use JavaScript and a canvas to draw a solid rectangle. Figure 2.7 shows what this canvas looks like in the browser.

Listing 2.8   Drawing a rectangle on a canvas

```
<canvas id="myCanvas"></canvas>
<script>
var myCanvas = document.getElementById('myCanvas');
var myContext = myCanvas.getContext('2d');
myContext.fillStyle = '#888';
myContext.fillRect(0,0,240,150);
</script>
```

In addition to drawing shapes, a canvas can also display images. These images can live either on the same server as the page, or on a different server. The canvas can display all images, regardless of whether or not the image comes from the same origin. The difference is that cross-origin images can taint the canvas.

Tainting a canvas means that data can no longer be extracted from the canvas. The <canvas> element exposes three methods for extracting data: toBlob, toDataURL, and getImageData. All three methods return the binary image data. When these methods are called on a canvas with a same-origin image, they work just fine. But when they are called on a canvas with a cross-origin image, the browser throws an error, as shown in figure 2.8.

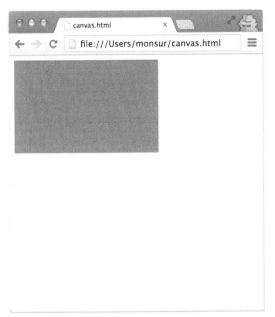

Figure 2.7   Example of drawing a rectangle on a canvas

To get around this error, the image must be labeled as "cross-origin." This is as simple as setting the image's crossOrigin attribute, as shown in the following listing.

Listing 2.9   Setting an image's `crossOrigin` attribute

```
<canvas id="myCanvas"></canvas>
<script>
var myCanvas = document.getElementById("myCanvas");
var myContext = myCanvas.getContext('2d');

var img = new Image();                          Setting image's
img.crossOrigin = 'anonymous';          ◁───── crossOrigin attribute.
img.onload = function() {
    myCanvas.width = img.width;                      Calling toDataURL works,
    myCanvas.height = img.height;                    even when the image is
    myContext.drawImage(img, 0, 0);                  on a different origin.
    console.log(myCanvas.toDataURL("image/png"));  ◁──┘
};
img.src = 'http://www.html5rocks.com/static/images/mastheads/h5r-shadow.png';

</script>
```

Q Elements Network Sources Timeline Profiles Resources Audits Console

⊘ ▽ <top frame> ▼

⊘ ▶ Uncaught SecurityError: Failed to execute 'toDataURL' on 'HTMLCanvasElement': Tainted canvases may not be exported.   canvas.html:12

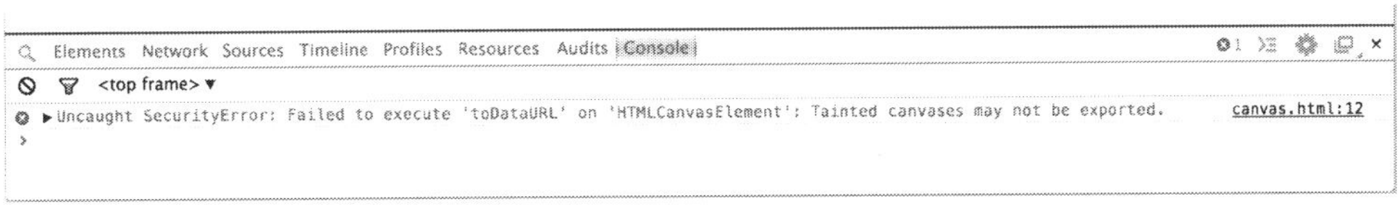

Figure 2.8   The error when trying to extract data from a tainted canvas

The crossOrigin attribute has two possible values: anonymous and user-credentials. If crossOrigin is set to user-credentials, any user credentials for that origin are included in the request. For example, if the origin has cookies, the cookies will be included with the image request. This is similar to setting the withCredentials property on the XMLHttpRequest object. Setting the crossOrigin attribute to anonymous will still make the request, but there won't be any cookies attached to the request. It's best to always use the anonymous value, unless you absolutely need the user's cookies to load the image.

Once the image's cross-origin property is set and the request is successful, the image can be manipulated in the same way as a same-origin image. That means that the toBlob, toDataURL, and getImageData methods will work on a canvas with a cross-origin image.

Note that the crossOrigin attribute alone isn't enough to avoid tainting the canvas. As with most of the other CORS features we've covered in this chapter, the server must indicate that cross-origin access to the image is allowed. If the server doesn't allow it, the image will still be displayed in the canvas, but none of the data extraction methods will work.

2.6   CORS requests from jQuery

JQuery is a popular JavaScript framework that powers many JavaScript apps. JQuery has a function named ajax for making HTTP requests. Under the hood, the ajax method uses the XMLHttpRequest object to make HTTP requests. The following listing modifies the Flickr API to use jQuery.

Listing 2.10   Using jQuery to make a cross-origin request

```
<!DOCTYPE html>
<html>
<body>
<div id="photos">Loading photos...</div>
<script src="http://ajax.googleapis.com/ajax/libs/jquery/2.1.1/
    jquery.min.js"></script>
<script>
function loadPhotos() {
  var api_key = '<YOUR API KEY HERE>';
  var method = 'GET';
  var url = 'https://api.flickr.com/services/rest/?' +
      'method=flickr.people.getPublicPhotos&' +
      'user_id=32951986%40N05&' +
      'extras=url_q&format=json&nojsoncallback=1&' +
      'api_key=' + api_key;

  $.ajax(url, {
    type: method,
    dataType: 'json',
    success: function(data, textStatus, jqXHR) {
      if (data.stat == 'ok') {
        $('#photos').empty();
```

**$.ajax method both
initializes and sends
an HTTP request.**

**json data type
indicates that
response should
be parsed as JSON.**

**success property is
used instead of onload.**

```
      $.each(data.photos.photo, function(i, photo) {
        var img = $('<img>').attr('src', photo.url_q);
        $('#photos').append(img);
      });
    } else {
      alert(data.message);
    }
  },
  error: function(jqXHR, textStatus, errorThrown) {       ◁──┐  error property is used
    alert('There was an error.');                            │  instead of onerror.
  }});
}

$(document).ready(loadPhotos);
</script>
</body>
</html>
```

The jQuery version looks similar to the original example, but the syntax varies slightly. Instead of distinct `open`, `send`, and `onload` methods, all the functionality is contained within the `ajax` method, and the HTTP request is made immediately when the `ajax` method is called.

JQuery's `dataType` property indicates that the response should be parsed as JSON. This saves the developer the additional step of using `JSON.parse` to parse the response text into a JSON object. The `XMLHttpRequest` object can do this as well by setting the `responseType` property to `'json'`. As of this writing, the `responseType` property isn't fully supported in all browsers. These are minor cosmetic differences; the functionality between the original sample and the jQuery version is the same.

While jQuery has full support for CORS, there are a few things to be aware of when using jQuery.

First, jQuery doesn't support synchronous cross-origin requests.

Second, the `ajax` method only supports `XMLHttpRequest`, and doesn't support `XDomainRequest`. This means if you're using jQuery and need support for CORS in Internet Explorer 8 or Internet Explorer 9, you'll need to write code to fall back on the `XDomainRequest` object, or use a jQuery plugin that supports `XDomainRequests`, such as the one at https://github.com/jaubourg/ajaxHooks/blob/master/src/xdr.js.

Third, if you need to set the `withCredentials` property, you'll need to use the `xhrFields` property, as shown in the following code snippet. The `xhrFields` property lets you set arbitrary fields on the `XMLHttpRequest` object:

```
$.ajax(url, {
  xhrFields: {
    withCredentials: true
  }
});
```

Fourth, jQuery doesn't set the X-Requested-With request header on cross-origin requests. JQuery traditionally sets the X-Requested-With header on HTTP requests.

This header is used by clients to indicate that a request is coming from an XMLHttp-Request object. The server receiving the request can look for the X-Requested-With header to determine where the request is coming from. JQuery always sets this header when making same-origin requests, but removes it from cross-origin requests. The reason is that setting custom request headers requires an additional server configuration step. Rather than force developers to make changes to their server, jQuery chose to drop this header. The following code snippet shows how to reenable the X-Requested-With header on cross-domain requests:

```
$.ajax(url, {
  headers: {'X-Requested-With': 'XMLHttpRequest'}
});
```

Note that if you add this header, you'll also need to update your server to allow this header on cross-origin requests. Chapter 4 shows how to add server-side support for this and other request headers.

2.7   *Summary*

This chapter explored ways to make cross-origin requests from the browser. Browsers can be divided into three tiers of CORS support:

- Tier 1—Browsers that fully support CORS
- Tier 2—Browsers that partially support CORS
- Tier 3—Browsers that don't support CORS

The browsers in tier 1 all use the XMLHttpRequest object to make cross-origin requests, while the browsers in tier 2 (Internet Explorer 8 and Internet Explorer 9) use the XDomainRequest object. JQuery can also be used to make cross-origin requests in tier 1 browsers.

In addition to these objects, the browser also uses CORS when loading cross-origin images in the <canvas> element. By default, a cross-origin image will taint a canvas, which prevents data from being extracted from the canvas. Setting the image's cross-Origin property to anonymous (or in some cases user-credentials) will allow data to be extracted.

This chapter gives you the foundation for issuing cross-origin requests from the browser. But it has glossed over the details of how the server responds to cross-origin requests. For a cross-origin request to succeed, the server must give its permission to make cross-origin requests. The next part will cover how to configure a server to support CORS. We'll start by learning how to identify and respond to simple CORS requests.

Part 2

CORS on the server

Part 1 looked at CORS from the perspective of a client making cross-origin requests. Part 2 examines CORS from the perspective of a server receiving a cross-origin request.

Chapter 3 takes a look at how to handle a simple CORS request. It begins by setting up a sample application that will be used throughout the rest of the book. Next, it covers the roles of that the client, the browser, and the server play in a cross-origin request. It then applies this knowledge back to the sample application, and shows how the server uses HTTP response headers to configure CORS behavior. In particular, chapter 3 introduces two key headers used by CORS: the Origin request header and the Access-Control-Allow-Origin response header.

Chapter 4 introduces the notion of a preflight request, which allows clients to ask permission before sending a cross-origin request. The preflight request ensures that servers aren't caught off-guard by unexpected requests. The server can give permissions to allow certain HTTP methods (via the Access-Control-Allow-Methods response header) and certain HTTP request headers (via the Access-Control-Allow-Headers response header). Finally, the chapter covers the preflight cache, which allows preflight requests to be cached for a certain period of time.

Chapter 5 rounds out your understanding of CORS by covering two remaining features: including user credentials such as cookies on cross-origin requests, and giving the client permission to view certain response headers.

Chapter 6 takes the knowledge from the previous three chapters and turns it into practical guidance for your own CORS implementation. It starts by looking at the different ways you can allow access to your API, from opening up to the public or limiting it to a certain subset of origins. This chapter also looks at common security issues, such as how to protect your API against CSRF attacks, and how you can use OAuth2 to give third-party services access to your API. Next, it looks at how to improve performance by minimizing preflight requests. Finally, it examines how CORS requests interact with HTTP redirects.

Handling CORS requests

This chapter covers

- How to set up the book's sample application
- What a CORS request looks like from a server's perspective
- What an origin is
- How to respond to CORS requests using the Access-Control-Allow-Origin header

Suppose you're the owner of a blog that you programmed yourself. To keep the site scalable, you've separated the blog data from the HTML code by introducing an API. The blog page queries the API to load the blog posts, then displays those posts on the page.

As your site becomes more popular, some of your more tech-savvy readers ask if they can use your data to create JavaScript mashups, or embed some of your data on their site by creating a JavaScript widget. They can do this now by screen-scraping the data from your site, but they would be a lot happier if they could plug into the same API you use to load the data for the site.

You love your readers, and think this is a great idea. But when you share your API code with them, it doesn't work. This is because the browser's same-origin policy prevents the API request from running from anywhere but your own web application.

CORS offers a way around this restriction by letting your server specify which kinds of requests are allowed. CORS gives you control over who can access which pieces of your API.

This chapter will take a closer look at how to handle CORS requests from the server's perspective. We'll start by setting up sample code for your blogging app. I'll then introduce the major players in CORS and you'll learn how they interact. You'll also learn about the basic building blocks of a CORS request and response.

3.1   Setting up the sample code

This section introduces the sample code that will be used throughout the rest of this book. You'll add new functionality to it as you learn more about how CORS works. The sample you'll be developing is a blogging app that displays a set of blog posts to the user. The app consists of a server that exposes two pieces of functionality:

1 An API endpoint that returns all the blog posts in JSON format
2 An HTML page that queries the API for the posts and then displays them on the page

Figure 3.1 shows what the blogging app will look like once you're done setting up the code in this section.

Appendix B explains how to set up the prerequisites for this sample. If you haven't already, take a moment to visit those requirements. After setting up the prerequisites, your development environment should have the following:

- Node.js
- Express
- A web browser that supports CORS

Once you've set up these prerequisites, you're ready to write code.

3.1.1   Setting up the sample API

Let's turn our attention to how to set up each piece of code. You'll start by building the API portion of the server, as highlighted in figure 3.2.

Add the JavaScript code in listing 3.1 to a file named app.js. This code creates a new server running on port 9999 of your computer. The code starts by creating a few

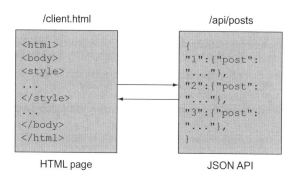

Figure 3.1   The sample blogging app consists of two parts: an API with blog data, and an HTML page to display the blog data.

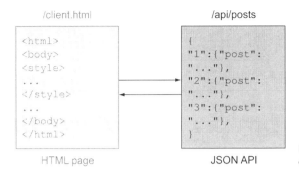

/client.html   /api/posts

HTML page   JSON API

Figure 3.2   The location of the API endpoint within the sample app

blog posts (these are just made-up sample posts for the app; a real blog would load these posts from a database). It then creates a new Express web server and adds the `express.static()` middleware. The `express.static()` middleware configures the web server to read files from your computer and serve them through the web server (this will come into play in the next section, where you'll add a client.html file).

Next, the code sets up the actual API. The API lives at the endpoint /api/posts. Requests to /api/posts will return a JSON object containing the sample blog posts. Now that the code has configured how the server behaves, it starts the server on port 9999. Finally, the code prints out a friendly startup message to verify that everything is working.

Listing 3.1   Sample server code

```
var express = require('express');

var POSTS = {
  '1': {'post': 'This is the first blog post.'},
  '2': {'post': 'This is the second blog post.'},
  '3': {'post': 'This is the third blog post.'}
};

var SERVER_PORT = 9999;
var serverapp = express();
serverapp.use(express.static(__dirname));
serverapp.get('/api/posts', function(req, res) {
  res.json(POSTS);
});
serverapp.listen(SERVER_PORT, function() {
  console.log('Started server at http://127.0.0.1:' + SERVER_PORT);
});
```

Serves static files from the same directory as app.js

Made-up blog posts for app

Creates a new Express-powered web server

Adds API endpoint to retrieve sample posts

Starts server

Displays a startup message once server is started

NOTE   If you are using Linux, you may have to invoke Node.js by typing `nodejs` rather than `node`.

You can run the server by opening a terminal window, navigating to the directory where your code lives, and typing `node app.js`. You should see the output in figure 3.3. You can stop the server by pressing Ctrl-C. Every time you make changes to the code in app.js, you'll need to stop and then start the server.

```
● ○ ○          listing-3.1 — node — 50×5
> node app.js
Started server at http://127.0.0.1:9999
```

Figure 3.3   Output from running the API server

Here is an overview of how to perform these tasks:

- *Stop the server.* If the server is running, press Ctrl-C in the terminal window to stop it.
- *Start the server.* If the server isn't running, type `node app.js` in the terminal window to start it.
- *Restart the server.* Stop the server, then start the server (that is, press Ctrl-C followed by typing `node app.js`).

You can verify that the server is working by visiting http://127.0.0.1:9999/api/posts in a browser. You should see a JSON response similar to figure 3.4. If you don't see this response or you receive an error, review the preceding steps to make sure everything is in order.

Now that you have a working API, let's build the page that uses this API.

3.1.2   *Setting up the sample client*

With the API in place, you're ready to add the client.html page that consumes the API, as highlighted in figure 3.5.

Copy the contents of listing 3.2 into a new file named client.html, and save it in the same directory as app.js. Client.html is the web page that reads the data from the API and displays it in the browser.

Chapter 2 covered the basics of how the client makes CORS requests, but here is a recap of the code in listing 3.2. The main functionality of client.html takes place in the `getBlogPost` function. The function starts by creating a new `XMLHttpRequest` object. `XMLHttpRequest` is the standard mechanism for making HTTP requests in

Figure 3.4   The response from a working server

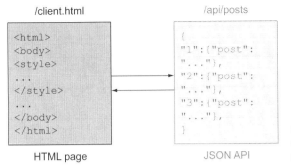

/client.html

/api/posts

HTML page

JSON API

Figure 3.5 Location of the client web page within the sample app

JavaScript, and will be used to load the posts from the API. Next, the code defines an onload function that executes when the HTTP response is received. This particular function parses the blog posts into a JSON object, then displays the posts on the page. After the request behavior is configured, the actual request is sent to the server. The getBlogPost function is called when the page loads, so that the posts are automatically displayed when the user visits the page. If there is an error when making the HTTP request, the page displays the word 'ERROR' on the page to let you know that something is wrong.

Listing 3.2 Sample client code

```
<!DOCTYPE html>
<html><body onload="getBlogPosts();">        ◁─┐ Gets posts when
<style>                                            page loads
.post {margin-bottom: 20px;}
</style>
<div id="output"></div>
<script>
var createXhr = function(method, url) {
  var xhr = new XMLHttpRequest();
  xhr.onerror = function() {                       Displays an error
    document.getElementById('output').innerHTML = 'ERROR';  ◁─┘ if request fails
  };
  xhr.open(method, url, true);
  return xhr;
};                                                           Creates a new
var getBlogPosts = function() {                              XMLHttpRequest
  var xhr = createXhr('GET', 'http://127.0.0.1:9999/api/posts'); ◁─ object
  xhr.onload = function() {
    var data = JSON.parse(xhr.responseText);
    var elem = document.getElementById('output');
    for (var postId in data) {                              Displays
      var postText = data[postId]['post'];                  posts on
      var div = document.createElement('div');              page
      div.className = 'post';
      div.appendChild(document.createTextNode(postText));
      elem.appendChild(div);
    }
  };
```

```
  xhr.send();
};
    </script>
</body></html>
```
◁─┐ **Makes HTTP**
   │ **request**

When making changes to the app.js server code, you'll need to reload the client.html page. This means clicking the browser's Reload button, or pressing Ctrl-R (Cmd-R on Macs) in the browser. Reloading the page ensures that the client page picks up the latest changes made on the server.

3.1.3 *Running the sample app*

Now that the server and client code are ready, let's fire up the sample app. Start the server by typing `node app.js` in the terminal window (or restart it if it's already running). Because the server also serves the client.html page, the server must be running for the client.html page to load. (If you encounter "file not found" errors on client.html, be sure to first check that the server is running.) Next, switch over to your web browser and visit the page at http://127.0.0.1:9999/client.html. You should see the blog posts as shown in figure 3.6.

The client.html page displays the sample posts defined in app.js. To do this, the client.html page sends an HTTP request to /api/posts. You can view this HTTP request and response (or any errors) by using the browser's JavaScript console. I'll be using Chrome for the screenshots throughout this book. You can open Chrome's JavaScript Console by pressing the keyboard shortcut Ctrl-Shift-J on Windows (Cmd-Option-J on Mac). You can also find it by navigating to the Tools > JavaScript Console menu option on Windows (or the View > Developer > JavaScript Console menu option on Mac). If you aren't using Chrome, don't worry. Most browsers have a built-in JavaScript Console that will give you the same information. Chapter 7 demonstrates how to open the JavaScript console in most major browsers.

You can view the details of the HTTP request by opening the JavaScript console, clicking the Network tab, and refreshing the client.html page. You should see two HTTP requests in the Network tab: one for client.html, the other for /api/posts. If you

**Figure 3.6   Client page
with a successful request**

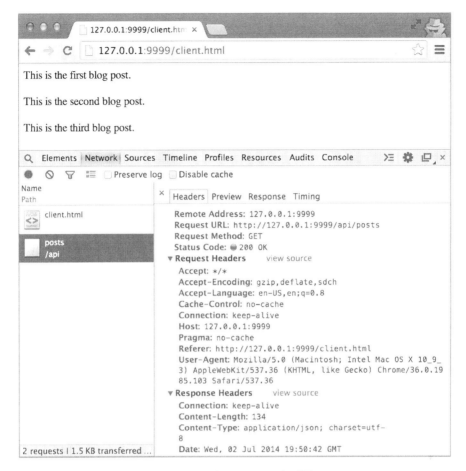

Figure 3.7 Viewing the HTTP request and response to the API

click the /api/posts request, then the Headers tab, you can see all the details of the request and response, as shown in figure 3.7.

The remainder of this book will make incremental updates to this sample code to demonstrate how the features of CORS work. You'll switch back and forth between the terminal and the browser depending on which part of the code we're looking at. Now that the sample app is up and running, let's introduce CORS to the mix.

3.2 Making a CORS request

The previous section created a sample app running on a single server at 127.0.0.1:9999. This sample app makes a same-origin HTTP request to load the blog data from the /api/posts endpoint. Now that the sample app is set up, let's modify it to make a cross-origin request.

You can make a cross-origin request by introducing a new server that sends requests to the API on 127.0.0.1:9999. Listing 3.3 modifies app.js to introduce a second server

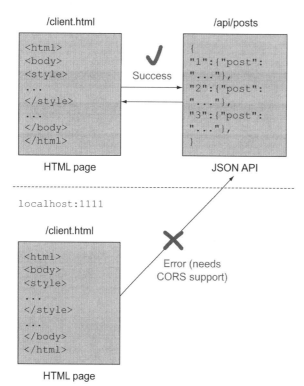

Figure 3.8   Topology of sample app with new server

running at localhost:1111. Requests from 127.0.0.1:9999 to localhost:1111 are cross-origin requests, because 127.0.0.1:9999 and localhost:1111 are different. Figure 3.8 shows what this new server configuration looks like.

Listing 3.3   Update app.js to add a new server running on localhost:1111

```
serverapp.listen(SERVER_PORT, function() {
  console.log('Started server at http://127.0.0.1:' + SERVER_PORT);
});

var CLIENT_PORT = 1111;
var clientapp = express();
clientapp.use(express.static(__dirname));
clientapp.listen(CLIENT_PORT, function(){
  console.log('Started client at http://localhost:' + CLIENT_PORT);
});
```

Code for second
server begins here

If you restart the server, then visit the page at http://localhost:1111/client.html, you'll receive an error in the browser as well as the JavaScript console, as shown in figure 3.9. Contrast this to the page at http://127.0.0.1:9999/client.html, which still works. Both pages are using the same client.html code, so what's the difference?

Figure 3.9   Error when making a cross-origin request

> **NOTE**   If you are using Internet Explorer 10 or above, you need to add http://
> localhost to your Trusted Sites for the sample to work. You do this by navigat-
> ing to Trusted Sites (located under Internet Options > Security > Trusted Sites
> > Sites) and adding http://localhost.

The difference is that the request from http://127.0.0.1:9999/client.html is a same-
origin request, while the request from http://localhost:1111/client.html is a cross-
origin request. The request from http://127.0.0.1:9999/client.html succeeds because the
request comes from the same location as the server (127.0.0.1:9999). The request
from http://localhost:1111/client.html fails because it crosses server boundaries, and
you haven't yet configured the server to accept these requests.

The rest of this chapter will work toward fixing that error. To do that, let's first discuss what happens behind the scenes when you make a CORS request.

3.3   Anatomy of a CORS request

Think about what happens when you want to withdraw money from an ATM. You
walk up to the machine, swipe your card, enter your PIN, and a few seconds later
you walk away with money in your wallet. Figure 3.10 shows each of the players in
this transaction.

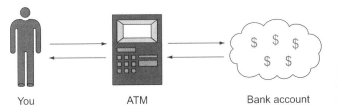

You   ATM   Bank account

**Figure 3.10   A bank withdrawal
consists of you, the ATM, and
your bank account**

The ATM acts as a trusted intermediary between you and the bank by verifying each step of the transaction. It checks things like whether you entered the correct PIN, or whether your bank account has enough money. Imagine if instead of an ATM there was a stack of money and the bank trusted everyone to take the right amount. That bank wouldn't be in business long!

Like this ATM transaction, a CORS request has its own group of players with similar functionality. The players in a CORS request are the client, the browser, and the server.

3.3.1 The players in a CORS request

The key players in a CORS request are the client, the browser, and the server. The client wants some piece of data from the server, such as a JSON API response or the contents of a web page. The browser acts as the trusted intermediary to verify that the client can access the data from the server. Table 3.1 shows how these players fit with the ATM analogy.

Table 3.1 A CORS request consists of the client, the browser, and the server

CORS player	ATM analogy	Description
Client	You	Wants data from the server
Browser	ATM	Manages the communication between the client and the server
Server	Bank account	Serves the data the client wants

CLIENT

In the same way that you want money from your bank account, the client wants data from the server. The client is a snippet of JavaScript code running on a website, and it's responsible for initiating the CORS request. It's served from a particular domain and usually consists of an XMLHttpRequest to a remote server. The following code snippet highlights the portion from the sample's client.html file that is responsible for making the CORS request:

```
var xhr = createXhr('GET', 'http://127.0.0.1:9999/api/posts');
xhr.onload = function() {
  ...
};
xhr.send();
```

Client versus user

Sometimes the words client and user are used interchangeably, but they are different in the context of CORS. A *user* is a person visiting a website, while a *client* is the actual code served by that website. Multiple users can visit the same website and be served the same JavaScript client code, as shown in figure 3.11. For the purposes of understanding CORS, we'll focus on the client and not on the user.

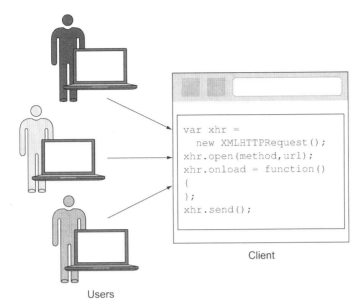

```
var xhr =
  new XMLHTTPRequest();
xhr.open(method,url);
xhr.onload = function()
{
};
xhr.send();
```

Client

Users

Figure 3.11 Multiple users interacting with a website's client code

BROWSER

The client code runs inside a web browser. The CORS spec calls the web browser a user agent, but we'll refer to it as the web browser. Just like the ATM, the browser is a trusted intermediary, and plays an active role in a CORS request in two ways:

- The browser adds additional information to the request so that the server can identify the client.
- The browser interprets the server's response and decides whether to send the request to the client or to return an error.

If the browser didn't do these things, a client could send any request to the server, and the protection introduced by the browser's same-origin policy would be broken. The browser ensures that both the client and the server play by the rules of CORS.

SERVER

The server is the destination of the CORS request. It's the bank account in the ATM analogy. The server stores the data that the client wants, and it has the final say as to whether the CORS request is allowed or not.

Now that you know who is involved in a CORS request, let's take a look at how they all work together.

3.3.2 Lifecycle of a CORS request

A full end-to-end CORS request flow is shown in figure 3.12. Although technically the client code runs inside the browser, figure 3.12 separates the client from the browser to make it easier to envision the flow. The steps in a CORS request, illustrated in the figure, are:

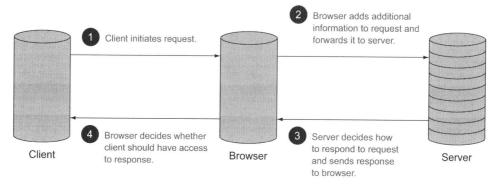

Figure 3.12 **Lifecycle of a CORS request**

1. The client initiates the request.
2. The browser adds additional information to the request and forwards it to the server.
3. The server decides how to respond to the request, and sends the response to the browser.
4. The browser decides whether the client should have access to the response, and either passes the response to the client or returns an error.

Like an ATM interacting with a bank account, the browser and the server "talk" to each other to determine whether the client can access the server's data. A hypothetical conversation between the browser and the server might go something like figure 3.13.

The browser and the server talk to each other through HTTP headers. HTTP headers carry the details of the CORS request, including whether or not the CORS request is allowed. Let's take another look at the conversation in figure 3.13, this time mapped onto a set of HTTP requests and responses. The bolded items show how the parts of the conversation map to the HTTP headers.

Figure 3.13 **Conversation between a browser and a server regarding CORS**

Browser: Hi server 127.0.0.1:9999! Please give me the data at /api/posts and let me know if the client at **localhost:1111** can access it.

```
GET /api/posts HTTP/1.1
User-Agent: Chrome
Host: 127.0.0.1:9999
Accept: */*
Origin: http://localhost:1111
```

Server: Here is the data. And, yup, **any client** can have access.

```
HTTP/1.1 200 OK
Access-Control-Allow-Origin: *
```

This conversation represents the simplest dialogue that can take place between a browser and a server during a CORS request. As you'll see in subsequent chapters, this conversation grows richer and new headers are added based on the client's needs.

CORS is built around many headers, but the two most important are:

- The Origin request header
- The Access-Control-Allow-Origin response header

These headers must be present on every successful CORS request. Without one or the other, the CORS request will fail. Let's dig deeper into the vocabulary of these two headers.

3.4   *Making a request with the Origin header*

The Origin header is central to CORS. The client identifies itself to the server by using the Origin header. Think of it as the client's calling card.

A CORS request must have an Origin header. There is no way around that. If there is no Origin header it isn't CORS. With that in mind, let's revisit the sample app and take a look at the actual Origin header.

3.4.1   *Viewing the Origin header*

The browser's Network tab lets you view the HTTP headers included on the request, including the Origin header. View this header by opening the Network tab in the browser's JavaScript console and reloading the page at http://localhost:1111/client.html.

After the page finishes loading, choose the request to /api/posts in the Network tab. This is the actual CORS request from localhost:1111 to the API server on 127.0.0.1:9999. On the right are the HTTP headers for the request (if there are no headers be sure the Headers tab is selected). You should see the Origin header in the list of headers, as shown in figure 3.14.

Notice how the console only shows the request headers, and no response headers. Because the CORS request is failing, the browser hides the response information from the console. Once the server is configured to support CORS, the response information will appear here as well.

Also notice that while the Origin header is present on the request, the code in client.html never added it to the request. The Origin header is silently added to the request by the browser. Next let's take a look at what the Origin header is and how it appears in the request.

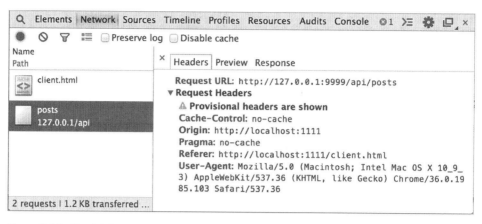

Figure 3.14   The Origin header on the HTTP request

3.4.2   *What is an origin?*

The origin defines where the client resource lives. The origin for the page at http://localhost:1111/client.html is http://localhost:1111. In other words, the origin is everything in the URL up until the path. In more formal terms, the origin is the scheme, host, and port of a URL, as shown in figure 3.15.

Table 3.2 shows the origins for various URLs (note that these are example URLs, and some won't actually work in your browser).

Table 3.2   Origin values for various example URLs

URL	Origin
http://localhost:1111	http://localhost:1111
http://localhost:1111/client.html	http://localhost:1111
https://localhost:1111/client.html	https://localhost:1111
http://localhost/client.html	http://localhost
file:///Users/hossain/ch02/client.html	null

The string `null` can also be a valid value for the origin, even though it doesn't follow the scheme/host/port pattern. Browsers use the value `null` when the origin of the client can't be determined. An example of this is opening a file in your browser. The file

Figure 3.15   The origin consists of the scheme, host, and port.

Figure 3.16 Request with null origin

exists on your local filesystem and isn't loaded from a remote server. Therefore it doesn't have an origin. You can see this in action by double-clicking the client.html file to open it in your browser. Looking in the Network tab, you'll see the Origin header set to `null`, as shown in figure 3.16. It's important to be aware of `null` origin values and respond to them appropriately. We'll cover this in more detail in chapter 6.

The term *origin* may be misleading in the context of CORS because it can be interpreted as the origin of the request. Origin has nothing to do with HTTP requests/responses in this case; it's only a property of a URL. Any URL can have an origin. When an origin refers to the client making the request, we call it the *client origin*. When an origin refers to the URL receiving the request, we call it the *server origin*. Table 3.3 shows the client and server origins for the sample app.

Table 3.3   Client and server origins for the sample app

	URL	Origin
Client	http://localhost:1111/client.html	http://localhost:1111
Server	http://127.0.0.1:9999/api/posts	http://127.0.0.1:9999

There isn't anything inherently special about an origin. It's merely what a browser uses to group content together. Servers use the origin to determine where a request is coming from. Browsers use the origin to define whether a request is same-origin or cross-origin, and exhibits different behavior for each.

SAME-ORIGIN VERSUS CROSS-ORIGIN REQUESTS

With the definition of origin in place, I can provide a more formal definition for same-origin and cross-origin requests. A request is a same-origin request when the client origin and the server origin are exactly the same. Otherwise the request is a cross-origin request.

This distinction between same-origin and cross-origin requests lies at the heart of CORS. When the client initiates the request, the browser extracts the server origin from the URL of the request. It then compares the server origin against the client origin to determine if the request is same-origin or cross-origin. Browsers allow clients to make same-origin requests without any restrictions. But if the request is cross-origin, the browser uses CORS to determine how to handle the request.

In the sample app, the origin of the page at http://127.0.0.1:9999/client.html is http://127.0.0.1:9999. This matches the origin of the API endpoint at http://127.0.0.1:9999/api/posts. Therefore the request is same-origin. On the other hand, the origin for the page at http://localhost:1111/client.html is http://localhost:1111, which doesn't match the origin http://127.0.0.1:9999. Table 3.4 shows example requests along with whether they are same-origin requests.

Table 3.4   Same-origin versus cross-origin requests

Client origin	Server origin	Same-origin request
http://127.0.0.1:9999	http://127.0.0.1:9999	Yes
http://127.0.0.1:9999	https://127.0.0.1:9999	No (different schemes)
http://localhost:1111	http://localhost:9999	No (different ports)
http://localhost:9999/	http://127.0.0.1:9999	No (different hosts)

The last example in table 3.4 might come as a surprise. The IP address for localhost is traditionally 127.0.0.1, so you'd expect http://localhost:9999 and http://127.0.0.1:9999

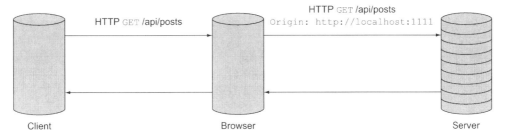

Figure 3.17   The browser adds the Origin header before sending the request to the server.

to be the same origin. But remember that the origin comparison only compares the string values of the scheme, host, and port, and knows nothing about what host an IP address maps to. In this example, "localhost" and "127.0.0.1" are different strings, and therefore the request isn't a same-origin request. Now that you know what an origin is, let's look at how the browser sets the Origin header on requests.

3.4.3   *Setting the Origin header*

The browser adds the Origin header to the HTTP request before sending the request to the server. The browser is solely responsible for setting the Origin header. The Origin header is always present on cross-origin requests, and the client has no way of setting or overriding the value. This is a requirement from a security standpoint: if the client could change the Origin header, they could pretend to be someone they aren't. Figure 3.17 shows how the browser adds the Origin header before sending the request to the server.

 Same-origin requests may sometimes have an Origin header as well. Chrome and Safari include an Origin header on same-origin non-GET requests. In these cases, the Origin header has the same value as the server's origin value. This is important to keep in mind. When identifying CORS requests, it's not enough to check that the Origin header exists. You should also check that the origin value is different from your server's origin value.

 In this section you learned what an Origin header is, where you can find it, and how it can be used to identify a CORS request. Next, let's update the server to respond to the CORS request by using the Access-Control-Allow-Origin response header.

3.5   *Responding to a CORS request*

Look back at the conversation between the browser and the server in figure 3.13. The Origin header got you to the first part of the conversation, where the browser identifies the client. Now let's turn our attention to the second part of the conversation, where the server responds to the browser. The server does this by adding the Access-Control-Allow-Origin header to the response. Let's take a look at how this header works.

3.5.1   *The Access-Control-Allow-Origin header*

The server uses the Access-Control-Allow-Origin response header to approve the request. This header must be present on every successful CORS response. It completes

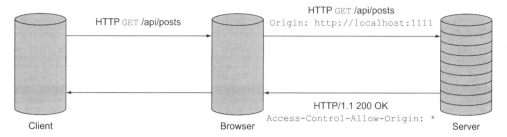

Figure 3.18   Responding to a CORS request using the Access-Control-Allow-Origin header

the conversation by saying "Yup, that client can have access." If this header isn't present, the CORS request will fail.

The Access-Control-Allow-Origin header is an additional response header layered onto the response. It shouldn't affect any other response parameters. If the resource can't be found and returns a 404 error, it should continue returning a 404, even with the Access-Control-Allow-Origin header. Figure 3.18 shows how a server can use the Access-Control-Allow-Origin header to respond to a CORS request.

The value of the Access-Control-Allow-Origin header can be either a wildcard or an origin value. The wildcard value says that clients from any origin can access the resource, while the origin value only gives access to a specific client. Here is an example of both header values.

```
Access-Control-Allow-Origin: *
Access-Control-Allow-Origin: http://localhost:1111
```

Let's look at how to use these header values.

3.5.2   *Access-Control-Allow-Origin with a wildcard (*) value*

An Access-Control-Allow-Origin header with the value * indicates that *any* client can access this resource. In fact, the simplest way to add CORS support to a server is to add `Access-Control-Allow-Origin: *` to every response. Let's modify the sample to do just that.

Listing 3.4 introduces a new piece of middleware to the server named `handleCors`. All CORS-related functionality will go in this middleware. The `handleCors` function adds an Access-Control-Allow-Origin header to the response, then calls `next()` to continue processing the request. (Calling `next()` is a standard pattern that all Express middleware components must follow to continue processing the request.) Finally, you attach the `handleCors` middleware to the server processing pipeline.

When you restart the server and reload the client at http://localhost:1111/client.html, you should see the blog posts loaded on the page. If you examine the request in the Network tab, you'll now see both the HTTP request and response, with the Origin header in the request and the Access-Control-Allow-Origin header in the response, as shown in figure 3.19. Congratulations—with that one line of code, you've added CORS support to the server!

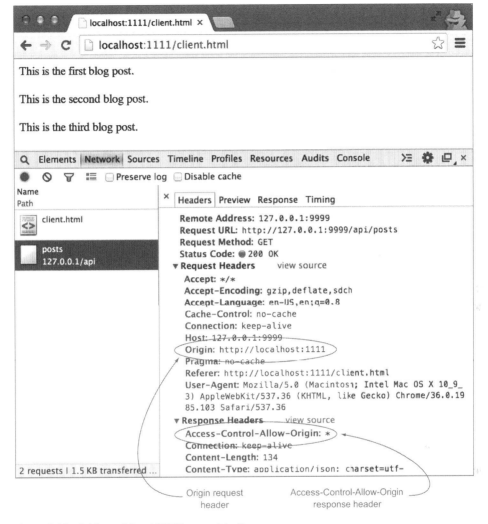

Figure 3.19 Adding wildcard CORS support to the server

Listing 3.4 Adding wildcard CORS support to the server

```
var handleCors = function(req, res, next) {
  res.set('Access-Control-Allow-Origin', '*');
  next();
};

var SERVER_PORT = 9999;
var serverapp = express();
serverapp.use(express.static(__dirname));
serverapp.use(handleCors);
serverapp.get('/api/posts', function(req, res) {
  res.json(POSTS);
});
```

Introduces new
handleCors middleware

Adds Access-Control-Allow-
Origin response header

Adds handleCors
middleware to server

Access-Control-Allow-Origin header
on HTML5rocks.com

Figure 3.20   html5rocks.com always adds the Access-Control-Allow-Origin: * header to responses.

The wildcard value is ideal for situations where anyone can access the data, regardless of the client. A good example is the HTML5Rocks.com website. The website itself is a public resource, accessible from any browser, without any authentication. If you make a request to HTML5rocks.com and examine the response in the console, you'll see the Access-Control-Allow-Origin header as shown in figure 3.20.

Note that although a resource has an `Access-Control-Allow-Origin: *` header, it doesn't necessarily mean that it's publicly accessible. There may be additional forms of authentication on the resource, as you'll see in chapter 6.

The wildcard is just one way to respond to CORS requests. Now let's look at using actual origin values in the Access-Control-Allow-Origin header.

3.5.3 *Access-Control-Allow-Origin with an origin value*

The Access-Control-Allow-Origin header can also have an actual origin as a value. For example:

```
Access-Control-Allow-Origin: http://localhost:1111
```

This header indicates that only clients from http://localhost:1111 can access the resource. Clients from other origins will be rejected.

Let's modify the example to respond with an origin value rather than a wildcard. This is pretty easy to do; simply replace the * value with `http://localhost:1111`, like in the following code snippet.

```
var handleCors = function(req, res, next) {
  res.set('Access-Control-Allow-Origin', 'http://localhost:1111');
  next();
};
```

Restart the server and reload the client at http://localhost:1111/client.html; you should still see the blog posts, with a successful response in the console.

The Access-Control-Allow-Origin header can have only a single origin value. You cannot specify multiple origins in the same header. If your server supports clients from different origins, the Access-Control-Allow-Origin header will have to contain only the origin for the specific client making the request.

Using the origin value is useful when you have a subset of servers, and you only want to allow CORS requests from those servers. For example, a mobile app may host its app on http://mobile.foo.com, but store its private API on http://api.foo.com. In this case a header with `Access-Control-Allow-Origin: http://mobile.foo.com` could be used to limit CORS requests to the http://mobile.foo.com origin only, as shown in figure 3.21.

You've learned of two ways to enable CORS on a server: using a wildcard value, or specifying a specific origin. But what if you want to prevent clients from certain locations from making CORS requests? The next section looks at how to reject CORS requests.

3.5.4 *Rejecting CORS requests*

So far we've covered what to do if you want to accept a CORS request. But what if you only want to allow CORS requests from certain origins and reject the others? CORS is strict in the sense that the Access-Control-Allow-Origin value must either be * or an exact match of the Origin header. Regular expressions or multiple origins aren't allowed; the Access-Control-Allow-Origin can only grant permissions to one origin at a time. If the Access-Control-Allow-Origin isn't * or an exact match of the Origin header, the browser rejects the request.

Table 3.5 summarizes the behavior for Origin and Access-Control-Allow-Origin header combinations. Rejecting a CORS request is as simple as:

- Sending an Access-Control-Allow-Origin header that doesn't match the Origin header
- Removing the Access-Control-Allow-Origin header entirely

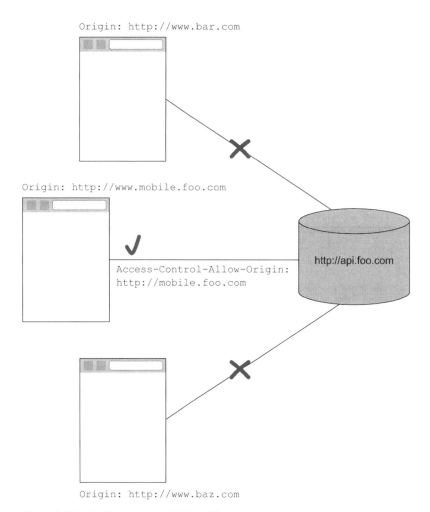

Origin: http://www.bar.com

Origin: http://www.mobile.foo.com

Access-Control-Allow-Origin:
http://mobile.foo.com

http://api.foo.com

Origin: http://www.baz.com

**Figure 3.21   The Access-Control-Allow-Origin only allows access from
http://mobile.foo.com.**

When you last modified the sample app, you updated the Access-Control-Allow-Origin
header to only allow cross-origin requests from http://localhost:1111. Requests from
any other origin will be rejected.

Table 3.5   How the browser reacts to server responses

Client request	Server response	Browser behavior
Origin: http:// localhost:1111	None	Error. No Access-Control-Allow-Origin header.
Origin: http:// localhost:1111	Access-Control-Allow-Origin: *	Success.

Table 3.5 How the browser reacts to server responses *(continued)*

Client request	Server response	Browser behavior
`Origin: http://` `localhost:1111`	`Access-Control-Allow-Origin:` `http://localhost:1111`	Success.
`Origin: http://` `localhost:1111`	`Access-Control-Allow-Origin:` `http://othersite.com`	Error. Access-Control-Allow-Origin header doesn't match Origin header.

What does it mean for the browser to reject the request? It means that the browser doesn't forward any of the response information to the client. The client only knows that an error occurred, but it doesn't receive any additional information about what the error was. This can be frustrating when debugging CORS requests, because it's hard to programmatically infer when a request fails due to CORS rather than some other reason. Chapter 7 delves more into how to debug failing CORS requests.

When the browser rejects the CORS request, it doesn't send the response to the client. But the actual HTTP request is still made to the server, and the server still sends back an HTTP response. It may seem a little odd for the browser to make an HTTP request only to have it rejected. But this must be done because the browser has no way of knowing whether or not CORS is supported without first asking the server by making the request. Figure 3.22 shows the CORS flow when the server rejects the CORS request. The request is still sent to the server ❶. When the browser notices that there is no Access-Control-Allow-Origin header (or the header doesn't match the origin), it triggers an error on the client, and doesn't forward the response details ❷.

Note that this mechanism for rejecting CORS requests also protects servers that know nothing about CORS. Any server that was operational before CORS was introduced needs to be protected from unauthorized CORS requests. If a server knows nothing about CORS, but it receives a CORS request, the server's response will not have an Access-Control-Allow-Origin header, and the request will be rejected. The CORS request will succeed only if the server explicitly opts-in to the request.

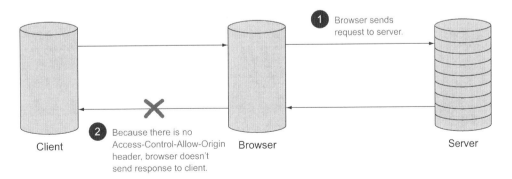

Figure 3.22 CORS flow for a rejected CORS request

There are a number of strategies for accepting and rejecting CORS requests, depending on how open or closed you'd like your server to be. We cover these strategies in chapter 6.

3.6   *Summary*

This chapter provided an overview of how CORS works from the server's perspective. I started by defining the players in a CORS request:

- The client, which initiates the cross-origin request
- The browser, which manages the communication between the client and the server
- The server, which serves data that the client wants

Next, I covered the HTTP headers needed for a basic CORS request:

- The browser sends the Origin header to indicate where a request is coming from.
- An origin is defined as the scheme, host, and port portion of a URL.
- The server responds with the Access-Control-Allow-Origin header if the request is valid.

Finally, you learned that the Access-Control-Allow-Origin header supports two values:

- Setting the Access-Control-Allow-Origin header to * allows cross-origin requests from any client.
- Setting the Access-Control-Allow-Origin header to a specific origin value only allows cross-origin requests from that specific client.

The techniques described in this chapter should give you a good understanding of how CORS works, and how to add simple CORS support to a server. But not all requests can be handled with only the Access-Control-Allow-Origin header. More complex HTTP requests, like PUT or DELETE, or requests with custom HTTP headers, will still fail. Any cross-origin request beyond the simplest request needs additional processing to succeed. We'll cover these new processing techniques in the next chapter.

Handling preflight requests

The previous chapter showed how to respond to CORS requests by using the Access-Control-Allow-Origin header. While this header is required on all valid CORS responses, there are some cases where the Access-Control-Allow-Origin header alone isn't enough. Certain types of requests, such as DELETE or PUT, need to go a step further and ask for the server's permission before making the actual request.

The browser asks for permissions by using what is called a *preflight* request. A preflight request is a small request that is sent by the browser before the actual request. It contains information like which HTTP method is used, as well as if any custom HTTP headers are present. The preflight gives the server a chance to examine what the actual request will look like before it's made. The server can then indicate whether the browser should send the actual request, or return an error to the client without sending the request.

This chapter will examine what a preflight request is and when it's used. Next it will introduce headers the server can use to respond to a preflight. It will then introduce the preflight cache, which is a browser optimization that helps limit the number of preflight requests that are made.

4.1 What is a preflight request?

Let's think about a preflight request in the context of the ATM example from chapter 3. Banks sometimes put their ATMs inside a room behind a locked door. The door can only be unlocked by swiping your ATM card (or if a kind person lets you in, but let's ignore that for now). Once you're inside, you can walk up to the ATM and withdraw money. The simple act of swiping your card to unlock the door doesn't automatically give you money, but it's a quick check to verify that you have permission to use the ATM.

In a similar fashion, a preflight request asks for the server's permission to send the request. The preflight isn't the request itself. Instead, it contains metadata about it, such as which HTTP method is used and if the client added additional request headers. The server inspects this metadata to decide whether the browser is allowed to send the request.

By asking for permission before making the request, the preflight introduces an additional processing step to CORS. Let's dig deeper into how this new step fits into your existing understanding of CORS.

4.1.1 Lifecycle of a preflight request

Chapter 3 framed CORS requests in the context of a conversation between the browser and the server. The preflight augments this conversation with additional dialogue, as shown in figure 4.1. This conversation is a bit longer than the conversation from chapter 3. It adds the first two lines, where the browser asks the server for permission to use the DELETE method. These two lines are the preflight request, while the last two lines are the CORS request.

Figure 4.2 expands figure 3.12 in chapter 3 to show how the preflight request fits into the lifecycle of a CORS request. The browser uses the server's response to the preflight to determine if the request can be made. If the server grants the right permissions on the preflight response, the browser sends the request to the server. The server can also decide not to approve the request, in which case the browser will return an error to the client, and the request will never be sent.

Now that you have a sense of what a preflight request is, let's discuss why it exists in the first place.

4.1.2 Why does the preflight request exist?

The concept of a preflight was introduced to allow cross-origin requests to be made without breaking existing servers that depend on the browser's same-origin policy. If the preflight hits a server that is CORS-enabled, the server knows what a preflight request is and can respond appropriately. But if the preflight hits a server that doesn't know or doesn't care about CORS, the server won't send the correct preflight response, and the actual request will never be sent. The preflight protects unsuspecting servers from receiving cross-origin requests they may not want.

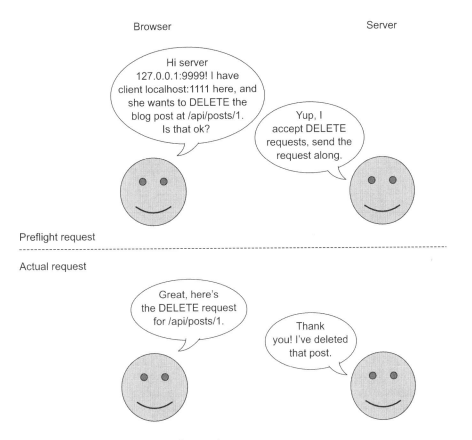

Figure 4.1 Preflight versus actual request

This is best conveyed by a story. Imagine it is is 2004. The web is still young, the term Web 2.0 was only recently coined, and you're the administrator of a small news site. Much like the sample app, this site uses XMLHttpRequests to load news data from an

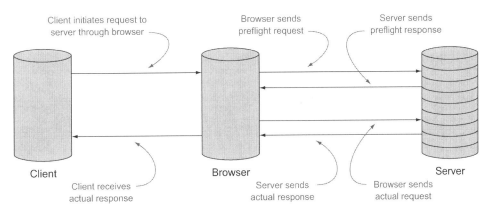

Figure 4.2 Lifecycle of a CORS request (with preflight)

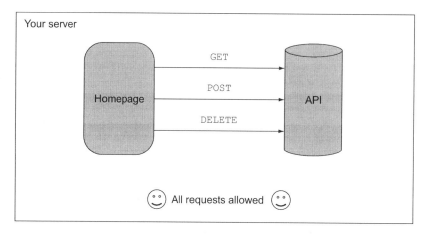

Figure 4.3   Your server, circa 2004. CORS doesn't yet exist, but your site and your API live under the same origin, so they can communicate.

API, as shown in figure 4.3. Because your site lives under the same origin as your API, it can make any type of HTTP request to the API.

Not only does this API fetch news stories, but it also lets you, the owner, edit and delete news items. While you have basic security measures in place, your code never checks which origin a request is coming from, because why should it? All browsers enforce the same-origin policy. There is no such thing as CORS (remember this is 2004), so there is no way for clients from other origins to access your API.

Now fast-forward to 2009. Your news site has become much more popular, and it's still humming along nicely, thanks to the clean architectural separation between your frontend and the API. But then late one night you read that Chrome 4.0 will be released soon, and it supports this new feature called Cross-Origin Resource Sharing that allows cross-origin requests.

You find this a bit troubling, and that night you have nightmares of your server being deluged with all sorts of requests from servers across the web, as shown in figure 4.4. You wake in a cold sweat wondering how you'll protect your server from these cross-origin requests. Will users suddenly be able to send DELETE requests without your permission? Why would browsers suddenly break the same-origin policy you have come to rely on?

Luckily, CORS answers these questions. The arrival of CORS didn't cause thousands of server administrators to wake in a cold sweat. In fact, browser support for CORS was a fairly painless rollout because when the CORS spec was being drafted, the spec authors recognized that CORS needed to be introduced in a way that was compatible with existing servers.

The answer to preserving backward compatibility was to introduce the preflight request. The preflight request is a way for the browser to ask the server if it's okay to send a cross-origin request before sending the actual request. The same-origin policy is still

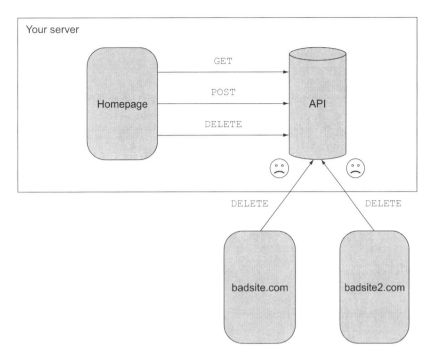

Figure 4.4 A CORS nightmare scenario. Cross-origin requests are made without any permission from the server. Thankfully this isn't how CORS is implemented.

preserved, because the request is never made unless the server grants permission. An existing server that knows nothing about CORS can safely ignore the preflight request, and the browser will not forward the actual request to the server, as shown in figure 4.5.

To return to the story, after learning about the CORS preflight request, you rest a little easier that night, knowing that your server won't receive any unauthorized requests from other people's servers.

This story demonstrates why the preflight was introduced: it allows cross-origin requests to be introduced to the web in a way that doesn't adversely affect existing servers. Now that you know why the preflight request exists, let's modify the sample code to trigger a preflight request.

4.2 Triggering a preflight request

Chapter 3 introduced a sample blogging app that loads blog posts using CORS. Let's modify that to let the user delete blog posts. The standard method for deleting data in a REST API is to use the HTTP DELETE method, so we'll use that here.

Listing 4.1 modifies client.html to display a Delete link next to each blog post. Clicking the link calls the deletePost JavaScript function. The deletePost function deletes a blog post by sending a DELETE request to the URL /api/posts/{ID}, where {ID} is the blog post's ID. For example, a request to /api/posts/1 would delete the blog post with an ID of 1. If the delete is successful, the post is removed from the page.

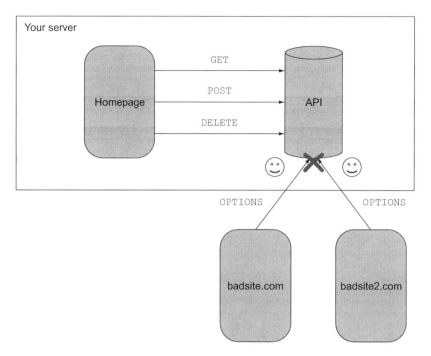

Figure 4.5   The CORS preflight request prevents unauthorized API requests from ever reaching your server.

Listing 4.1   Adding a function to delete posts

```
var getBlogPosts = function() {
  var xhr = createXhr('GET', 'http://127.0.0.1:9999/api/posts');
  xhr.onload = function() {
    var data = JSON.parse(xhr.responseText);
    var elem = document.getElementById('output');
    for (var postId in data) {
      var postText = data[postId]['post'];
      var div = document.createElement('div');
      div.className = 'post';
      div.id = 'postId' + postId;
      div.appendChild(document.createTextNode(postText));

      var a = document.createElement('a');
      a.innerHTML = 'Delete post #' + postId;
      a.href = '#';
      a.onclick = function(postId) {
        return function() {
          deletePost(postId);
        };
      }(postId);
      div.appendChild(document.createTextNode(' '));
      div.appendChild(a);
```

**Adds a Delete link
next to blog post**

```
        elem.appendChild(div);
      }
    };
    xhr.send();
  };
                                                          Processes
                                                          delete request
  var deletePost = function(postId) {
    var url = 'http://127.0.0.1:9999/api/posts/' + postId;
    var xhr = createXhr('DELETE', url);
    xhr.onload = function() {
      if (xhr.status == 204) {
        var element = document.getElementById('postId' + postId);
        element.parentNode.removeChild(element);
      }
    };
    xhr.send();
  };
```

This listing modifies the client code. Now let's turn our attention to the server code to respond to the DELETE request. Listing 4.2 modifies the app.js server code to handle the incoming DELETE request. It listens for DELETE requests on the /api/posts/{ID} URL. When it receives a DELETE request, the code deletes the post with the corresponding ID and returns the HTTP 204 status code. HTTP 204 means that the request was successful, but the body has no content; it's the traditional response code used for DELETE requests in REST APIs.

Listing 4.2 Adding server support for deleting posts

```
serverapp.get('/api/posts', function(req, res) {
  res.json(POSTS);                                        Listens for delete
});                                                       requests on
serverapp.delete('/api/posts/:id', function(req, res) {  /api/posts/{ID}
  delete POSTS[req.params.id];
  res.status(204).end();                                 Returns
});                                                       HTTP 204
serverapp.listen(SERVER_PORT, function() {
  console.log('Started server at http://localhost:' + SERVER_PORT);
});
```

Deletes blog post

After making the changes in listings 4.1 and 4.2, restart the server and reload the client.html page. You should see a Delete link next to each blog post, as shown in figure 4.6.

The code looks like it should work, because you added CORS support to your server in the previous chapter. But if you click a Delete link, you'll see the error message shown in figure 4.7. What is going on here?

Looking at the error in figure 4.7, one inconsistency should stand out: although the code is making a DELETE request ❶, the error is on an OPTIONS request ❷. The browser never sends the DELETE request. This certainly looks weird, but this isn't a bug. What you're seeing is the preflight request.

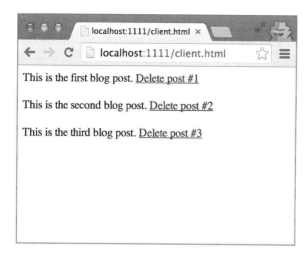

Figure 4.6   Adding a Delete link next to each blog post

Seeing the preflight on the DELETE request may lead you to ask, why didn't the GET request to load posts also have a preflight? The preflight request is only sent some of the time. The next section looks at when a preflight request is sent.

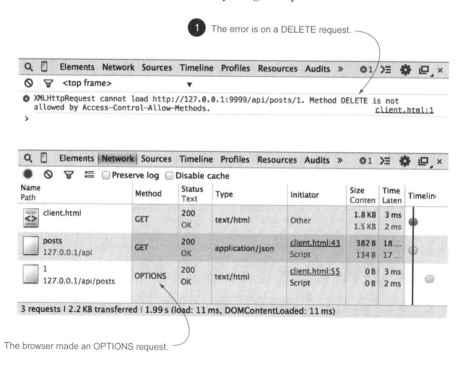

Figure 4.7   Error message when trying to delete a post

4.2.1 When is a preflight request sent?

Even with the same-origin policy in place, there are ways to make some types of cross-origin requests from the browser. Appendix D goes into more details about these techniques, but here are two ways the client can circumvent the same-origin policy:

- *A web page can easily make GET requests to another origin.* Every `<script>` tag or `<img>` tag issues a `GET` request.
- *A web page can make POST requests via the <form> tag.* The `<form>` tag also allows the Content-Type header to be set to `application/x-www-form-urlencoded`, `multipart/form-data`, or `text/plain`.

The following listing shows the code that can be used to make these cross-origin requests. (You don't need to download or run this listing, it's only meant as an example.)

Listing 4.3 Making cross-origin requests without CORS

```
<html><body>                                            Using HTML to make GET
                                                        request for an image
<img src="http://example.com/image.jpg">  ←─┘

<form enctype="text/plain" method="post" action="http://example.com/
    form_submit" id="myform">                ←─┐
  <input type="submit" value="Submit" />        Using HTML to make POST request
</form>                                          with a Content-Type header

<script>
                                                Using JavaScript to make
var img = document.createElement('img');        GET request for an image
img.src = 'http://example.com/image.jpg';  ←─┘

var myform = document.getElementById('myform');
myform.submit();                           ←─   Using JavaScript to make POST
                                                request with a Content-Type header
</script>
</body></html>
```

These techniques existed long before the concept of CORS and preflights. Because the browser can make these requests without CORS, the preflight doesn't provide any additional value. For example, if there were a preflight on a `GET` request, the client could always use a `script` tag to get around the preflight. The browser skips the preflight in cases where the client can already make the cross-origin request through other means.

This gives a general overview of when a preflight is used. To state it more concretely, a preflight request is issued when a request meets any of the following criteria:

- It uses an HTTP method other than `GET`, `POST`, or `HEAD`
- It sets the Content-Type request header with values other than
  a `application/x-www-form-urlencoded`
  b `multipart/form-data`
  c `text/plain`

- It sets additional request headers that are not
  - a Accept
  - b Accept-Language
  - c Content-Language
- The `XMLHttpRequest` contains upload events (section 4.5 shows an example using upload events)

The CORS spec collectively refers to these HTTP methods as *simple methods*, and the HTTP headers as *simple headers*. If these rules seem like a bit of a hodgepodge, it's because they are. There isn't any rhyme or reason as to why those rules are defined that way. It's a result of how the web has evolved over the past 20 years. But how these rules were defined isn't as important as identifying and responding to preflight requests. The next section modifies the sample app to respond to the preflight for the `DELETE` request.

4.3   *Identifying a preflight request*

In the context of the CORS lifecycle diagram, the preflight request is the first request sent from the browser to the server, as shown in figure 4.8. If a preflight request is just another HTTP request, how do you distinguish it from actual requests? The first thing you need to do is figure out what a preflight request looks like.

There are three characteristics of a preflight request, as shown in figure 4.9 it uses the HTTP `OPTIONS` method ❶, it has an Origin request header ❷, and it has an Access-Control-Request-Method header ❸.

Figure 4.9 shows the preflight request from the sample with each of these three characteristics highlighted. All three characteristics must exist on the request for it to be a preflight request. If any one of these pieces is missing, the request isn't a preflight. Let's dig deeper into what each of these pieces is.

4.3.1   *Origin header*

In chapter 3 you learned that every CORS request must have an Origin header. The preflight is no different. Without the Origin header, the request isn't a CORS request, and therefore it can't be a preflight request.

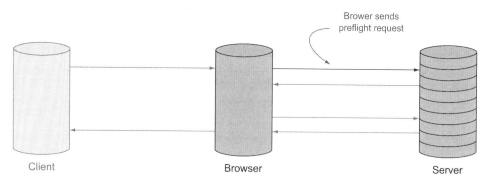

Figure 4.8   Preflight request

Brower sends preflight request

Client   Browser   Server

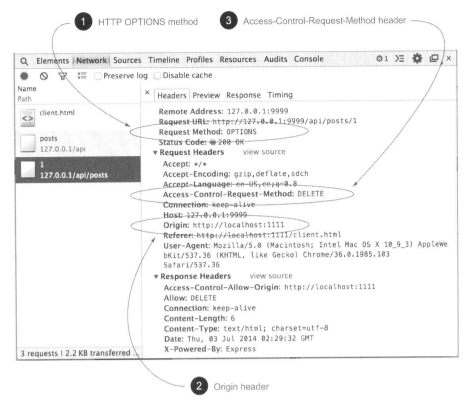

Figure 4.9   The pieces of a preflight request

The Origin header tells you where the request is coming from. The value of the Origin header on a preflight request is the same value as the Origin header on the actual request. So if you're making a CORS request from http://localhost:1111, the Origin header on the preflight request will also have the value http://localhost:1111.

4.3.2   HTTP OPTIONS method

A preflight request must be made via the HTTP OPTIONS method, which is defined by the HTTP spec and isn't specific to CORS. The HTTP spec (RFC2616) defines an OPTIONS request as "a request for information about the communication options available on the request/response chain." This means that even before CORS, clients could use the OPTIONS method to learn more about an endpoint. When used outside of CORS, the OPTIONS method traditionally conveys which HTTP methods are supported on a particular URL. Table 4.1 shows an example of a non-CORS OPTIONS request to a server. The Allow response header is used to indicate which HTTP methods are supported at the /api/posts endpoint, without triggering an actual request to the /api/posts endpoint.

Table 4.1   What an HTTP OPTIONS **request and response might look like in a pre-CORS world**

HTTP request	HTTP response
OPTIONS /api/posts HTTP/1.1 User-Agent: Chrome Host: 127.0.0.1:9999 Accept: */*	HTTP/1.1 200 OK Allow: GET, POST

> **NOTE**   You may have noticed that the preflight request itself is a cross-origin request. This was deemed acceptable by the CORS spec authors, because the preflight request is used in the way OPTIONS requests are intended.

An OPTIONS request with an Origin header is not necessarily a preflight request. To distinguish a regular OPTIONS request from a preflight OPTIONS request, a preflight request will always contain an Access-Control-Request-Method header, as discussed next.

4.3.3   *Access-Control-Request-Method header*

The Access-Control-Request-Method request header asks the server for permission to make a request using a particular HTTP method. The preceding example of deleting a post uses the HTTP DELETE method. Therefore, the Access-Control-Request-Method header would be set to DELETE:

```
Access-Control-Request-Method: DELETE
```

The Access-Control-Request-Method header is always set to the value of the HTTP method for the actual request, as shown in table 4.2. Because an HTTP request must have an HTTP method, a preflight request must have an Access-Control-Request-Method header.

Table 4.2   Mapping the actual request method to the preflight

Preflight request	Actual request
OPTIONS /data HTTP/1.1 User-Agent: Chrome Host: localhost:10009 Accept: */* Origin: http://localhost:10007 **Access-Control-Request-Method: DELETE**	**DELETE** /data HTTP/1.1 User-Agent: Chrome Host: localhost:10009 Accept: */* Origin: http://localhost:10007

To recap, a preflight request must have an HTTP OPTIONS method, and it must contain an Origin and Access-Control-Request-Method header. Now that you know what comprises a preflight request, let's modify the sample code to detect these three characteristics.

4.3.4 *Putting it all together*

Listing 4.4 adds an `isPreflight` method to the sample app that detects whether an incoming request is a preflight request. The `isPreflight` method checks three things:

- Is the request an HTTP OPTIONS request?
- Does the request have an Origin header?
- Does the request have an Access-Control-Request-Method header?

Listing 4.4 Checking if the request is a preflight

Does the request have an Access-Control-Request-Method header?

Is the request an HTTP OPTIONS request?

Does the request have an Origin header?

```
var isPreflight = function(req) {
  var isHttpOptions = req.method === 'OPTIONS';
  var hasOriginHeader = req.headers['origin'];
  var hasRequestMethod = req.headers['access-control-request-method'];
  return isHttpOptions && hasOriginHeader && hasRequestMethod;
};

var handleCors = function(req, res, next) {
  res.set('Access-Control-Allow-Origin', 'http://localhost:1111');
  if (isPreflight(req)) {
    console.log('Received a preflight request!');
    res.status(204).end();
    return;
  }
  next();
};
```

If request is a preflight, stops processing it and displays a message.

If all three criteria are true, the request is a preflight. If you reload the sample and click a Delete link, you should see the text "Received a preflight request!" in the server's terminal window, as shown in figure 4.10.

```
> node app.js
Started server at http://127.0.0.1:9999
Started client at http://localhost:1111
Received a preflight request!
```

Figure 4.10 The server successfully received a preflight request.

This verifies that the server has detected a preflight request. But the request still fails because you aren't responding to the preflight. Next you'll learn how to respond to the preflight.

4.4 *Responding to a preflight request*

Now that you have detected the preflight request, the server needs to respond so that the browser can make the actual request. The server's preflight response, shown in figure 4.11, grants permissions to make the HTTP request. These permissions are granted by setting HTTP headers on the response. This section will show which HTTP headers the server needs to set to respond to a preflight, and how to reject a preflight if the request isn't allowed.

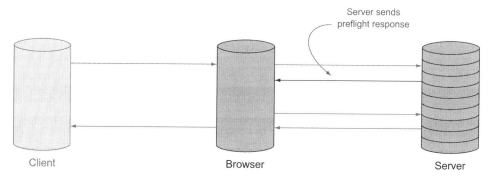

Figure 4.11   After receiving a preflight request, the server sends a preflight response that may grant permissions to make the actual HTTP request.

4.4.1   *Supporting HTTP methods with Access-Control-Allow-Methods*

Thinking back to the conversation between the browser and the server in figure 4.1, responding to a preflight involves telling the browser that the server accepts DELETE requests from different origins. The server does this by setting the Access-Control-Allow-Methods response header as follows:

```
Access-Control-Allow-Methods: DELETE
```

This header indicates that the server grants permissions to the client to make a DELETE request to that URL. The Access-Control-Allow-Methods header may look a lot like the Access-Control-Request-Method header, but they're quite different. The Access-Control-Request-Method is a single value that asks permission to use a specific HTTP method. The Access-Control-Allow-Methods header grants permissions to use one or more HTTP methods, and it can have multiple values. If you wanted to open your API endpoint to all HTTP methods, you can put the following values in the Access-Control-Allow-Methods header:

```
Access-Control-Allow-Methods: HEAD, GET, POST, PUT, DELETE
```

Let's turn back to the sample code and update it to respond to the preflight request.

UPDATING THE SAMPLE TO SUPPORT DELETE

The following listing modifies the sample code to respond to the preflight request. If the request is a preflight, the code adds an Access-Control-Allow-Methods header to the response.

> **Listing 4.5   Modifying `handleCors` to respond to a preflight**

```
var handleCors = function(req, res, next) {
  res.set('Access-Control-Allow-Origin', 'http://localhost:1111');
  if (isPreflight(req)) {
    res.set('Access-Control-Allow-Methods', 'GET, DELETE');   ⟵   Adds Access-Control-
    res.status(204).end();                                          Allow-Methods
    return;                                                          response header
  }
```

```
   next();
};
```

Now, finally, if you restart the server, reload the page, and click a Delete link, the blog post will be deleted. The deleted post will disappear from the page as a confirmation that the delete was successful. Figure 4.12 shows the two HTTP requests being made to delete the post.

NOTE If this were a real app, the corresponding blog post would be permanently deleted from the database. Because the sample doesn't have a database, the deleted posts will reappear when you restart the web server.

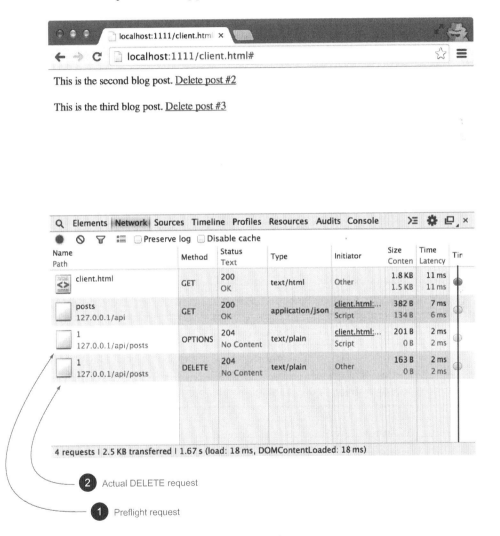

Figure 4.12 The preflight followed by the `DELETE` request

In addition to the Access-Control-Allow-Methods header, the preflight response should have the following characteristics:

- *The HTTP response status should be in the 200 range.* This is defined by the CORS spec (although some browsers still process the response correctly if the status isn't in the 200 range). The sample code uses response code 204, which indicates the response is valid, but contains no body.

- *The response shouldn't have a body.* There isn't anything in the CORS spec regarding the body of the preflight response, but having a body could cause confusion for the developer, because he or she then must know how to parse and interpret the body. It's better to keep things simple and stick to the CORS headers only.

- *If a method is a simple method, it doesn't need to be listed in the Access-Control-Allow-Methods header.* (Recall from section 4.2 that the CORS spec defines simple methods as `GET`, `POST`, and `HEAD`.) If the client sends an `Access-Control-Request-Method: GET` request header, the server doesn't need to include the Access-Control-Allow-Methods header in the response. But this can be confusing. For consistency, the rest of the samples in this chapter will always include the Access-Control-Allow-Methods header, even for simple HTTP methods.

With the changes done so far, the server can now support CORS for various HTTP methods. But we aren't done with the preflight quite yet. A preflight request is also sent when the client adds additional headers to a request. The next section covers how to respond to those requests.

4.4.2 *Supporting request headers with Access-Control-Allow-Headers*

The previous section taught you how the server can respond to a preflight request to grant permissions to use HTTP methods. But this isn't the only type of preflight a server can receive. A browser may also send a preflight if the request contains additional HTTP headers from the client. The modified browser/server conversation is shown in figure 4.13.

TRIGGERING A PREFLIGHT FOR REQUEST HEADERS

To see this in action, let's modify the `getBlogPost` method to include a couple of additional headers when loading the blog posts. It really doesn't matter what the headers are, so let's make some up:

- *Timezone-Offset*—The user's time zone offset in minutes. This can be calculated from JavaScript.

- *Sample-Source*—The name of this book, *CORS in Action*.

The following listing adds these headers to the sample code. Again, the actual values of these headers aren't important; they are needed only to see how CORS behaves.

Listing 4.6   Adding headers to the request

```
var getBlogPosts = function() {
  var xhr = createXhr('GET', 'http://127.0.0.1:9999/api/posts');
```

```
xhr.setRequestHeader('Timezone-Offset',
                     new Date().getTimezoneOffset());
xhr.setRequestHeader('Sample-Source',
                     'CORS in Action');
xhr.onload = function() {
...
```

When you reload the client page, none of the posts will load, and you'll see an error message similar to the one you saw with the DELETE method, as shown in figure 4.14. Only this time the error is about the new headers and not the HTTP method. If you inspect the request in the Network tab as shown in figure 4.15, you can see that the preflight request has a new Access-Control-Request-Headers header with the additional header values.

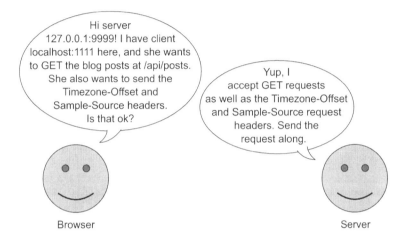

Preflight request

Figure 4.13 Conversation between browser and server for additional headers

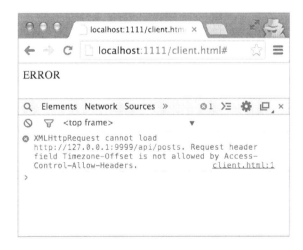

Figure 4.14 Error when trying to add additional headers to a request

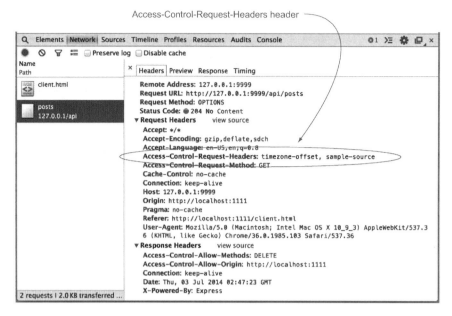

Access-Control-Request-Headers header

Figure 4.15   Preflight request has a new Access-Control-Request-Headers header

NOTE   It may be surprising to see that the preflight request is sent even though the request is a GET request. After all, didn't we add support for GET requests in chapter 3? Adding custom headers to a cross-origin request is a new functionality that wasn't possible before CORS. Therefore, it needs a preflight, even if the HTTP method wouldn't normally trigger a preflight.

In the same way that the Access-Control-Request-Method header asks permission to use a particular HTTP method, the Access-Control-Request-Headers header asks permission to send additional headers to the server. Table 4.3 shows how the request maps onto the Access-Control-Request-Headers header.

Table 4.3   Mapping the actual request headers to the preflight

Preflight request	Actual request
OPTIONS /api/posts HTTP/1.1 User-Agent: Chrome Host: 127.0.0.1:9999 Accept: */* Origin: http://localhost:1111 **Access-Control-Request-Method: GET** **Access-Control-Request-Headers: Timezone-** **Offset, Sample-Source**	GET /api/posts HTTP/1.1 User-Agent: Chrome Host: 127.0.0.1:9999 Accept: */* Origin: http:// localhost:1111 **Timezone-Offset: 300** **Sample-Source: Cors in Action**

The Access-Control-Request-Headers header serves a similar purpose as its Access-Control-Request-Method counterpart, but there are differences. While the Access-Control-Request-Method header can have only one value, the Access-Control-Request-Headers header can have multiple values separated by a comma. And while a preflight request will always have an Access-Control-Request-Method header, the Access-Control-Request-Headers header is optional, and is only present if the client adds headers to the request.

ALLOWING CUSTOM HEADERS ON THE REQUEST

The server responds to the preflight request by adding the Access-Control-Allow-Headers header. The Access-Control-Allow-Headers header contains a list of headers that are allowed in requests. The following response header indicates that the client has permission to include the Timezone-Offset and the Sample-Source headers on requests:

```
Access-Control-Allow-Headers: Timezone-Offset, Sample-Source
```

If all the values in the Access-Control-Request-Headers request header match the values in the Access-Control-Allow-Headers response header, the browser is granted permission to make the request. If the browser requested a header, and that header isn't present in the Access-Control-Allow-Headers header, the request is rejected. Table 4.4 shows an example of a valid and an invalid Access-Control-Allow-Headers header.

Table 4.4 Responding to Access-Control-Request-Headers by using Access-Control-Allow-Headers. All requested headers must also be in the response for the CORS request to succeed.

Response header	Preflight request status
Access-Control-Allow-Headers: Timezone-Offset, Sample-Source	Accepted. Timezone-Offset and Sample-Source were requested, and both are present in the Access-Control-Allow-Headers header.
Access-Control-Allow-Headers: Timezone-Offset, Sample-Source, Anything-Else	Accepted. Same as the previous case. Even though the Anything-Else header is not present in the request, it's okay to specify additional values in the Access-Control-Allow-Headers header.
Access-Control-Allow-Headers: Timezone-Offset	Rejected. Both Timezone-Offset and Sample-Source were requested, but only Timezone-Offset is present in the Access-Control-Allow-Headers header.

Listing 4.7 recaps how the browser translates additional headers from code into the preflight request, and how these headers flow from preflight request to preflight response to actual request. The preflight starts in the developer's JavaScript code, which adds new headers to the XMLHttpRequest ❶. The browser notices that there are additional headers and puts them in the Access-Control-Request-Headers header in the preflight ❷. The server responds by including those same headers in the Access-Control-Allow-Headers response ❸. Finally, the browser validates that the headers match those requested by the developer, and sends the request to the server ❹.

Listing 4.7 Flow of additional headers on CORS requests

JavaScript code: ←
```
var xhr = new XMLHttpRequest();
xhr.setRequestHeader('Timezone-Offset');
xhr.setRequestHeader('Sample-Source');
```

Preflight request: ◁─❷

```
OPTIONS /api/posts HTTP/1.1
User-Agent: Chrome
Host: 127.0.0.1:9999
Accept: */*
Origin: http://localhost:1111
Access-Control-Request-Method: GET
Access-Control-Request-Headers: Timezone-Offset, Sample-Source
```

Preflight response: ◁─❸

```
HTTP/1.1 204 No Content
Access-Control-Allow-Origin: http://localhost:1111
Access-Control-Allow-Methods: GET, DELETE
Access-Control-Allow-Headers: Timezone-Offset, Sample-Source
```

Actual request: ◁─❹

```
GET /api/posts HTTP/1.1
User-Agent: Chrome
Host: 127.0.0.1:9999
Accept: */*
Origin: http://localhost:1111
Timezone-Offset: 300
Sample-Source: Cors in Action
```

> **NOTE**   If the requested header is a simple header, it's not required to be
> included in the Access-Control-Allow-Headers response header. But I recom-
> mend including simple headers to avoid confusion.

Listing 4.8 modifies the sample code to respond to the Access-Control-Request-Headers
header. The code sets the Access-Control-Allow-Headers header to the value of the
headers you support. It also adds the GET method to the list of allowed HTTP methods,
because the custom headers are sent on a GET request. The sample will work fine even
without adding GET to the Access-Control-Allow-Methods header (because GET is a
simple method), but I like to include it to avoid confusion. Restart the server and
reload the page, and the blog posts should reappear.

Listing 4.8   Responding to Access-Control-Request-Headers

```
var handleCors = function(req, res, next) {
  res.set('Access-Control-Allow-Origin', 'http://localhost:1111');     Adds GET to the
  if (isPreflight(req)) {                                               Access-Control-
    res.set('Access-Control-Allow-Methods', 'GET, DELETE');       ◁─   Allow-Methods
    res.set('Access-Control-Allow-Headers',             ◁─┐            response header
            'Timezone-Offset, Sample-Source');
    res.status(204).end();
    return;                                      Adds Access-Control-Allow-
  }                                              Headers to preflight response
  next();
};
```

After the server responds to the preflight request, the browser inspects the preflight
response and verifies that the server is granting the appropriate permissions. If the
preflight response checks out, the browser sends the actual request to the server.

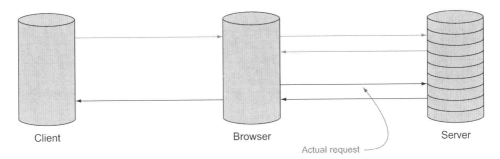

Figure 4.16   Sending the actual request

4.4.3   *Sending the actual request*

Once the browser receives a successful preflight response, it sends the actual request to the server, as shown in figure 4.16.

In the blogging app, once the browser receives the preflight response, it sends the HTTP DELETE request to delete the blog post. The DELETE request can be handled using the same technique you learned in chapter 3: add an Access-Control-Allow-Origin header.

The following listing highlights the code that adds the Access-Control-Allow-Origin header to the response. This code is from chapter 3. You don't need to write any new code—the Access-Control-Allow-Origin header is added to both preflight and actual responses.

Listing 4.9   Adding the Access-Control-Allow-Origin header to all CORS responses

```
var handleCors = function(req, res, next) {
  res.set('Access-Control-Allow-Origin', 'http://localhost:1111');    ⟵   The Access-
  if (isPreflight(req)) {                                                   Control-Allow-
    res.set('Access-Control-Allow-Methods', 'GET, DELETE');               Origin header is
    res.set('Access-Control-Allow-Headers',                               added to both
            'Timezone-Offset, Sample-Source');                            preflight and
    res.status(204).end();                                                actual CORS
    return;                                                               requests.
  }
  next();
};
```

We've spent a lot of time talking about how to successfully respond to a preflight request. But there may be times when you don't want a request to be made. Next, let's turn our attention to rejecting a preflight request.

4.4.4   *Rejecting a preflight request*

We've explored how to successfully respond to a preflight request. But there may also be times when you want to reject a CORS request. Perhaps your server doesn't support the DELETE method at a particular endpoint. How do you tell the browser that the request isn't allowed?

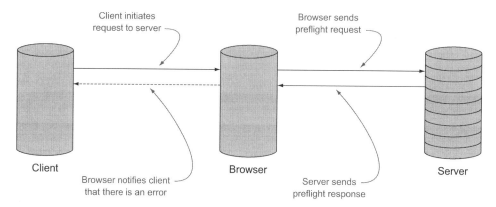

Figure 4.17   If the server rejects a preflight request, the browser returns an error to the client without ever sending the actual request.

Rejecting a CORS request "short-circuits" the request, as shown in figure 4.17. The browser makes the preflight request to the server, and when the server rejects the request, the browser notifies the client code that the request was rejected. The client code doesn't receive the actual preflight response, nor does it receive any additional data about why the request failed (even though the console log shows this information).

As mentioned in chapter 1, servers must opt-in to CORS. That means if a server's response doesn't exactly match what the browser expects, the browser plays it safe and rejects the request. With that in mind, there are many ways for a server to reject a preflight request, including:

- Leave out the Access-Control-Allow-Origin header (if the requested method is not a simple method).
- Return a value in Access-Control-Allow-Methods that doesn't match the Access-Control-Request-Method header.
- If the preflight request has an Access-Control-Request-Headers header:
  - Leave out the Access-Control-Allow-Headers header.
  - Return a value in the Access-Control-Allow-Headers header that doesn't match the Access-Control-Request-Headers header.

Returning a non-200 HTTP response code as the preflight response will not reject the request in some browsers. This may sound surprising, because a non-200 status code is used to signal that something isn't right. But in this case, even though the CORS spec explicitly states that the preflight response should be in the 200 range, some browsers still allow non-200 responses. It's still a good idea to stick to the HTTP 200 or 204 status code, because it adheres to the spec, which won't change.

Table 4.5 shows ways to reject the preflight request. Suppose someone tries to send a request header named `Shady-Status` to the sample app. You don't want your server to receive this header, so the server code should reject the preflight.

```
OPTIONS /api/posts HTTP/1.1
Origin: http://localhost:1111
Access-Control-Request-Method: DELETE
Access-Control-Request-Headers: Shady-Status
```

Table 4.5 Various ways to reject a CORS preflight request

Response	Reason
`HTTP/1.1 200 OK`	No Access-Control-Allow-Origin header
`HTTP/1.1 200 OK` `Access-Control-Allow-Origin: *`	No Access-Control-Allow-Methods header

`HTTP/1.1 200 OK`
`Access-Control-Allow-Origin: *`
`Access-Control-Allow-Methods: DELETE`
	No Access-Control-Allow-Headers header

`HTTP/1.1 200 OK`
`Access-Control-Allow-Origin: *`
`Access-Control-Allow-Methods: DELETE`
`Access-Control-Allow-Headers: Foo`
	Access-Control-Allow-Headers doesn't match

`HTTP/1.1 200 OK`
`Access-Control-Allow-Origin: *`
`Access-Control-Allow-Methods: GET`
`Access-Control-Allow-Headers: Shady-`
`Status`
	Access-Control-Allow-Methods doesn't match

As you can see, there are a lot of ways to reject a preflight request. Which one should you choose? Chapter 6 provides guidance for rejecting CORS requests.

The last few sections threw a lot of information your way. The next section takes a step back and reviews what you've learned so far.

4.5   Recapping preflights

The first thing you may have noticed is that there are a lot of different headers involved when working with preflights. Table 4.6 recaps these headers and what they mean.

Table 4.6 Preflight request headers and their corresponding response headers

Request header	Details	Response header	Details
Access-Control-Request-Method	Indicates the HTTP method for the actual request	Access-Control-Allow-Methods	Indicates which HTTP methods are supported at that endpoint Can contain multiple values
Access-Control-Request-Headers	Indicates additional headers on the request Can contain multiple values Optional	Access-Control-Allow-Headers	Indicates which HTTP headers are supported at that endpoint Can contain multiple values

A simple way to distinguish these headers is to remember that any header starting with "Access-Control-Request-" is a request header added by the browser asking the server for permissions, and any header starting with "Access-Control-Allow-" is a response header sent by the server that grants permissions.

Figure 4.18 revisits the end-to-end flow from figure 4.2, except this time it includes the header and code that is exchanged among the client, browser, and server. The

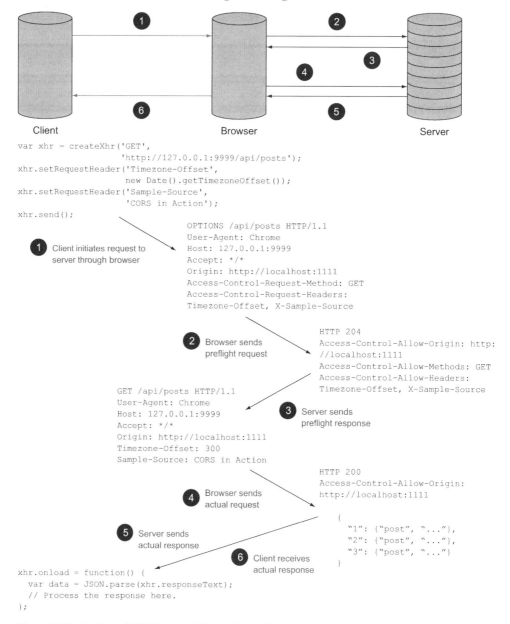

Figure 4.18   End-to-end CORS request flow (with preflight)

JavaScript code initiates the request by calling the XMLHttpRequest's send method ❶. The browser intercepts the request and initiates a preflight request ❷. If the server provides a valid preflight response ❸, the browser follows up by sending the actual request ❹. The server responds to the actual request ❺. This actual request is then sent to the calling JavaScript code for further processing ❻.

Let's wrap up our discussion on preflights by looking at a few things to keep in mind about preflight requests.

SUCCESSFUL PREFLIGHT != SUCCESSFUL REQUEST

The preflight response doesn't provide any insight into the success or failure of the actual request. A preflight could be successful, but the request could still fail for many reasons, such as a file not found, an authorization error, or a server issue. The preflight only ensures that the browser can make a cross-origin request to the server, and nothing more. The server is still free to reject the request for other reasons.

Think of an HTTP request as a set of Russian nesting dolls. Each doll contains a set of request headers that define the request behavior. Figure 4.19 shows how an HTTP request maps to this Russian nesting doll analogy.

The outermost doll is the CORS doll, and it contains the Origin header. The inner dolls can contain a variety of information, such as a cookie validating the user (cookie support in CORS will be covered in the next chapter). Even if the outermost CORS layer succeeds, the request may still fail while processing through one of the inner layers (for example, the cookie may have expired).

JAVASCRIPT CODE AND PREFLIGHTS

The preflight takes place solely between the browser and the server. There is no way for the JavaScript code to intercept the preflight response or get updates on its status. From the client code's perspective, the preflight is invisible. A failing preflight is akin to the actual request failing, even though the actual request is never made.

This is a useful feature, because it hides the complexity of preflight requests from the developer writing the client code. Figure 4.20 shows how both the client and the server view a CORS request with a preflight. There is complexity in answering a preflight

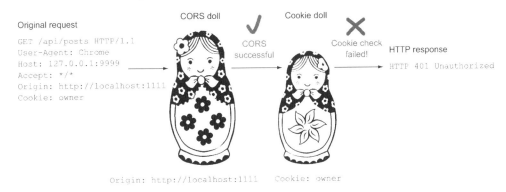

Figure 4.19 An HTTP request as a set of Russian dolls. Requests may fail for various reasons, and a successful preflight doesn't imply a successful request.

CORS from the client's perspective

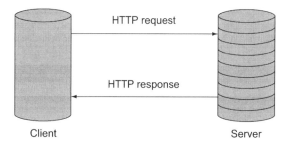

Client   Server

CORS from the server's perspective

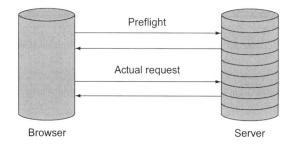

Browser   Server

Figure 4.20   A CORS request (with preflight) looks like a regular HTTP request from the client's perspective.

request, but only the server developer needs to worry about this complexity. From the client developer's perspective, a cross-origin request looks the same as any HTTP request.

PREFLIGHTS ARE STATELESS

Both the preflight and the actual request are stateless. This means that there is no additional information connecting the actual request back to the preflight request that preceded it. To get a sense of what this means, table 4.7 compares a preflight request with its partner request.

Table 4.7   The actual request has no information about the preflight request

Request type	HTTP request
Preflight	OPTIONS /api/posts HTTP/1.1 User-Agent: Chrome Host: 127.0.0.1:9999 Accept: */* Origin: http://localhost:1111 Access-Control-Request-Method: GET Access-Control-Request-Headers: Timezone-Offset, Sample-Source
Actual	GET /api/posts HTTP/1.1 User-Agent: Chrome Host: 127.0.0.1:9999 Accept: */* Origin: http://localhost:1111 Timezone-Offset: 300 Sample-Source: Cors in Action

Looking at the actual request, there is no information that connects it to the original preflight request. This can be confusing because we think of the preflight plus the actual request as occurring in tandem. If your server receives the actual request, you have to trust that the browser did the right thing and sent the preflight request before it. This highlights how crucial the browser is when making a CORS request.

Because the preflight request is stateless, it's important that all CORS responses include the Access-Control-Allow-Origin header. It's not enough to include the Access-Control-Allow-Origin header on just the preflight response. Both the preflight response and the actual response need the Access-Control-Allow-Origin header, as shown in table 4.8.

Table 4.8 **Both the preflight response and the actual response need the Access-Control-Allow-Origin header.**

Response type	HTTP response
Preflight	HTTP/1.1 204 No Content **Access-Control-Allow-Origin: *** Access-Control-Allow-Methods: GET, DELETE Access-Control-Allow-Headers: Timezone-Offset, Sample-Source
Actual	HTTP/1.1 200 OK **Access-Control-Allow-Origin: *** Content-Type: application/json

If neither the preflight response nor the actual response has an Access-Control-Allow-Origin header, the CORS request will be rejected.

PREFLIGHT REQUESTS AND UPLOAD EVENTS

The discussion in this chapter has been focused on making HTTP requests, but a preflight request can also be issued on upload events. Upload events provide progress information about an upload. The following code shows how to use upload events to show a status message for an upload:

```
function uploadFile(file) {
  var xhr = new XMLHttpRequest();
  xhr.open('POST', '/upload', true);

  xhr.upload.onprogress = function(e) {
    console.log('Upload progress: ' ((e.loaded / e.total) * 100));
  };

  xhr.send(file);
}
```

The request needs to have a preflight because upload events are a new concept. Before upload support in XMLHttpRequests existed, the traditional way of doing an upload was through a form. While the form would upload a file, it couldn't provide additional information, such as how far the upload has progressed. The upload event introduces a functionality that wasn't available before CORS; therefore it requires a preflight request.

Upload events are a purely client-side feature: the browser fires the event, and doesn't need to make a server request for more information. But the upload request still requires a preflight because it's introducing functionality that didn't exist before CORS. On the other hand, if you upload a file using XMLHttpRequest, but without using upload events, the request doesn't need a preflight (again, this makes sense, because without upload events, the upload behaves the same as a form upload). Table 4.9 shows the distinction between the two types of uploads.

Table 4.9   Uploading with and without upload events. Uploading without upload events doesn't need a preflight.

JavaScript code	Preflight status
```var xhr = new XMLHttpRequest();``` ``` ``` ```xhr.open('POST', '/upload', true);``` ``` ``` ```xhr.upload.onprogress = function(e) {``` ``` console.log('Upload progress: ' ((e.loaded / e.total)``` ```* 100));``` ```};``` ``` ``` ```xhr.send(file);```	Uses upload events; requires a preflight
```var xhr = new XMLHttpRequest();``` ```xhr.open('POST', '/upload', true);``` ```xhr.send(file);```	Doesn't use upload events; no preflight necessary

While this section has done its best to catalog all the cases where a preflight request is made, there may be new types of requests in the future that issue a preflight. But as long as your server is armed with the Access-Control-Allow-Methods and Access-Control-Allow-Headers headers, you'll be prepared to answer any preflight request that comes your way.

4.6   *Preflight result cache*

One downside of the preflight request is that it issues two HTTP requests, one for the preflight and a second for the actual request. This can be a performance concern because HTTP requests are expensive, especially on resource-constrained devices like smartphones. To help reduce the number of preflight requests, preflight responses can be cached in a preflight result cache.

The preflight result cache stores the responses to a preflight request for a particular URL. If a request is made to the same URL, the browser first checks the preflight result cache to see if there is already a response. If the browser finds a response in the cache, it skips the preflight request and goes straight to the actual request. If there is no response in the cache, the browser sends the preflight, and then stores the response of that preflight in the cache. Figure 4.21 shows how responses flow through the preflight result cache.

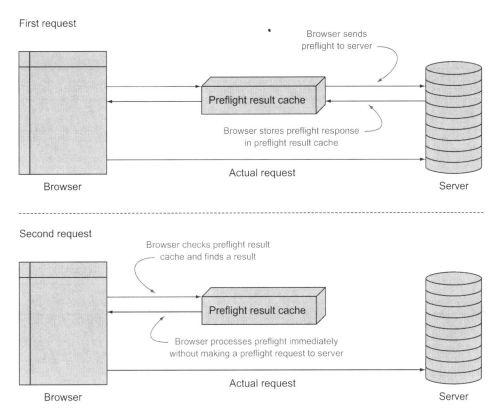

Figure 4.21 Using the preflight cache. The first request sends a preflight to the server, but the second request grabs the preflight response from the preflight cache.

You can see the preflight cache in action by reloading the page a few times. The first time you reload the page, you'll see the preflight OPTIONS request in Chrome's Network tab. But subsequent reloads will skip the preflight request and go straight to the actual request. Figure 4.22 shows three GET requests fired one after the other, with only one preflight request. The preflight is sent for the first request only; the other two requests take advantage of the preflight result cache.

> **NOTE** To isolate just the CORS requests in figure 4.22, I selected the Preserve Log Upon Navigation option, which is the fifth icon from the left along the bottom of the console log. I also selected only to show XHR requests, so the requests to client.html are filtered out.

The cache stores entries by URL plus origin. Requests from different origins to the same URL all have different cache entries. Likewise, requests from the same origin to different URLs all have different cache entries. Because the preflight result cache can only store entries based on origin and URL, you can't take shortcuts and specify a preflight response for an entire domain. Each URL in your domain that supports CORS will need to be able to respond to a preflight request.

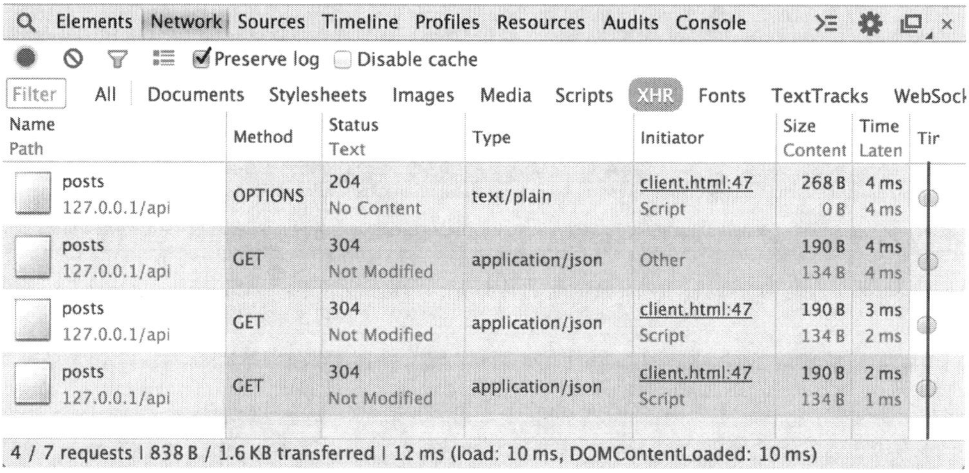

Figure 4.22   Multiple GET requests to the same URL using the preflight result cache

While you can examine network traffic to see whether a preflight request was sent, there is no way to view the contents of the preflight request cache. The cache is a black box that is maintained internally by the browser. But you can have some control over how long items stay in the cache by using the Access-Control-Max-Age header.

SETTING THE CACHE TIME WITH ACCESS-CONTROL-MAX-AGE

CORS gives servers some control over how long a preflight response is cached through the Access-Control-Max-Age response header. The Access-Control-Max-Age header indicates how long, in seconds, a response can stay in the cache.

The following listing modifies the sample app to cache preflight requests for two minutes. This means that after the first preflight response is cached, the browser will check the cache before every request to the same URL for the next two minutes. After those two minutes are up, the browser will send a preflight request again.

Listing 4.10   Adding the Access-Control-Max-Age response header

```
var handleCors = function(req, res, next) {
  res.set('Access-Control-Allow-Origin', 'http://localhost:1111');
  if (isPreflight(req)) {
    res.set('Access-Control-Allow-Methods', 'GET, DELETE');
    res.set('Access-Control-Allow-Headers',
            'Timezone-Offset, Sample-Source');
    res.set('Access-Control-Max-Age', '120');          ◁─┐ Setting cache
    res.status(204).end();                               │ expiration to
    return;                                              │ two minutes
  }
  next();
};
```

The Access-Control-Max-Age value is only a suggestion for how long an item should be cached. Browsers may cache for a shorter amount of time. Firefox doesn't allow items to be cached for longer than 24 hours, while Chrome, Opera, and Safari cache items for a maximum of five minutes. If the Access-Control-Max-Age header isn't specified, Firefox doesn't cache the preflight, while Chrome, Opera, and Safari cache the preflight for five seconds.

> **NOTE** The preceding browser-specific numbers were pulled from looking at the browser's source code, and this behavior may change in the future. It's not clear how Internet Explorer's preflight cache behaves, because it isn't documented and Internet Explorer's code is not open source.

4.7 Summary

This chapter introduced the concept of a CORS preflight request:

- The browser sends a preflight request to ask the server for permission to make the actual request.
- The preflight request protects servers from receiving unexpected requests.
- The preflight request asks permissions to make requests with certain HTTP methods and/or add custom HTTP headers to the request.
- The preflight request takes the form of an HTTP OPTIONS method with an Origin and Access-Control-Request-Method header.
- The server can grant permissions to use certain HTTP methods by using the Access-Control-Allow-Methods header. The server can also grant permission to use certain HTTP headers by using the Access-Control-Allow-Headers header.
- The preflight result cache is a performance optimization that helps reduce the number of preflight requests made to a particular endpoint.

The previous chapter and this one introduced you to the headers to handle most types of CORS requests. But there are still some features, such as cookie support, that are not covered by the headers in this chapter. Chapter 5 takes a look at how to support these remaining features on CORS requests.

Cookies and
response headers

This chapter covers

- Including cookies with requests
- Understanding how client and server settings interact to control cookie behavior
- Exposing response headers to clients

Chapter 4 introduced the concept of preflight requests. Preflight requests enable the browser to ask for the server's permission before making requests with certain HTTP methods and headers. This permissions model puts the server in charge of how cross-origin requests behave.

In the same way, there are additional features that also require special permissions in CORS. The first is user credential support. By default, CORS doesn't attach user credentials, such as cookies, on requests. The second is response headers support. The browser doesn't reveal all response headers to the client code. If your server responds with an X-Powered-By response header, the JavaScript client code won't be able to read its value without permission.

Luckily CORS has ways to support these features. As with all the other CORS features you've learned about, the server is in charge of enabling them, and it does so by using HTTP headers. This chapter will introduce two new response headers:

Access-Control-Allow-Credentials, which indicates that cookies may be included with requests, and Access-Control-Expose-Headers, which indicates which response headers are visible to the client.

We'll start by having you add a login page to the sample blogging app. The login page will include a cookie that needs to be validated in order to delete blog posts. Next, you'll modify the sample to display a response header on the page. By setting the Access-Control-Allow-Credentials and Access-Control-Expose-Headers headers on the response, the sample app will enable support for each of these features.

5.1 Supporting cookies in CORS requests

The sample app has a pretty glaring security hole: anyone visiting the site can delete a blog post! The server code doesn't verify whether the user deleting the post has permission to do so. Regardless of whether you're the blog author or a casual reader, clicking the Delete link will delete a post. This is obviously something that needs to be fixed.

The app needs a way to identify the user, and the standard way of identifying a user on the web is to use cookies. Cookies are small bits of information exchanged between the server and the browser. For example, when a user logs in to Facebook, the Facebook server sets a cookie with a unique user ID. As the user browses the site, each request to the server contains the cookie. The server can read the cookie from the request and load user-specific data, such as the user's timeline.

> **NOTE** The CORS spec uses the term *user credentials* to describe any bits of information the browser sets on a request to identify the user. This includes cookies, basic HTTP authentication, and client-side SSL. While the techniques described in this section apply to all of these types of user credentials, the text will focus only on cookies to keep things simple.

As you can see from this example, using cookies revolves around two actions: setting the cookie and reading it. A login page can be used to validate the user and set the appropriate cookie. Once the cookie is set, any user-specific activity should first read the cookie and validate the user. Let's modify the sample app to support these two actions. We'll start with the login page.

5.1.1 Setting cookies with a login page

The sample app currently only has one page, client.html, where users can view blog posts. In this section you'll add a second page called login.html. This login page will collect the user's username and password and set a cookie on his or her behalf.

> **NOTE** This code is only meant as an example. It's not a best practice for implementing security for your own site.

Figure 5.1 shows how the login page integrates with the rest of the app. The login page lives on 127.0.0.1:9999, along with the API. Because the login page lives on 127.0.0.1:9999, the cookie will be set on that domain as well.

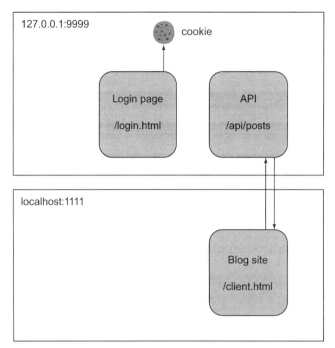

Figure 5.1   Topology of the sample app

Listing 5.1 shows the code for the login page. Save this code to a file called login.html in the same directory as the sample app. The login page displays a form asking for the user's username and password. When the user clicks Login, the page sets a cookie identifying the user, then redirects to the main blog at client.html. The value of the cookie is set to the username. (Of course, a real app should verify the username and password against a database, and set the cookie to an ID rather than the username.)

Listing 5.1   Adding a login page to the sample app

```
<html><body>
<form onsubmit="handleLogin(); return false;">          Shows login
    Username: <input type="text" id="username"></input>   form
    Password: <input type="password" id="password"></input>
    <input type="submit" id="btnSubmit" value="Login"></input>
</form>
<script>
var handleLogin = function() {
    var username = document.getElementById('username').value;   Sets cookie
    document.cookie = 'username=' + username;
    window.location = 'http://localhost:1111/client.html';    Redirects to
}                                                              blog site
</script>
</body></html>
```

You can test the login page by restarting the server and visiting the page at http://127.0.0.1:9999/login.html. Enter owner as the username, any value for the password

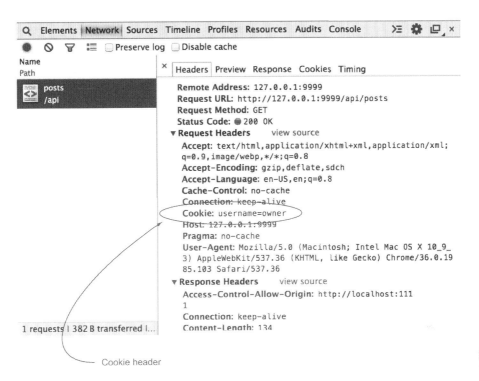

Figure 5.2   Request headers for a request to the API

(because we aren't validating the password, any password will do), and click the Login button. Once you've logged in, you can see the cookie being passed to the API by visiting http://127.0.0.1:9999/api/posts. If you view this request in the Network tab, you'll see the Cookie header included as part of the request, as shown in figure 5.2.

Now that the cookie is set, let's turn our attention to reading the cookie on the server.

5.1.2   *Reading the cookie on the server*

Let's update the server to delete the post only if the blog owner is making the request. Express provides a useful piece of middleware to manage cookies called cookie-parser. The cookie-parser middleware parses all of a site's cookies into an easy-to-use JavaScript object. We'll use cookie-parser to handle the minutiae of parsing cookies so that you can focus on CORS.

Listing 5.2 modifies the server code to only delete posts if the username is `owner`. First you'll add the cookie-parser middleware to the server. When the server receives a delete request, the username is pulled from the cookie and compared against the string owner. If the values match, the post is deleted. Otherwise, the server returns a 403 error (indicating that a user doesn't have permission to perform an action).

Listing 5.2 Modifying the server code to read the cookie

```
var express = require('express');
var cookieParser = require('cookie-parser');

var SERVER_PORT = 9999;
var serverapp = express();                          Adds cookie-parser
serverapp.use(cookieParser);                        middleware to server
serverapp.use(express.static(__dirname));
serverapp.use(handleCors);
serverapp.get('/api/posts', function(req, res) {
  res.json(POSTS);
});
serverapp.delete('/api/posts/:id', function(req, res) {    Checks username to
  if (req.cookies['username'] === 'owner') {               see if it's the owner
    delete POSTS[req.params.id];
    res.status(204).end();                          If user is valid,
  } else {                                           deletes post
    res.status(403).end();                      ...otherwise, returns
  }                                               a 403 forbidden error
});
serverapp.listen(SERVER_PORT);
```

NOTE You may also have to install the cookie-parser middleware for this sample to work. You can do so by running npm install cookie-parser.

With this code in place, restart the web server and visit http://127.0.0.1:9999/login.html. Enter the username owner and any password (remember you aren't validating passwords because this is a sample), and click the Login button. Once you're redirected to the blog, click a Delete link.

NOTE The login page resides at 127.0.0.1:9999 and not localhost:1111. The login page from localhost:1111 will not set the correct cookie.

After clicking the Delete link, you'd expect the request to succeed. The previous section verified that cookies are included on API requests, but the sample will once again fail with the error shown in figure 5.3. Switching over to the Network tab as shown in figure 5.4 reveals that the cookie isn't included in the request.

Where is the cookie you just set? This is once again a distinction between same-origin and cross-origin requests. Cookies are always included with same-origin requests, but they aren't included on cross-origin requests by default. Because clicking the Delete link triggers a cross-origin request, the request goes through but the cookies don't. Luckily CORS offers a solution for including cookies with requests.

Figure 5.3   Server returns a 403 forbidden error when deleting a post

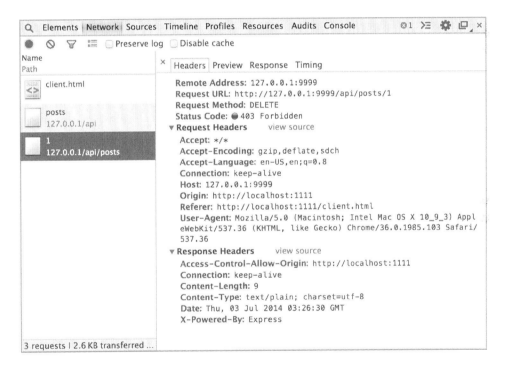

Figure 5.4   No Cookie header on the request

5.1.3   Including cookies in CORS requests

Like all other CORS features, the server uses an HTTP response header to define cookie behavior. But unlike other CORS features, there is a client-side component to cookie support. Cookies will only work when both the client and the server are in agreement.

SERVER-SIDE COOKIE SUPPORT

The server indicates that it can receive cookies on CORS requests by setting the Access-Control-Allow-Credentials response header. Setting that header to `true` means that the server allows cookies on the CORS request.

If the request includes a preflight request, the Access-Control-Allow-Credentials header must be present on both the preflight and the actual request. But the cookie will only be sent on the actual request; the preflight request will never have a cookie.

The following listing modifies the server code to enable cookie support by adding the Access-Control-Allow-Credentials header.

Listing 5.3   Adding the Access-Control-Allow-Credentials header

```
var handleCors = function(req, res, next) {
  res.set('Access-Control-Allow-Origin', 'http://localhost:1111');
  res.set('Access-Control-Allow-Credentials', 'true');          ◁┐
  if (isPreflight(req)) {                                          │ Sets Access-Control-
    res.set('Access-Control-Allow-Methods', 'GET, DELETE');       │ Allow-Credentials
    res.set('Access-Control-Allow-Headers',                       │ header on both the
            'Timezone-Offset, Sample-Source');                    │ preflight and actual
    res.set('Access-Control-Max-Age', '120');                     │ request
    res.status(204).end();
    return;
  }
  next();
};
```

But even with this server-side support, the delete request still fails. This is because the client needs to be configured to send cookies with the request. Let's update the client to do that.

CLIENT-SIDE COOKIE SUPPORT

In addition to setting a server-side response header, you have to set a property in the client's JavaScript code to include the cookie with the request. Chapter 2 introduced the `withCredentials` property, which controls cookie behavior. The default value for this property is `false`, which indicates that cookies aren't included on requests. Setting the `withCredentials` property to `true` includes cookies on cross-origin requests (this property has no effect on same-origin requests, which always include cookies). The following listing updates the client code to set the `withCredentials` property to true.

Listing 5.4   Setting `withCredentials` to `true` in the client code

```
var deletePost = function(postId) {
  var url = 'http://127.0.0.1:9999/api/posts/' + postId;
  var xhr = createXhr('DELETE', url);
  xhr.withCredentials = true;                       ◁┐ Indicates that cookies are
  xhr.onload = function() {                            │ included with the request
    if (xhr.status == 204) {
      var element = document.getElementById('postId' + postId);
      element.parentNode.removeChild(element);
    }
```

```
  };
  xhr.send();
};
```

After these updates to the client code, you're finally ready to process cookies on CORS requests! Reload the client.html page, and try clicking a Delete link. Figure 5.5 shows the page after the user clicks the Delete link. The cookie is now included with the request, and the post is deleted.

Having two different settings with two different Boolean values leads to four combinations for the `withCredentials` property and Access-Control-Allow-Credentials header. These combinations can get confusing, so the next section explores how a request behaves when these properties are set to different values.

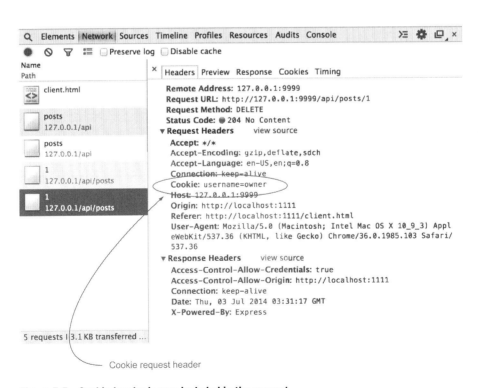

Figure 5.5 Cookie header is now included in the request

> ### Why do cookies need a client-side property?
>
> Why do user credentials require a client-side component while all other CORS features don't? The answer is, again, safety. Because user credentials are often used to perform sensitive actions (such as identify a user or update a user's personal data), the CORS spec needs to be absolutely certain that credentials should be included in the request. Having the client opt-in along with the server adds another layer of caution when adding sensitive data such as user credentials.

5.1.4   *How withCredentials and Access-Control-Allow-Credentials interact*

Supporting user credentials requires that the `withCredentials` property work in tandem with the Access-Control-Allow-Credentials header. Each can either be set to `true` or `false` (or the property can't be set at all, which is the same as setting it to `false`). This leads to four combinations of properties. This can get confusing, and it may not be clear what a particular combination means. Table 5.1 summarizes how the values interact.

Table 5.1   Behavior for various values of the `withCredentials` property and Access-Control-Allow-Credentials header

withCredentials	Access-Control-Allow-Credentials	Status	Caveats
false	false	Allowed	Cookies *aren't* included in the request
true	true	Allowed	Cookies *are* included in the request
false	true	Allowed	Cookies *aren't* included in the request
true	false	Rejected	Invalid because cookies are sent on the request, but the server doesn't allow them

As you can see, only one combination leads to a rejection. But the other combinations lead to subtly different behavior, as indicated by the Caveats column in the table.

Let's examine these four combinations in more detail in the following tables.

Table 5.2   Client code and server HTTP response when `withCredentials` and Access-Control-Allow-Credentials aren't set

Client code	Server HTTP response

`var xhr = new XMLHttpRequest();`
`xhr.open('GET',`
`    'http://127.0.0.1:9999/api/posts');`
`xhr.send();`
	`HTTP/1.1 200 OK`
	`Access-Control-Allow-Origin:`
	`    http://localhost:1111`

If `withCredentials` and Access-Control-Allow-Credentials aren't set, cookies aren't included on the request. You've seen how CORS requests behave when these properties aren't set. All the examples from chapters 3 and 4 behave this way. Because those examples didn't set any cookies, withCredentials and Access-Control-Allow-Credentials weren't necessary.

Table 5.3 Client code and server HTTP response when withCredentials **and Access-Control-Allow-Credentials are both** true

Client code	Server HTTP response

`var xhr = new XMLHttpRequest();`
`xhr.open('GET',`
`'http://127.0.0.1:9999/api/posts');`
`xhr.withCredentials = true;`
`xhr.send();`
	`HTTP/1.1 200 OK`
	`Access-Control-Allow-Origin:`
	`   http://localhost:1111`
	`Access-Control-Allow-Credentials:`
	`true`

This section already covered what happens when both withCredentials and Access-Control-Allow-Credentials are true. There is really not much more to say here: if a cookie exists, it will be included with the CORS request. But things get a little more interesting for the next two cases, where one property is set and the other isn't.

Table 5.4 Client code and server HTTP response when withCredentials **isn't set but Access-Control-Allow-Credentials is** true

Client code	Server HTTP response

`var xhr = new XMLHttpRequest();`
`xhr.open('GET',`
`'http://127.0.0.1:9999/api/`
`posts');`
`xhr.send();`
	`HTTP/1.1 200 OK`
	`Access-Control-Allow-Origin:`
	`   http://localhost:1111`
	`Access-Control-Allow-Credentials:`
	`true`

In this case, the server sets the Access-Control-Allow-Credentials header to true, even though the client doesn't set the withCredentials property. Although the values of the two don't match, the request still succeeds.

Here is how this combination works. When the server responds with an Access-Control-Allow-Credentials: true header, it's saying that it's okay to send cookies with the request. But because the withCredentials property isn't set, the CORS request doesn't include the cookie. From the server's perspective, the request looks like a normal CORS request without any cookies. The Access-Control-Allow-Credentials header isn't saying that cookies must be included in the request. It's merely suggesting that cookies can be included in the request. The client, armed with the withCredentials property, has the final say in whether or not cookies are included.

Setting withCredentials to true without an Access-Control-Allow-Credentials header is the only combination that returns an error (table 5.5). Because withCredentials is set to true, the cookies will be included with the request. But because Access-Control-Allow-Credentials isn't set, the server declares that cookies aren't allowed on the request. There is a conflict in expectations, and the request is rejected.

Table 5.5   Client code and server HTTP response when `withCredentials` **is** `true` **but Access-Control-Allow-Credentials isn't set**

Client code	Server HTTP response

`var xhr = new XMLHttpRequest();`
`xhr.open('GET',`
`    'http://127.0.0.1:9999/api/posts');`
`xhr.withCredentials = true;`
`xhr.send();`
	`HTTP/1.1 200 OK`
	`Access-Control-Allow-Origin:`
	`    http://localhost:1111`

As you can see, there is a lot of subtlety involved when setting the values for the `with-Credentials` and Access-Control-Allow-Credentials. As a rule, it's best not to set these values unless you need the cookie on cross-origin requests. Requests without cookies are safer and easier to debug, because they don't contain any user-specific information.

This section took a comprehensive look at the `withCredentials` property and Access-Control-Allow-Credentials header. But there are still a few more caveats to be aware of when using these settings, which we'll cover next.

5.1.5   *Caveats to cookie support*

While the Access-Control-Allow-Credentials header allows cookies to be set on CORS requests, there are still a few caveats to how they are used.

COOKIES ON THE CLIENT

JavaScript's `document.cookie` property allows programmatic access to a site's cookies. Using `document.cookie`, JavaScript code can read and write the value of a cookie, as shown in the following code snippet. You can print the value of the cookie to the console using

```
console.log(document.cookie);
```

and you can set the cookie value using

```
document.cookie = 'newcookie=1';
```

But the preceding code will not work with cross-origin cookies. The `document.cookie` property can't read or write the value from another origin. Calling `document.cookie` from the client will return only the client's own cookies, not the cross-origin cookies.

This is because cookies themselves have a same-origin policy similar to the same-origin policy for HTTP requests. Each cookie has a path and a domain, and only pages from that path and domain can read the cookie. So while the cookie is included in the CORS request, the browser still honors the cookie's same-origin policy, and keeps the cookie hidden from client code.

COOKIES WHEN THERE IS NO PREFLIGHT REQUEST

Based on the previous discussion, you may think that if a server doesn't want cookies, all it needs to do is omit the Access-Control-Allow-Credentials header. However this isn't quite true. Cookies may still be sent to the server in the case where the request doesn't have a preflight. To understand why, look at how cookies behave with and without a preflight.

Figure 5.6 shows how cookie processing differs on a preflight request versus an actual request. Preflight requests never include the cookie. When the browser makes the preflight request, it doesn't include the cookie in the preflight, even though the

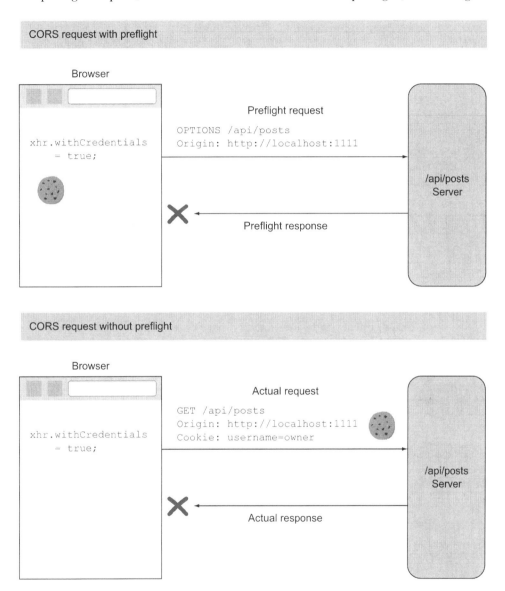

Figure 5.6 Differences in cookie behavior for requests with and without preflights. The preflight request will never include the cookie, but a request without a preflight might. This is true even if the server doesn't include the Access-Control-Allow-Credentials header and the request is rejected (as indicated with the X).

browser may have a cookie connected to that server. If the server rejects the request, the browser never sends the actual request with the cookie, and the cookie never reaches the server.

But things are different if there is no preflight. If the client has `withCredentials` set to `true`, and there isn't a preflight, the cookie will be sent to the server. This is because the browser has no way of predicting what the value of the Access-Control-Allow-Credentials header will be before sending the actual request. When the browser sees that the Access-Control-Allow-Credentials header isn't set, it will throw an error in the client. But because the client set the `withCredentials` property, the cookie was already sent to the server in the request.

So you can have situations where the server explicitly states that it doesn't want cookies, but the browser sends them anyway. This may sound unintuitive and a bit scary, until you remember that this is already how requests behave, even without CORS. If a client makes a JSON-P request to a server, and the browser has a cookie for that server, the cookie will be included as part of the JSON-P request.

This behavior isn't new to the web. There is a whole class of attacks that can arise from this request-plus-cookie combination called cross-site request forgery (CSRF), and CORS isn't immune to them. Therefore, standard security precautions such as CSRF prevention should be used when making CORS requests. The next chapter will look at what CSRF is and how to prevent it.

USER CREDENTIALS AND ACCESS-CONTROL-ALLOW-ORIGIN

If the Access-Control-Allow-Credentials header is set to `true`, the * value can't be used in the Access-Control-Allow-Origin header. Recall that the value * in the Access-Control-Allow-Origin header indicates that any origin can make a cross-origin request.

If the Access-Control-Allow-Credentials header is set to `true`, the server must provide an actual origin value in the Access-Control-Allow-Origin header. If the browser sees the header `Access-Control-Allow-Origin: *` used in conjunction with `Access-Control-Allow-Credentials: true`, it will reject the request. Table 5.6 compares the valid and invalid header combinations.

Table 5.6 Valid and invalid combinations for the Access-Control-Allow-Origin and Access-Control-Allow-Credentials headers

Valid	Invalid
`Access-Control-Allow-Origin: http://localhost:1111` `Access-Control-Allow-Credentials: true`	`Access-Control-Allow-Origin: *` `Access-Control-Allow-Credentials: true`

Allowing cookies to be sent on all requests is insecure and can lead to CSRF vulnerabilities. The CORS spec authors wisely chose to avoid the security risk entirely by disallowing this header combination.

SETTING THE COOKIE FROM CORS

The rules described in this section also apply to setting the cookie from the server. If the `withCredentials` property and Access-Control-Allow-Credentials header are both `true`, the server can set a cookie on the client. This cookie still can't be read from JavaScript code, but it will be included on subsequent requests to the server.

This section introduced a lot of new code to both the server and the client. Here is a recap:

1 The login.html page sets a cookie identifying the user.
2 The client sets the `withCredentials` property to indicate it would like to send cookies on CORS requests.
3 The server validates the user in the cookie before deleting a post.
4 The server sets the Access-Control-Allow-Credentials header to indicate that cookies are okay on CORS requests.

By including both a client- and server-side component, the developer has a lot of flexibility and control over when cookies are included in requests.

5.2 *Exposing response headers to the client*

All the CORS-specific headers introduced so far handle how an incoming request behaves. The Access-Control-Allow-Methods header specifies the valid request methods, while the Access-Control-Allow-Headers header specifies the valid request headers. Now we'll turn our attention to the HTTP response behavior. Specifically, you'll learn how client JavaScript code can access the response headers.

By now you may be discerning a pattern to how CORS works: for the client to do anything, the server must first give its permission. This behavior extends to the headers in the HTTP response. Response headers are the headers the server sends back to the client. Figure 5.7 shows a request from the sample's client.html page to the API. The response headers are the headers from the API back to the client.

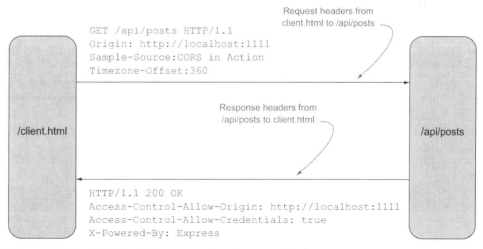

Figure 5.7   The distinction between request and response headers

The `XMLHttpRequest` object exposes two methods for reading the response headers: `getResponseHeader` and `getAllResponseHeaders`. Same-origin requests can use these methods to read headers from the response. But cross-origin requests have limitations on which response headers can be viewed by the client. By default, only a few response headers are visible to clients on cross-origin requests (these are called simple response headers; see the sidebar "Simple response headers" later in the chapter for more details). The server must give its permission to read any of the other response headers. Let's modify the sample app to read one of these headers.

5.2.1   Reading a response header

The X-Powered-By header is often used by servers to highlight the underlying technology that powers the server. Values for this header could be `ASP.NET` (for a server running on ASP.NET) or `PHP/5.2.4` (for a server running on PHP). By default, Express sets the X-Powered-By header to `Express`. Figure 5.8 shows where to find the X-Powered-By header in the API response.

Because the X-Powered-By header exists on every response, let's display it in the sample app. The following listing reads the header using `XMLHttpRequest`'s `getResponseHeader` method. If the header exists, it's displayed on the page.

Listing 5.5   Reading the X-Powered-By response header

```
xhr.onload = function() {
  var data = JSON.parse(xhr.responseText);
  var elem = document.getElementById('output');

  var xPoweredBy = xhr.getResponseHeader('X-Powered-By');   ◁──┐ Reads X-Powered-
  if (xPoweredBy) {                                               By header from
    var xpbDiv = document.createElement('div');                   HTTP response
    xpbDiv.className = 'post';
    xpbDiv.innerHTML = 'X-Powered-By: ' + xPoweredBy;
    elem.appendChild(xpbDiv);                               ◁──┐ Displays header
  }                                                              on page

  for (var postId in data) {
```

If you reload the page, you'd expect to see the X-Powered-By header displayed on the page. Since this is a cross-origin request, the header comes up empty. (Some browsers such as Chrome even display a helpful error message in the console log: `Refused to get unsafe header "X-Powered-By"`). So let's update the server to give you access to that header.

5.2.2   Adding response header support

The server needs to specify that it's okay for the client to read the X-Powered-By header. The server does this by using the Access-Control-Expose-Headers header. The Access-Control-Expose-Headers header contains a list of headers that the client code can read.

This shouldn't be confused with the Access-Control-Allow-Headers header that was covered in chapter 4. While they are similar, there is no connection between the two.

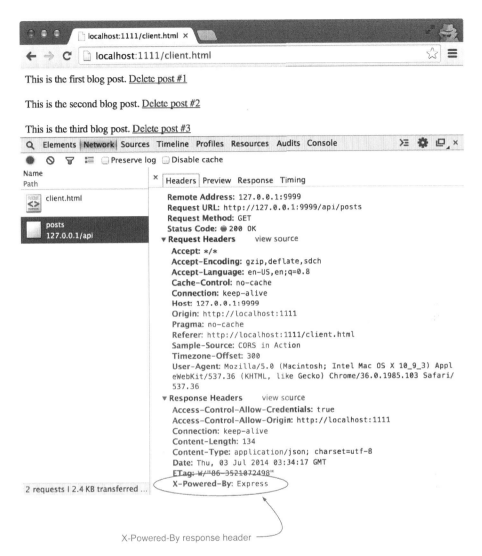

Figure 5.8 X-Powered-By response header

The Access-Control-Allow-Headers header is used by the preflight to indicate which headers are allowed on the request. The Access-Control-Expose-Headers header is used by the actual response to indicate which response headers are visible to the client.

The following listing adds the Access-Control-Expose-Headers header to the server. Once this is included in the response, the X-Powered-By header will be visible to the getResponseHeader method.

Listing 5.6 Adding the Access-Control-Expose-Headers header

```
var handleCors = function(req, res, next) {
  res.set('Access-Control-Allow-Origin', 'http://localhost:1111');
```

```
res.set('Access-Control-Allow-Credentials', 'true');
if (isPreflight(req)) {
  . . .
} else {
  res.set('Access-Control-Expose-Headers', 'X-Powered-By');    ◁──┐
}
```

Sets Access-Control-Expose-Headers header on the actual response

NOTE The Access-Control-Expose-Headers header need only be included if the request isn't a preflight request. This is because the header only takes effect on the actual request. It doesn't hurt to put it on the preflight, but it doesn't provide any benefit either.

After making the changes in listing 5.6 and reloading the sample, the X-Powered-By header should be displayed on the page, as shown in figure 5.9.

Simple response headers

Not all response headers need the Access-Control-Expose-Headers header. Some response headers are always visible to the client, regardless of whether or not the Access-Control-Expose-Headers header is present. These headers are called *simple response headers*. There isn't any documented reason why these specific headers are special; they are just the result of the evolution of the web over many years. The simple response headers are defined as:

- Cache-Control
- Content-Language
- Content-Type
- Expires
- Last-Modified
- Pragma

The server doesn't need to do anything for the client to view these headers. The client can always read these response headers.

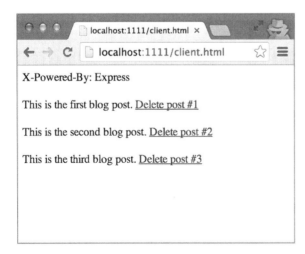

Figure 5.9   Displaying the X-Powered-By response header on the page

It may seem like overkill for the server to weigh in on response headers. After all, what harm can the X-Powered-By header do? But like the other CORS headers, the Access-Control-Expose-Headers header exists to protect the server's data from unexpected access. Accessing response headers is a new capability introduced by CORS. Before CORS existed, clients had no way of reading the response headers. Because a server may depend on this behavior, CORS needs to be careful not to break this assumption. The Access-Control-Expose-Headers header ensures that the client code can only read the response headers intended by the server.

5.3 Summary

This chapter rounded out your understanding of CORS by introducing a few additional features:

- The Access-Control-Allow-Credentials header can be used in conjunction with `XMLHttpRequest`'s `withCredentials` property to include cookies on cross-origin requests.
- The Access-Control-Expose-Headers header can be used to expose response headers to the client.

These features are the tools in your CORS toolbox. But the tools alone aren't enough; you also need to know how to use them. The flexibility offered in CORS means that there are a lot of ways of configuring a server, and there sometimes isn't any clear guidance on which way is preferred. The next chapter offers guidance and best practices for using CORS on your own server.

Best practices 6

This chapter covers

- Opening up your API to public CORS requests
- Limiting CORS requests to a whitelisted set of origins
- Ensuring your CORS responses are properly handled by proxy servers
- Protecting against cross-site request forgery (CSRF) vulnerabilities
- Configuring and minimizing preflight requests

The previous chapters showed how Access-Control prefixed HTTP headers can dictate the behavior of CORS requests. There are six CORS-specific response headers, each with its own set of valid values. This can lead to myriad ways in which the server response can be configured. While the previous chapters explained what these HTTP headers do, they didn't offer a lot of guidance on how to best use these headers. How should you configure your server if you want to whitelist certain clients? How can your server accept cookies while still remaining secure?

This chapter will answer these questions and show you how to configure these headers in a way that makes sense for your server needs. If HTTP headers are the language of CORS, this chapter aims to improve your CORS grammar.

The chapter starts by refactoring the sample code from chapter 5 to be more configurable. It then takes a closer look at each of the CORS response headers and offers practical guidance on how to use them. By the end of this chapter, the sample code will become something you can incorporate into your own server to handle CORS requests.

6.1 Refactoring the sample code

The sample code from the previous three chapters did a good job of covering various CORS topics. But it falls far short of being a general-purpose CORS library. The code has hard-coded values geared toward explaining particular concepts, and isn't flexible or configurable. Concepts like the Timezone-Offset and Sample-Source request headers were made up to demonstrate CORS. If you were to copy and paste the sample code into your own server, it wouldn't match up with your own needs.

The goal of this chapter is to build a flexible CORS server that can be used with a variety of configurations. To do this, we'll first refactor the sample code so that it can be configured in different ways. The configuration options will allow the code to be used in various circumstances. The following listing shows the result of this refactoring.

Listing 6.1 Modifying the `handleCors` method to accept configuration options

Declares new configuration options object (to be used later in chapter)

handleCors returns a new middleware function based off configuration options.

```
var corsOptions = {};

var handleCors = function(options) {
  return function(req, res, next) {
    res.set('Access-Control-Allow-Origin', 'http://localhost:1111');
    res.set('Access-Control-Allow-Credentials', 'true');
    if (isPreflight(req)) {
      res.set('Access-Control-Allow-Methods', 'GET', 'DELETE');
      res.set('Access-Control-Allow-Headers',
              'Timezone-Offset, Sample-Source');
      res.set('Access-Control-Max-Age', '120');
      res.status(204).end();
      return;
    } else {
      res.set('Access-Control-Expose-Headers', 'X-Powered-By');
    }
    next();
  }
};

var SERVER_PORT = 9999;
var serverapp = express();
serverapp.use(cookieParser());
serverapp.use(express.static (__dirname));
serverapp.use(handleCors(corsOptions));
serverapp.get('/api/posts', function(req, res) {
  res.json(POSTS);
});
```

Adds new middleware to server.

The listing starts by declaring the `corsOptions` variable which will store the configuration options we'll add throughout this chapter. This variable will grow as you learn ways to configure CORS requests. The `handleCors` method is updated to accept an `options` object, and returns a new middleware object. The `corsOptions` variable is passed to the `handleCors` method, and you receive a fully configured middleware.

Now that the sample code framework is in place, you can focus on tips for setting each individual header in the CORS pipeline. But before doing that, let's take a few moments to think about your own server configuration.

6.2   Before you begin

Before writing a single line of code, take a step back and think about what you're trying to achieve by adding CORS support to your server. Here are a few questions you should consider:

- Why are you adding support for cross-origin requests?
- Are you adding CORS support to a new service or an existing server?
- Which clients should have access to the site?
- What devices/browsers will they be accessing the site from?
- Which HTTP methods and headers will your server support?
- Should the API support user-specific data? If so, will cookies be used to authenticate the user?

The answers will guide you through the rest of this chapter. For example, an API that needs Internet Explorer 8 or Internet Explorer 9 support will need to be built differently from an API that only needs to be supported on mobile devices. An API that is open to the public will have different needs than an API built for internal use. Here are some common server configurations that may benefit from CORS support:

- *Providing a public API that users can access from JavaScript.* Most Google APIs support CORS, including the popular Drive API and YouTube API.
- *Unifying various properties behind a single API.* If you own a mobile, tablet, and website, and each is hosted under a different origin, they can all talk to the same underlying API using CORS.

By having an understanding of what you're trying to achieve with CORS, you can make better choices on how to configure CORS for your server. Now that you have a sense of how your own CORS implementation should behave, let's turn our attention to the most important CORS header: Access-Control-Allow-Origin.

6.3   Setting the Access-Control-Allow-Origin header

The Access-Control-Allow-Origin header indicates which origins can access a resource via a cross-origin request. This header can either use the * value to give access to everyone, or it can set a specific origin value to give access to a specific client. Table 6.1 gives an overview of the valid values for the Access-Control-Allow-Origin header. The rest of this chapter delves deeper into these values, and explores different use cases.

Table 6.1 Valid values for the Access-Control-Allow-Origin header

Access-Control-Allow-Origin value	Effect on the response
`<no header>`	CORS isn't supported for any origins
`*`	CORS is supported for all origins
`null`	CORS is supported for unknown origins (such as accessing from a file rather than a website)
`<origin value>`	CORS is supported on a specific origin

6.3.1 Allowing cross-origin access for everyone

If you want to allow cross-origin requests to the widest audience, use the * value for the Access-Control-Allow-Origin header. The * value indicates that any client can make a cross-origin request to this resource.

An example of a site that sets the * value is the HTML5Rocks.com website. This website contains a wealth of articles and tutorials for using HTML5. HTML5Rocks.com sets the `Access-Control-Allow-Origin: *` header on every page. This allows other JavaScript developers to use CORS to consume and parse any page on the HTML5Rocks .com site.

The * value works best in the cases where

- The resource should be accessible to as wide a range of users as possible.
- You don't know ahead of time which origins and clients will access the resource.
- No authentication or individualization is required.

Turning to the sample code, it's easy to enable the * value on all pages, as shown in the following code:

```
var handleCors = function(options) {
  return function(req, res, next) {
    res.set('Access-Control-Allow-Origin', '*');
```

Note that just because the * value is enabled, it doesn't mean that the request will be successful. The request may fail for other reasons, such as a 404 Not Found or a 500 Internal Server Error. The * value only indicates that a client can make cross-origin requests, and nothing more.

BE CAREFUL WITH CONTENT BEHIND A FIREWALL

Setting the * value comes with a caveat: you should be careful when setting it on content behind a firewall. A firewall is set up specifically to allow access to a certain set of users. For example, your company may maintain a firewall so that only employees can access certain pages on the intranet. The * value can be used to bypass these restrictions and broadcast the data to unintended users.

Figure 6.1 illustrates the dangers of allowing all origins over a VPN. Suppose there are some private internal documents on your company's intranet, which happens to have the `Access-Control-Allow-Origin: *` header set. As an employee, because you're

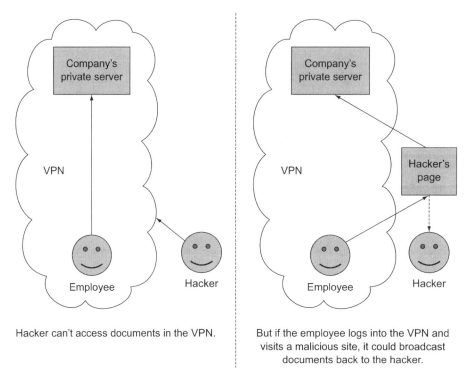

Hacker can't access documents in the VPN.

But if the employee logs into the VPN and visits a malicious site, it could broadcast documents back to the hacker.

Figure 6.1   An example of how a hacker could take advantage of an `Access-Control-Allow-Origin: *` **response over a VPN**

able to connect to the firewall, you're able to access these documents using CORS. Now suppose some malicious hacker would like to access this document as well. He knows the URL, but he can't make a request to the document because he isn't on the firewall.

But he can create a special HTML file that makes a CORS request to grab the contents of the document, and then uploads the contents to the hacker's own server. Even though he has this specially crafted HTML file, the hacker still can't use it because he isn't connected to the firewall. But if he can somehow trick an employee to visit the web page while the employee is connected to the intranet, the CORS request will succeed and the hacker will get the contents of the document.

This example contains a lot of steps, but a determined hacker will use any tools at his disposal to get at the information he wants. If a document or API needs to be accessible to a group of users, it's best to limit the set of origins. The next section looks at how to do this.

6.3.2   *Limiting CORS requests to a set of origins*

Suppose you're in the early days of building your blogging service. While you know you'd like the mobile, tablet, and web versions of the site to be driven by the same API, you aren't yet comfortable exposing the API to external users. In this case, the * value

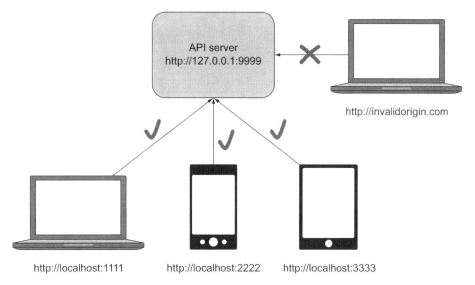

Figure 6.2   Accepting requests from specific origins

for the Access-Control-Allow-Origin header isn't quite right because this could open up your API to unexpected requests.

If you'd like to limit which clients can access your server, the Access-Control-Allow-Origin header also accepts a client origin value. Building off the preceding example, suppose your API is at http://127.0.0.1:9999, and you'd like to allow access to the API from your website at http://localhost:1111, your mobile site at http://localhost:2222, and your tablet site at http://localhost:3333, as shown in figure 6.2.

Chapter 3 showed you how to set the Access-Control-Allow-Origin header to a single origin value. For example, to allow access from a desktop client, the header would be set as

```
Access-Control-Allow-Origin: http://localhost:1111
```

This is fine if you only want to give access to a single origin. But what if instead of only http://localhost:1111, you'd like to give access to a range of origins? Suppose you have mobile, tablet, and web versions of the same website, and you'd like to give them all access to your API. In this case, using a single origin value isn't enough, and the Access-Control-Allow-Origin header doesn't support more than one value. You'll need to write code to process the incoming origin value against a whitelist.

USING A WHITELIST TO SPECIFY THE ORIGIN
A whitelist is a list of origins that are allowed to make requests to the server. In the example from figure 6.2, the whitelist would include the origins http://localhost:1111, http://localhost:2222, and http://localhost:3333. If the origin of the incoming request matches one of these values, then the client is allowed access to the resource.

The code in the following listing creates a function to validate an origin value against a whitelist.

Figure 6.3   Example of using a whitelist to find a valid and an invalid Origin header

Listing 6.2   Creating a whitelist validator function in app.js

```
var createWhitelistValidator = function(whitelist) {
  return function(val) {
    for (var i = 0; i < whitelist.length; i++) {
      if (val === whitelist[i]) {
        return true;
      }
    }
    return false;
  }
};
```

The `createWhitelistValidator` function returns a function that validates an origin value against a whitelist of acceptable origins. The `createWhitelistValidator` function doesn't do the validation itself; it only creates a function that can be used to do the validation later on, when the client sends a request. The validation function loops through each value in the whitelist. If there is a match, the function returns `true`. If the function loops through all the whitelist values without finding a match, it returns `false`. Figure 6.3 provides a visualization of what the whitelist check looks like.

Armed with the `createWhitelistValidator` function, let's validate the origin against the whitelist values. The following listing updates the sample code to validate origins against a whitelist.

Listing 6.3   Using the whitelist validator

```
var originWhitelist = [
  'http://localhost:1111'        ◁─┐  Defines valid origin
];                                   │  values in whitelist

var corsOptions = {
  allowOrigin: createWhitelistValidator(originWhitelist)  ◁─┐  Creates a new
};                                                            │  function to
                                                             │  validate origin
var handleCors = function(options) {
  return function(req, res, next) {
```

```
              if (options.allowOrigin) {
                  var origin = req.headers['origin'];
                  if (options.allowOrigin(origin)) {
                      res.set('Access-Control-Allow-Origin', origin);
                  }
              } else {
                  res.set('Access-Control-Allow-Origin', '*');
              }
              ...
          };
```

Checks if allow-Origin option exists

Runs allowOrigin function against origin header

Sets Access-Control-Allow-Origin header if origin is valid

If allowOrigin option isn't specified, allows all origins

The code starts by creating an array of valid client origins. Because the sample code accepts cross-origin requests only from http://localhost:1111, this is the only value in the whitelist. The code then defines a new `allowOrigin` option which uses the `create-WhitelistValidator` function to create a function to validate the origin.

Now that you've created the `allowOrigin` option, you need to read that value from your middleware. The code starts by checking if the `allowOrigin` option exists. If it doesn't, the code sets the Access-Control-Allow-Origin header to *, as it did originally. But if the `allowOrigin` does exist, the code runs the validator function against the value of the origin header. If there is a match, the origin is allowed to make cross-origin requests, and you can set the Access-Control-Allow-Origin header to the value of the Origin header. Otherwise, the client isn't allowed to make cross-origin requests, and the Access-Control-Allow-Origin header is never set.

A whitelist is an easy way to manage cross-origin access to your server. You can easily add values to the `originWhitelist` array to give access to more servers. But it also requires constant management to make sure it's up-to-date.

OTHER WAYS TO VALIDATE THE ORIGIN

A whitelist is not the only way you can validate client origin values. You can also modify listing 6.3 to use a regular expression or issue a database call to validate the origin. Suppose instead of just three clients you want to allow any client from http://localhost, regardless of port, to access your API. You could use a regular expression to validate this origin, as follows:

```
var createRegexpValidator = function(re) {
  return function(origin) {
    return re.test(origin);
  }
};
```

createRegexpValidator creates a function to validate an origin using a regular expression.

```
var corsOptions = {
  allowOrigin: createRegexpValidator(
      /^http:\/\/localhost(:\d+)?$/i)
};
```

This regular expression matches a request to any port on http://localhost.

This code snippet introduces a new `createRegexpValidator` function. The `create-RegexpValidator` function works in the same way as the `createWhitelistValidator` function from listing 6.2, except instead of a whitelist check, this function runs a regular expression. Any client of the form http://localhost:PORT (where PORT is the port

A single regular expression:

```
var re = /^http:\/\/localhost(:\d+)?$/i;
```

Matches all these whitelist values:

```
var originWhitelist = [
    "http://localhost",
    "http://localhost:1",
    "http://localhost:10",
    "http://localhost:100",
    "http://localhost:200",
    "http://localhost:300",
    "http://localhost:400",
    "http://localhost:1000",
    "http://localhost:1111",
    "http://localhost:2000",
    // And on and on and on...
;]
```

Figure 6.4   Regular expression versus a whitelist

number) can access the API. If you had hundreds of clients, each living on a different port, you can see how a single regular expression would be easier to manage than a whitelist with hundreds of entries, as shown in figure 6.4.

A regular expression is just one example of using a custom function to validate the origin. Table 6.2 shows more ways to validate the origin, along with the pros and cons of each.

Table 6.2   Pros and cons of validation techniques

Validation technique	Description	Pros	Cons
Whitelist	Maintains a list of valid origins	Clearly indicates which origins are allowed Works well for small lists of origins	Difficult to maintain as the list grows larger
Regular expression	Writes a regular expression that matches all the valid origins	Works well for a range of origins that follow a pattern	Need to verify that the regular expression doesn't accidentally match an invalid origin
Database query	Stores the list of valid origins in a database	Provides a central location for storing origin information Works well for a large number of origins without any common pattern Good for maintaining a consistent CORS policy across different servers	Database calls can be slow (may need a caching layer to speed up things)
Blacklist	The opposite of a whitelist: maintains a list of origins that aren't valid	Easier to maintain if you'd like to allow all but a few origins	Easy for clients to bypass (just pick a new origin that isn't in the blacklist)

Regardless of which technique you choose to validate the origin, the steps of the validation are the same:

1 Grab the value from the Origin header.
2 Validate the origin value using your chosen technique.
3 If the origin is valid, set the Access-Control-Allow-Origin header.

6.3.3 CORS and proxy servers

One side effect of validating origins against a whitelist is that the value of the Access-Control-Allow-Origin header can vary between requests. For example, a request from the origin http://localhost:1111 will return the header `Access-Control-Allow-Origin: http://localhost:1111`, but a request from http://localhost:2222 to the same server will return the header `Access-Control-Allow-Origin: http://localhost:2222`. These different response headers from the same servers can sometimes cause caching issues. If your server can return different Access-Control-Allow-Origin headers to different clients, you should also set the Vary HTTP response header to `Origin`, like so:

```
Vary: Origin
```

Without the Vary header, proxy servers may cache responses for one client and send them as responses to a different client. This issue is notoriously difficult to debug, because it may not be reproducible from clients who aren't behind the same proxy servers.

A *proxy server* is a server that sits between the client and the destination server. The proxy server forwards the request from the client to the server. Along the way, it may also provide additional functionality, such as caching data to speed up response time. Figure 6.5 shows two separate requests passing through a proxy server; the first request hits the destination server, while the second request is cached.

It's this caching functionality that is relevant to CORS. Proxy servers use some, but not all, of the HTTP request headers when deciding whether or not to cache a response. Because the Origin header is a fairly new HTTP header, not all proxy servers take the Origin header into account when deciding whether to cache a response.

Suppose it's Monday morning and coworkers Bob and Alice are at work catching up on the highlights from yesterday's game. They both get the scores from ESPN, but

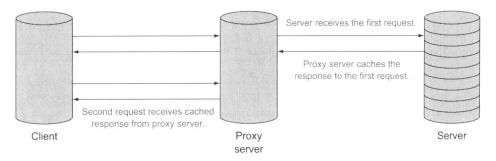

Figure 6.5 Example of a proxy server making two requests

Alice's request from http://tablet.espn.com

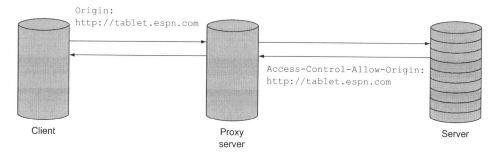

Bob's request from http://mobile.espn.com

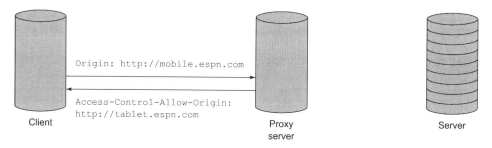

Figure 6.6   Example of how a proxy server could mix up Access-Control-Allow-Origin headers through caching

Bob is using his iPhone and visits http://mobile.espn.com, while Alice is using her tablet and visits http://tablet.espn.com. Because both Alice and Bob are at work, their requests flow through the company's proxy server.

When Alice makes the first request to http://tablet.espn.com, the tablet site makes a CORS request to load the scores from http://api.espn.com. The API responds with the header `Access-Control-Allow-Origin: http://tablet.espn.com`, and the proxy server caches the response.

Next, Bob makes his request to http://mobile.espn.com, and the mobile site grabs the scores from the same API. The proxy server notices that the request is to the same server that the tablet requested, and so it returns the cached response. Unfortunately, the cached response has the `Access-Control-Allow-Origin: http://tablet.espn.com` header set. This header causes a request from http://mobile.espn.com to fail, because the Origin header doesn't match the Access-Control-Allow-Origin header (figure 6.6).

Luckily, there is a way to fix this. The Vary header tells the proxy server that the Origin header should be taken into account when deciding whether or not to send cached content. With the `Vary: Origin` header in place, the proxy server will treat a request with `Origin: http://mobile.espn.com` differently from a request with `Origin: http://tablet.espn.com`.

The following listing shows a simple one-line change for adding the Vary header to the sample.

Listing 6.4   Listing 6.4 Setting the Vary response header

```
if (options.allowOrigin) {
  var origin = req.headers['origin'];
  if (options.allowOrigin(origin)) {
    res.set('Access-Control-Allow-Origin', origin);
  }
  res.set('Vary', 'Origin');                          Setting Vary:
} else {                                              Origin header
  res.set('Access-Control-Allow-Origin', '*');
}
};
```

The Vary header is only necessary when the Origin header causes changes in the response. You don't need it when you return `Access-Control-Allow-Origin: *`, because the * value is the same regardless of what the value of the Origin header is. The Vary header should also be present even if the Access-Control-Allow-Origin header isn't in the response. If a request's origin is http://example.com, the response will not have an Access-Control-Allow-Origin header, because http://example.com isn't in the list of whitelisted headers. But the response should still contain a Vary header, because the response can change, based on the Origin header value.

6.3.4 Null origin

So far we've only discussed origins in terms of URLs with a scheme, host, and port. But when configuring the acceptable origin values, it's important to keep in mind that `null` is also a valid origin value. A `null` origin value typically indicates that the request is coming from a file on a user's computer, rather than from a website. It can also mean the request came from a redirect (which we'll cover in more detail later).

Making requests from a file on your computer (which I'll refer to as a *local file*) is useful if you want to test CORS requests without uploading files to a live server. It can be a lot easier to test locally than to upload new code every time you'd like to test a request. Testing code is an iterative process: the developer writes code, tests the results, and writes more code based on the results. When working with a local file, a developer can iterate very quickly: trying new code is as easy as saving a file and refreshing the web browser.

In contrast, if CORS requests required an actual origin for every request, the developer velocity would be much slower. Each change would need to be uploaded to a web server, which can be slow (at least when compared with saving a file locally). The developer would also need a separate test server to test changes on, because uploading to the live server could break other users. Even if you don't anticipate using this technique to test your own API, opening up your API to `null` origins can make it easier for your users to test their code against your API.

The * value allows all origins to make cross-origin requests, including the `null` origin. If your server returns *, there is nothing more you need to do to support local files. If you're using the whitelist method, be sure to add the `null` value to your whitelist, as follows:

```
var originWhitelist = [
  'null',                          ⟵  Allows Origin: null to make
  'http://localhost:1111'              cross-origin requests
];
```

Adding `null` to the whitelist means that the server will return the following header in the response:

```
Access-Control-Allow-Origin: null
```

Along with the * and origin value, `null` is a valid value for the Access-Control-Allow-Origin response header.

6.3.5 *Origin header on same-origin requests*

Up until this point we've only discussed the Origin header in the context of cross-origin requests. But it turns out that some browsers will include the Origin header on same-origin requests as well. Chrome and Safari include the Origin header on same-origin POST, PUT, and DELETE requests. Firefox, Internet Explorer, and Opera don't include the Origin header on same-origin requests.

The good news is that although Chrome and Safari sometimes include the Origin header, they don't require any CORS-specific headers on the response. Same-origin requests will always work (figure 6.7), regardless of whether or not they have an Access-Control-Allow-Origin header. You don't need to explicitly whitelist your same-origin requests (although it won't hurt to do so).

You usually won't need to worry about this distinction between same-origin and cross-origin requests. If you're building an API for external users, you probably won't expect same-origin requests. And even if your API accepts both same-origin and cross-origin requests, as long as your API behaves exactly the same for both request types, you won't have to distinguish between the two.

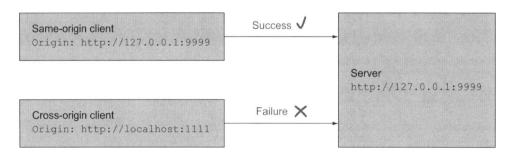

Figure 6.7   Response status when the server responds without an Access-Control-Allow-Origin header. The same-origin request succeeds, even though it has an Origin header. The cross-origin request fails.

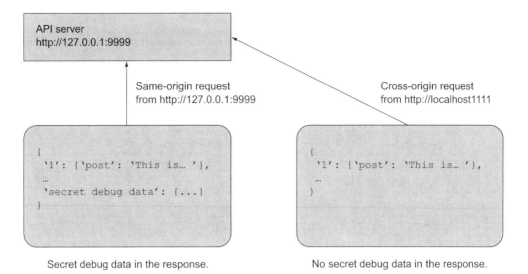

Figure 6.8   Different data is sent to same-origin and cross-origin requests

But if same-origin requests behave differently from cross-origin requests, the distinction between the two becomes relevant. Suppose you have an API that accepts requests from your own web page (a same-origin request) as well as requests from other clients (a cross-origin request). The request from your own web page receives additional debug information, which you don't want to share with cross-origin clients, as shown in figure 6.8. In this case, you want to differentiate between same-origin and cross-origin requests; otherwise cross-origin requests could receive data they aren't supposed to see.

In these cases, you can compare the Origin header against the Host header to see if they match. The Host header is an HTTP request header that contains the host and port of the server receiving the request. Because the Origin header contains the scheme, host, and port of the client sending the request, if the Origin and the Host headers match, the request is a same-origin request.

The following code snippet shows a function for detecting whether the request is a same-origin request. The `isSameOrigin` function returns `true` if the request is a same-origin request, and `false` otherwise.

```
var isSameOrigin = function(req) {
  var host = req.protocol + '://' + req.headers['host'];
  var origin = req.headers['origin'];
  return host === origin || !origin;
};
```

The `isSameOrigin` function extracts the client origin from the Origin header and compares it to the server's origin, which is derived from the Host header. Note that the Host header doesn't include any scheme information, so it's up to you to decide which scheme to use. The preceding code snippet uses the `req.protocol` property to

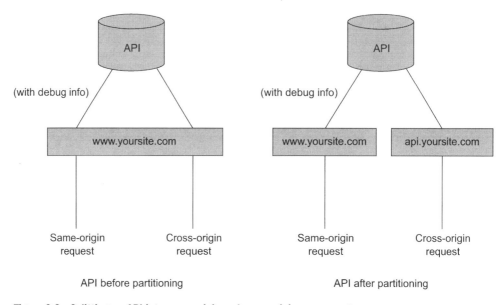

Figure 6.9   Splitting an API into same-origin and cross-origin components

figure out the scheme of the request. Calling `req.protocol` returns either `http` or `https`, and calculating the scheme is as easy as appending `://` to the protocol (for example, if the URL's protocol is "http", the scheme is "http://"). This `protocol` property is only available in Express. If you use Node without Express, you may need to find some other way of getting the request's scheme.

A better alternative to the Host header method is to separate same-origin traffic from cross-origin traffic (figure 6.9). If your same-origin and cross-origin traffic all funnels through www.yoursite.com, consider separating API requests into two different servers: www.yoursite.com for same-origin traffic, and http://api.yoursite.com for cross-origin traffic. You don't have to implement two completely different APIs, you just need to channel the requests differently. It's like having two doors to enter a bank: one door is for the public, and the second is for employees only.

Hopefully this section has given you a more comprehensive understanding of how to use the Access-Control-Allow-Origin header to manage cross-origin requests to your API. Although the Access-Control-Allow-Origin header helps dictate who gets access to your server, it shouldn't be the sole security mechanism for your API. The next section looks at the security issues related to CORS.

6.4   *Security*

The previous section presented strategies for accessing a server from different origins. At one end of the spectrum, any client can make cross-origin requests by setting the `Access-Control-Allow-Origin: *` header. At the other end of the spectrum, a server administrator can limit cross-origin requests to specific clients only. But regardless of which strategy you choose, there is one thing to always keep in mind: CORS isn't security.

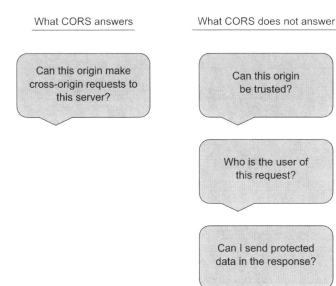

Figure 6.10 Questions CORS does and doesn't answer

This is an important enough point to state again: CORS isn't security. The Access-Control-Allow-Origin header only indicates which clients are allowed to make cross-origin requests. It shouldn't also be used to protect a site's content.

Figure 6.10 shows some questions that CORS does and doesn't answer. Don't be disheartened if you see a question that you'd like answered. Just because CORS doesn't answer a particular question doesn't mean it can't be answered at all. There are other mechanisms to answer these questions, which this section will explore.

To demonstrate why CORS shouldn't be used for security, consider that it's possible to use tools to spoof the Origin header. The following curl command shows how to send a request to your API with the Origin header set to somerandomorigin.com (if you don't know what curl is, don't worry; it will be covered in the next chapter).

```
curl -H "Origin: somerandomsite.com" http://127.0.0.1:9999/api/posts
```

This request is obviously not coming from somerandomsite.com, and your server shouldn't trust only the Origin header. This is why the Access-Control-Allow-Origin header should only be used to specify the cross-origin policy.

Spoofing CORS requests

The preceding curl request may have set off a red flag: What is the point of CORS if an Origin header can be spoofed? To answer this, it's important to keep in mind that users can use tools like curl to make an HTTP request to any server, regardless of whether or not the server has CORS enabled. CORS doesn't introduce any new security holes; it only ensures that cross-origin requests from a browser are performed in a safe manner.

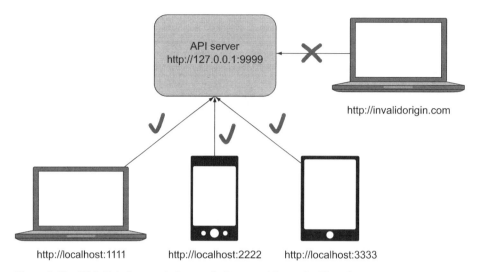

Figure 6.11   Whitelisted requests from a desktop, mobile, and tablet client

So if CORS shouldn't be used for security, how can you protect the content on your site when enabling cross-origin requests? The rest of this section explores ways to keep your site secure while still using CORS.

6.4.1   *Including cookies on requests*

Cookies aren't included on CORS requests by default, but they can be enabled by setting the Access-Control-Allow-Credentials header to `true`. If you're thinking about enabling cookies on your API, you should really consider whether you need cookie support. Cookies make requests harder to debug, and expose a new attack vector. So if you don't need cookies, don't enable them.

Cookies work best in situations where

- You want to authorize users within your own ecosystem of clients and servers.
- You know exactly which clients will be accessing your server.

This means that you control both the clients and the servers, and you don't accept CORS requests from external clients. The web/tablet/mobile scenario shown in figure 6.11 is a good example. In this scenario, CORS access is limited to a select few whitelisted origins. Because you're in charge of both the server and the clients, you have control over where the requests are coming from.

The following listing shows how to configure the sample code to allow cookies.

> **Listing 6.5   Enabling cookies on requests**

```
var corsOptions = {
  allowOrigin: createWhitelistValidator(originWhitelist),
  allowCredentials: true
};
```
Sets allowCredentials option to true

```
var handleCors = function(options) {
  return function(req, res, next) {
    ...
    if (options.allowCredentials) {
      res.set('Access-Control-Allow-Credentials', 'true');   ◁
    }
    ...
};
```

Reads allowCredentials option to set Access-Control-Allow-Credentials header

The code introduces a new `allowCredentials` option. Setting this value to `true` means that cookies are allowed on requests.

If you allow credentials on requests, the Access-Control-Allow-Origin header must be set to an actual origin value. The `*` value isn't valid when using credentials, and the browser will reject any response that has Access-Control-Allow-Credentials set to `true` but Access-Control-Allow-Origin set to `*`.

Using similar code as the previous section, you could write code to always echo the Origin header value when `allowCredentials` is set to `true`. This would allow any client (internal or external) to include cookies on requests. But while this is technically possible, it's not advisable. By enabling cookies to be always included on requests, you open your server up to a class of vulnerabilities called cross-site request forgery (CSRF). Appendix C goes into more details on CSRF. The rest of this section explores how to protect against CSRF vulnerabilities.

VALIDATING THE ORIGIN

The simplest way to protect against CSRF is to return an error if the origin is invalid. This ensures that only valid origins are allowed, and that the request stops processing if the origin is invalid. The previous section showed you how to use a whitelist to validate the origin, but it continued to process the request even when it encountered an invalid origin. The following listing repeats the origin validation code from the previous section.

> **Listing 6.6   Only whitelisted origins can make CORS requests**

```
var originWhitelist = [
  'null',
  'http://localhost:1111'
];

var corsOptions = {
  allowOrigin: createWhitelistValidator(originWhitelist),
  allowCredentials: true
};

var handleCors = function(options) {
  return function(req, res, next) {

    if (options.allowOrigin) {
      var origin = req.headers['origin'];
      if (options.allowOrigin(origin)) {
        res.set('Access-Control-Allow-Origin', origin);      ◁
      }
```

Nothing happens if origin is invalid, and request continues processing.

```
    res.set('Vary', 'Origin');
  } else {
    res.set('Access-Control-Allow-Origin', '*');
  }
```

Even though the code in the listing checks if the origin is valid, there is no `else` block to define how the request behaves with an invalid origin. Without defining this behavior, the code continues processing the request, even if the request is from an unauthorized origin. This means that even if the origin is invalid, the request's action, such as returning the user's blog posts, will go through.

What you really want to do is short-circuit the request in the CORS handler and return an error to the user. By stopping the request at the CORS-level, you prevent any other request code from running. The following listing introduces a new option to short-circuit the request.

Listing 6.7   Short-circuiting the request on invalid origins.

```
var originWhitelist = [
  'null',
  'http://localhost:1111'
];

var corsOptions = {
  allowOrigin: createWhitelistValidator(originWhitelist),
  allowCredentials: true,
  shortCircuit: true                          ◁──┐  Introduces a new
};                                                 │  shortCircuit option.

var handleCors = function(options) {
  return function(req, res, next) {

    if (options.allowOrigin) {
      var origin = req.headers['origin'];
      if (options.allowOrigin(origin)) {
        res.set('Access-Control-Allow-Origin', origin);
      } else if (options.shortCircuit) {
        res.status(403).end();            ◁──┐  If origin is invalid, stops
        return;                                │  processing request and
      }                                        │  returns an HTTP 403 response.
      res.set('Vary', 'Origin');
    } else {
      res.set('Access-Control-Allow-Origin', '*');
    }
```

The code begins by introducing a new `shortCircuit` option that controls this new behavior. Next, the code returns an HTTP 403 status if the origin is invalid, and stops processing the request.

ADDITIONAL CSRF PROTECTION

Validating the origin is a nice way to verify that the request meets your expectations and for most use cases, this should be a sufficient form of CSRF protection. However, it is not foolproof. As we saw earlier, tools like curl could be used to spoof the origin of a request. If you want stronger protection, you will need a *CSRF token*.

A simple definition is that a CSRF token is an unguessable secret shared between the client and the server. If a CSRF token is invalid, the request fails. Appendix C goes into more details about CSRF tokens and how they are used.

There are many packages available for adding CSRF token support to same-origin requests. Appendix C also includes an example that uses the CSURF middleware package to add CSRF token support to a sample server. This is easier to do on same-origin requests, where the client and server are the same machine, or share the same code.

Implementing CSRF token support is a bit trickier for cross-origin requests because in order for CSRF tokens to work, the server and client must agree upon a CSRF token format. A cross-origin request's client and server may live on separate servers and have separate codebases, which makes it hard to sync secrets. Another issue is that the CSRF token usually has embedded user information, such as a user ID or session ID. On same-origin requests, the user info can be derived from the cookie. On cross-origin requests, the client doesn't have access to the server's cookies.

These issues make it difficult to add CSRF protection to CORS requests. One possible way to do this is to have the client embed an iframe from the server. The server can place the CSRF token in this iframe, and then give it to the client via `postMessage`.

Security is very difficult to get right. If you need CSRF protection on CORS requests, here are a few things to keep in mind:

- *Consider whether you need CSRF protection.* CSRF protection is only needed if you are requesting protected data that includes the cookie.
- *Validate the Origin header.* This is a good form of CSRF protection, and it may be sufficient for your needs. While tools such as curl can spoof the Origin header, spoofing along with the cookie is harder (curl wouldn't have access to the cookie). Older browsers that allow the Origin header to be set don't support CORS.
- *Consider same-origin requests instead.* If you have a particular feature that requires CSRF protection, such as posting a new weblog, consider making it a same-origin feature instead. Same origin requests have proven mechanisms for protecting against CSRF. Part of using CORS successfully is understanding its limits, and you may save yourself a headache or two by using same-origin requests in this particular case.
- *Use something other than a cookie to validate the user.* If you're building a public API, or need to provide authorized access to all origins, an authorization mechanism like OAuth2 might be a better fit for your needs.

The next section explores the last bullet point in-depth by looking at what OAuth2 is and how it works.

6.4.2   *Authorizing requests using OAuth2*

Suppose you store all your calendar data in Google Calendar. One day you discover a cool new startup app that uses your calendar data to determine when is the best time to schedule a massage. This is a revolutionary idea! No longer do you need to worry about scheduling your own massages—this new app will do it for you.

There is only one problem. This hot new startup app needs your Google Calendar data in order to work. How can the startup get data from a different company such as Google? Well, you could give your Google password to this startup app, and the startup app could then log into your Google account and read your calendar data.

Of course sharing your password is a horrible, horrible idea. Your password is the key not only to your calendar data, but to any data you store in Google. By giving your password to a third-party startup, you trust that third party not to do anything bad with your data (like accidentally delete your calendar entries). And even if you do trust them, their systems could be hacked and your password could land in the hands of a hacker. Passwords are just too valuable to share.

So if you can't share your password, how can the startup app gain access to your data? OAuth2 can save the day. OAuth2 is an open authorization standard. It's a popular authorization mechanism for APIs. APIs from Dropbox, Facebook, GitHub, and Google (to name a few) all use OAuth2. The goal of OAuth2 is to allow a site to get user data from a different site without asking for the user's password. This keeps the user's password safe, and puts the user in control of when and how his or her data is used.

If the startup app implements OAuth2, instead of asking for your password, it will redirect you to a special page hosted on Google. Figure 6.12 shows an example of what this authorization page looks like.

Google then asks you if it's okay to share your data with this hot new startup. If you click Accept, Google gives a token to the hot new startup app. The startup app can then include this token in the request to load Google Calendar data. No passwords need to be shared to make this work.

This token method is a much better option than sharing your password. The token is "scoped," meaning that it can only be used to load calendar data, and can't change or delete calendar data. And if you, the user, decide you don't want the startup app to access your data after all, you have the power to revoke the token. Revoking the token prevents the startup app from using the token to access your data.

Once the third-party app has a token, it can use the token to make requests to the Google Calendar API for a particular user's data. When making a request for data, the token is included in the Authorization header of the request, as shown in figure 6.13. Because the Authorization header is added to the request by the client (rather than passively included on requests like cookies), a malicious user can't trigger a cross-site request forgery attack.

If you're using OAuth2 with CORS, it's important to remember to whitelist the Authorization header on preflight requests. Because the Authorization header isn't a

Figure 6.12 Example of a Google authorization page asking for your permission to share your calendar data with a third-party app

simple request header, it will always require a preflight request, even on GET and POST requests. Table 6.3 shows an example of making a request with an Authorization header. The Authorization header carries the token in the request. The request requires a preflight request because Authorization is a custom header.

Adding support for OAuth2 is beyond the scope of this book. It can be a difficult technology to work with, but luckily there are libraries for most major server languages.

Figure 6.13 Making an authorized request to the Google Calendar API

Table 6.3   Making a CORS request with an OAuth2 token.

Preflight request	Preflight response
OPTIONS /api/posts HTTP/1.1 Host: 127.0.0.1:9999 Origin: http://localhost:1111 Access-Control-Request-Method: GET **Access-Control-Request-Headers:** **Authorization**	HTTP/1.1 204 No Content Access-Control-Allow-Origin: http:// localhost:1111 Access-Control-Allow-Methods: GET, POST, PUT, DELETE **Access-Control-Allow-Headers:** **Authorization**

Actual request	Actual response

GET /api/posts HTTP/1.1
Host: 127.0.0.1:9999
Origin: http://localhost:1111
Authorization: Bearer <OAUTH2
TOKEN>
	HTTP/1.1 200 OK
	Date: Sat, 05 Apr 2014 20:28:05 GMT
	Content-type: application/json;
	charset=UTF-8
	Content-length: 123
	
	{
	  "data": "..."
	}

The node-oauth project has a popular OAuth2 implementation; it can be found at https://github.com/ciaranj/node-oauth. The OAuth2 website at http://oauth.net/2/ has more information on how OAuth2 works, as well as pointers to various server implementations. *Getting Started with OAuth2* by Ryan Boyd (O'Reilly Media, 2012) is also a great resource for learning how OAuth2 works.

This section introduced a lot of different security concepts. Here is a recap of each of these concepts, and how they're used:

- *Origin header*—Identifies where the client's request originates. Should only be used to verify that cross-origin requests from the origin are allowed.
- *Authorization cookies*—Can be used to identify the user making the request to the server. Cookies are always included on same-origin requests, and must be opted into by both the server and the client on cross-origin requests. But once opted in to, cookies can be vulnerable to CSRF attacks.
- *CSRF token*—Guards against CSRF attacks. Ensures that a request is coming from the user, not from a different page that is trying to trick the user into making a request.
- *Authorization header*—Used to add OAuth2 authorization information to the request. Authorizes a client to use a third-party API on behalf of a user, without the user giving their third-party username and password to the client.

Next, let's turn our attention to best practices for handling preflight requests.

6.5 Handling preflight requests

In the beginning of the chapter we talked about simple CORS requests. But if your server handles anything beyond simple GETs or POSTs, you also need to respond to preflight requests. Chapter 4 introduced the basics of handling preflight requests. As covered in that chapter, preflight requests are a necessary part of the CORS flow, and help protect servers from unsupported requests. But a preflight request can be a performance hit, because it requires two HTTP requests. This can especially be an issue on resource-constrained systems, like mobile phones. This section investigates strategies for both handling and reducing preflight requests.

6.5.1 Whitelisting request methods and headers

The preflight request is issued to verify that the server allows certain HTTP methods and headers. In the blogging sample, a preflight request is issued before a post can be deleted to ensure that HTTP DELETE requests are allowed.

Earlier in this chapter we used a whitelist to validate the origin header. You can use a similar whitelist to specify valid HTTP methods and headers. The code in the following listing updates the blogging sample application in app.js with two new options for configuring preflight requests, called allowMethods and allowHeaders.

Listing 6.8 Allowing HTTP methods and headers

```
var corsOptions = {
  allowOrigin: createWhitelistValidator(originWhitelist),
  allowCredentials: true,
  shortCircuit: true,
  allowMethods: ['GET', 'DELETE'],                              Configuration options
  allowHeaders: ['Timezone-Offset', 'Sample-Source']           for allowed HTTP
};                                                              methods and headers

var handleCors = function(options) {
  return function(req, res, next) {
    ...
    if (isPreflight(req)) {
      if (options.allowMethods) {
        res.set('Access-Control-Allow-Methods',
          options.allowMethods.join(','));                      Sets preflight-specific
      }                                                         headers to
      if (options.allowHeaders) {                               configuration values
        res.set('Access-Control-Allow-Headers',
          options.allowHeaders.join(','));
      }
```

The allowMethods and allowHeaders options contain the whitelisted HTTP methods and headers that are allowed by the server. The server uses these values to set the corresponding preflight headers on the response. Now that the code is configured to set the preflight headers, the far more interesting question is: what values do you choose for the whitelist?

ALLOWING HTTP METHODS

When it comes to the HTTP method, there are only a handful of acceptable values, the most common of which are HEAD, OPTIONS, GET, POST, PUT, PATCH, and DELETE. If you'd like to allow all types of cross-origin requests, you can set the Access-Control-Allow-Methods header to all of these values, as follows:

```
var corsOptions = {
  allowMethods: ['HEAD', 'OPTIONS', 'GET', 'POST',
                 'PUT', 'PATCH', 'DELETE']
};
```

A better approach is to consider which types of requests your server allows, and only accept those types of requests. If your server only allows GET and DELETE requests, you should only set those values on the preflight:

```
var corsOptions = {
  allowMethods: [GET', DELETE']
};
```

Accurate preflight headers protect your server from unexpected requests, and serve as useful documentation for your clients. If your server doesn't allow PUT requests, there is no reason to accept them in the first place, only to have them fail on the actual request. From the client's perspective, if they try to make a PUT request and it fails on the preflight, the developer can look at the error message and clearly understand why the request is failing, as shown in figure 6.14. If the PUT request is accepted by the preflight request but then fails on the actual request, the developer may be misled into thinking that the PUT request is failing for some other reason.

Unlike HTTP methods, which have a small set of acceptable values, clients can send any HTTP header. Let's look at how to configure custom request headers.

ALLOWING HTTP HEADERS

It can be a bit tougher to know which HTTP headers to allow on requests because there are so many different request headers. If you have control over both the server and the client, you can control exactly which headers are included on requests. Because you control the server code, it's easy to add a new header to the allow-Headers whitelist.

If you're building an API for external clients, it can be harder to know which headers to allow. JavaScript libraries and frameworks may add their own custom headers to requests. Table 6.4 lists a few common HTTP request headers.

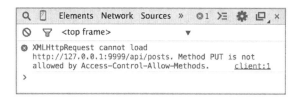

Figure 6.14 **Example of a failing PUT request. The error message clearly indicates why the request is failing.**

Table 6.4 Common HTTP request headers

Request header	Description
Authorization	The credentials for making an authenticated request. If the server uses OAuth2 to authorize users, the token would be set in this header.
Content-Type	The MIME type of the request body. The MIME type indicates the data type of the body. If the body were JSON, the MIME type would be `application/json`.
If-Match	The ETag value of the corresponding resource. Used during updates to ensure that the update doesn't conflict with a different update. Also used for requests with the Range header to make sure the new part matched the previously downloaded parts.
If-Modified-Since	Similar to the If-None-Match header, but with a date instead of ETag. The server only returns a response body if the resource has been modified since the date in this header. Otherwise, the server returns an HTTP 304 Not Modified status.
If-None-Match	The ETag value of the corresponding resource. Used when retrieving a resource. If the resource's ETag matches the request ETag, the resource hasn't changed since the previous retrieval, and the server returns an HTTP 304 Not Modified status (without a response body).
If-Unmodifed-Since	Similar to If-Match. Used during updates to ensure that the update doesn't conflict with a different update and to check if a Range request makes sense. Uses date instead of ETag.
Range	Specifies a range of bytes to download from the server (rather than the entire response). Used during resumable downloads to specify where to start the downloading.
X-Requested-With	Indicates where an AJAX request originates. Set by many JavaScript clients (although JQuery disables this header when making CORS requests).

Some of these headers are tied to certain features. For example, the If-Match and If-None-Match headers are tied to ETag support, so those headers need only be allowed if your server supports ETags. Table 6.4 is a good place to start if you're trying to decide which HTTP headers to support.

It's not easy to configure HTTP headers because there can literally be an infinite number of custom response headers. As a server administrator, you don't want to continually update your server configuration every time a client sends a new header. If you find yourself in this situation, the next section shares code to allow all request headers through.

ALLOWING ALL REQUEST HEADERS

As a server administrator, it can be overwhelming to manage all the headers a client may send. You may not even care about which headers a client includes on the request. In these cases, it would be helpful if the Access-Control-Allow-Headers header supported a * value that let all request headers through. The CORS spec doesn't define a * value for the Access-Control-Allow-Headers header, but you can mimic this behavior through the code in the following listing.

Listing 6.9   Adding all requested headers on preflight

```
var corsOptions = {
  allowHeaders: function(req) {                                    ◁──┐  Sets allowHeaders
    return req.headers['access-control-request-headers'];            │  option to a function
  }
};

var handleCors = function(options) {
  return function(req, res, next) {
    ...
    if (isPreflight(req)) {
      ...
      if (typeof(options.allowHeaders) === 'function') {          ┌── Sets value of Access-
        var headers = options.allowHeaders(req);                  │   Control-Request-
        if (headers) {                                            │   Headers header
          res.set('Access-Control-Allow-Headers', headers);
        }
      } else if (options.allowHeaders) {
        res.set('Access-Control-Allow-Headers',
            options.allowHeaders.join(','));
      }
    }
  }
```

The previous listing introduces an option that lets users define a function for setting the Access-Control-Allow-Headers header. The header is set to whatever value is returned by the function. This allows the user to customize the Access-Control-Allow-Headers header in any way (if the `allowHeaders` option isn't a function but an array, the code falls back on the original behavior of setting the header to the array).

In listing 6.9, the function in the `allowHeaders` option just returns the value of the Access-Control-Request-Headers header. This means that any header that is requested will be allowed. While the code itself is simple, the consequences are powerful. Any header the client sets on a request will be sent to your server. If you use this technique, you should be absolutely sure that your server is prepared to handle all incoming request headers.

Because the `allowHeaders` option can be a function, the developer isn't limited to allowing all request headers, and can define any type of behavior. For example, the function in the following listing will allow only those header values prefixed with X-.

Listing 6.10   Only allowing request headers prefixed with X-

```
  allowHeaders: function(req) {
    var reqHeaders = req.headers['access-control-request-headers'];
    if (!reqHeaders) {
      return null;
    }
    reqHeaders = reqHeaders.split(',');
    resHeaders = [];
    for (var i = 0; i < reqHeaders.length; i++) {
      var header = reqHeaders[i].trim();
```

```
      if (header.toLowerCase().indexOf('x-') === 0) {
        resHeaders.push(header);
      }
    }
  }
  return resHeaders.join(',');
}
```

This function is different from the one before because it actually parses and looks at the values in the Access-Control-Request-Headers header. It only returns those requested header values that start with an X-. For example, if the client sends the following request header:

```
Access-Control-Request-Headers: X-One, Two, Three, X-Four
```

the server will reply with the following response header:

```
Access-Control-Allow-Headers: X-One, X-Four
```

`X-One` and `X-Four` are allowed because they begin with `X-`, while header values `Two` and `Three` don't. If a developer inspects the preflight request and response, he or she can easily see which header values were requested and which were allowed.

This is just one example of the nuanced ways you can control the Access-Control-Allow-Headers header. If your own server has different request header requirements, you can tailor it any way you see fit.

6.6 *Reducing preflight requests*

While preflight requests are an important form of server protection, the additional HTTP request can be a performance hit. This is especially true for resource-constrained environments where HTTP requests are expensive, such as mobile devices. Therefore, it's useful to try to limit the number of preflight requests a client has to make. Now that your server is configured to respond to all types of preflight requests, let's look at ways to reduce the number of preflight requests.

> **NOTE** Some of these suggestions are also useful for supporting CORS on Internet Explorer 8 and Internet Explorer 9. If you'll recall from chapter 2, Internet Explorer 8 and Internet Explorer 9 use a special `XDomainRequest` object to make limited CORS requests.

6.6.1 *Maximizing the preflight cache*

The simplest way to avoid preflight requests is to take advantage of the preflight result cache. The cache exists for the specific purpose of avoiding multiple preflight requests to the same URL. You can increase the cache time by using the Access-Control-Max-Age header, as shown in the following listing.

Listing 6.11 Configuring the Access-Control-Max-Age header

```
var corsOptions = {
  allowOrigin: createWhitelistValidator(originWhitelist),
```

```
    allowCredentials: true,
    shortCircuit: true,
    allowMethods: ['GET', 'DELETE'],
    allowHeaders: ['Timezone-Offset', 'Sample-Source'],
    maxAge: 120
};

var handleCors = function(options) {
  return function(req, res, next) {
    ...
    if (isPreflight(req)) {
      ...
      if (options.maxAge) {
        res.set('Access-Control-Max-Age', options.maxAge);
      }
      ...
    };
```

◁── **Introduces new maxAge configuration option**

If maxAge option exists, sets Access-Control-Max-Age header

The Access-Control-Max-Age indicates the maximum number of seconds to cache a preflight request. For example, setting the header to a value of 120 will wait two minutes before issuing a new preflight request to the URL.

It's tempting to set the Access-Control-Max-Age value to something really high, like 604800 (the number of seconds in a week). But the Access-Control-Max-Age value is more of a suggestion, because browsers have their own caps on how long a preflight request can be cached for. Chrome, Safari, and Opera cache preflight requests for up to five minutes, while Firefox caches preflight requests for up to 24 hours.

The client origin and the server URL are part of the unique cache key used to determine if a preflight request has been cached. Because the cache key takes both the URL and origin into account, the cache can't be used to set blanket caching rules across sites. For example, because the cache applies to a specific URL, there is no way to specify a caching policy for an entire domain. Each URL under a domain has its own cache value. At the same time, there is no way to specify caching rules for a URL across all origins. If you make a request to a URL from origin http://foo.com, and then make a request to that same URL from http://bar.com, you'll have to issue a new preflight. Table 6.5 summarizes the cases where preflight requests are cached.

Table 6.5 Various requests and whether their preflight requests are cached

Request URL	Request origin	Is preflight cached?	Why?
/api/posts	http://localhost:1111	No	First request, there is nothing in the cache
/api/posts	http://localhost:1111	Yes	Preflight request was cached from the previous request
/api/posts/1	http://localhost:1111	No	Request sent to a different URL
/api/posts	http://localhost:2222	No	Request is from a different origin

Because the criteria for caching a preflight request are so limited, the preflight result cache provides narrow value. The preflight result cache is only useful for multiple requests to the same URL from the same origin, within a five-minute span. Most requests to an API will probably fall outside of this window. Luckily, there are still changes you can make to your API to reduce preflight requests.

6.6.2 Changing your site to reduce preflight requests

The key to reducing preflight requests is to reduce the conditions that result in preflight requests. Recall from chapter 4, a preflight is issued in cases where:

- The request method is something other than GET or POST.
- The request contains custom HTTP headers.

Eliminating these conditions will eliminate the need for a preflight. The following section looks at ways in which you can do this. Note that some of these suggestions fly in the face of what is considered good API design. You should weigh your need to eliminate preflight requests against the need to have a sane, structured RESTful API before implementing these suggestions.

REDUCING CUSTOM HEADERS

If your API includes custom headers on requests, eliminating or moving these headers can remove the need for a preflight. The Content-Type request header indicates what data type is in the body of a request. If you have a JSON API, it's tempting to set the value of the Content-Type request header to application/json. In fact, there are some libraries that will automatically set this value for you. But setting the Content-Type to application/json triggers a preflight, because the only allowed values for Content-Type are application/x-www-form-urlencoded, multipart/form-data, or text/plain. By removing this header from the request, you avoid the need to issue a preflight.

If you need the information from a particular header, you could consider moving the value from a header to a query parameter. The sample code in chapter 4 introduced the Timezone-Offset and Sample-Source custom headers to demonstrate how preflight requests work. Instead of custom headers, you could use query parameters to convey the same information. Table 6.6 shows two ways to convey the time zone and sample source data introduced in chapter 4.

Table 6.6 Moving custom headers into the query parameter. Eliminating the custom headers eliminates the need for a preflight request.

Original request (requires a preflight request due to custom headers)	New request (no custom headers, so no preflight request)

`GET /api/posts HTTP/1.1`
`Host: 127.0.0.1:9999`
`Origin: http://localhost:1111`
`Timezone-Offset: 300`
`Sample-Source: CORSInAction`
	`GET /api/posts?`
	`    timezoneOffset=300&`
	`    sampleSource=CORSInAction`
	`    HTTP/1.1`
	`Host: 127.0.0.1:9999`
	`Origin: http://localhost:1111`

The server-side code that reads these values would also have to change to read from the query parameter rather than the request headers.

REDUCING HTTP METHODS

Another way to reduce preflight requests is to reduce the types of HTTP methods used. If your API supports PUT or DELETE requests, these requests must have a preflight request. There is no way to work around a preflight on PUT and DELETE requests.

But if the request were a POST instead of a PUT, it wouldn't need a preflight request (so long as it didn't also have custom headers). Certain protocols, such as JSON-RPC, are built entirely around GET and POST requests only. (JSON-RPC also gives excellent preflight caching because all requests are made to a single endpoint.) If avoiding preflight requests is important, you may want to investigate an alternative protocol.

This section covered strategies for handling preflight requests. It started by discussing common methods and headers that should be whitelisted. It then described a technique to give more fine-grained control over what types of request headers are allowed (a technique that can be expanded to allow any request header).

Next it discussed strategies for reducing preflight requests. Because preflight requests issue an additional HTTP request, reducing them can lead to performance gains, especially on resource-constrained devices such as mobile. A preflight request is issued whenever a request uses methods other than GET or POST, or when it uses custom headers. Reducing the need for either reduces the need for preflight requests.

This discussion of preflight requests rounds out the basic building blocks of a CORS server. But there are still a few more odds and ends to CORS requests. The next sections look into exposing headers to clients, and handling HTTP redirects.

6.7   *Exposing response headers*

The last remaining CORS feature is the ability to expose response headers to the client. Chapter 5 described how the Access-Control-Expose-Headers header could be used to indicate which, if any, response headers are visible to the client. It's not a critical CORS header in that the request will still succeed if this header isn't present, but it's useful if clients need to read response headers. If the server wants to give the client the ability to read the X-Powered-By response header, it would set the following header on the response:

```
Access-Control-Expose-Headers: X-Powered-By
```

Using the technique similar to the Access-Control-Allow-Headers header, the sample code in the following listing adds an option to set the Access-Control-Expose-Headers header.

Listing 6.12   Exposing response headers to the client

```
var corsOptions = {
  allowOrigin: createWhitelistValidator(originWhitelist),
  allowCredentials: true,
  shortCircuit: true,
```

```
    allowMethods: ['GET', 'DELETE'],
    allowHeaders: ['Timezone-Offset', 'Sample-Source'],
    maxAge: 120,
    exposeHeaders: ['X-Powered-By']                 ◁─┐  New exposeHeaders option
};                                                      specifies which headers to expose

var handleCors = function(options) {
  return function(req, res, next) {
    ...
    if (isPreflight(req)) {
      ...
      res.status(204).end();
      return;
    } else if (options.exposeHeaders) {                   Sets Access-Control-
      res.set('Access-Control-Expose-Headers',            Expose-Headers on
          options.exposeHeaders.join(','));               nonpreflight responses
    }
```

The exposeHeaders option specifies the response headers that should be exposed to the client. If the exposeHeaders property exists and the request isn't a preflight request, the Access-Control-Expose-Headers header is set to the values in the expose-Headers array.

Table 6.7 summarizes common response headers that may be useful to clients. If your server sets one of the headers listed in the table, it may be useful to expose these to clients.

Table 6.7   Common response headers

Response header	Description
Content-Length	The number of bytes in the response body.
Date	The date the server sent the response.
ETag	A unique identifier that identifies a particular version of a resource. Used in conjunction with the If-Match and If-None-Match request headers to determine whether a resource has changed.
Expires	The date after which the resource is considered stale. Can be used in conjunction with the ETag or Date header to retrieve fresh content from the server.
Last-Modified	The date the resource was last modified.

It would be convenient to support a * value for the exposeHeaders option (similar to how you did for the allowHeaders option). A * value would mean that all response headers should be exposed to the client. To do this, the code needs to keep track of all the headers in the response. Unfortunately, NodeJS and Express don't provide convenient mechanisms for reading the response headers before the response is sent to the client. Other platforms, such as Java servlets, provide a mechanism for doing this. If you're using a language that supports this feature, you can use it to configure the Access-Control-Expose-Headers header.

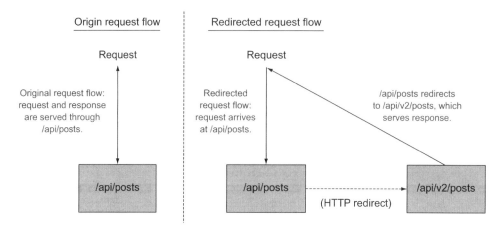

Figure 6.15   Sample server before and after introducing a redirect

6.8   *CORS and redirects*

When performing an HTTP redirect, both the server initiating the redirect and the server receiving the redirect must have the correct CORS headers. If either server doesn't have the correct CORS configuration, or doesn't support CORS at all, the request will fail.

As an API evolves, it may have the need to use HTTP redirects. While we like to think that our API design is perfect from the beginning, the truth is that APIs change based on user's needs and feedback, and it's sometimes necessary to create a whole new URL endpoint. In these cases, HTTP redirects give the server a mechanism for connecting the old URL to the new URL. Visitors to the old URL are seamlessly redirected to the new one. This ensures that old URLs will continue to work even as an API evolves.

Suppose you want to introduce a new API version living at /api/v2/posts. After a lot of testing and bug fixes, you decide that the API is ready for everyone to use, including users of the previous version. So you set up an HTTP redirect from /api/posts (the old endpoint) to /api/v2/posts (the new endpoint). Figure 6.15 shows what your new API would look like.

The following snippet shows the code that implements a redirect which consists of two parts: the HTTP status code and the Location header. The status code indicates that the response is a redirect. There are two valid status codes for redirects: 301, which indicates that a resource has permanently moved to a new URL, and 302, which indicates a temporary move. (An example of a temporary redirect is if a server is down and you want to redirect the visitor to a status page for the duration of the outage.) The Location header indicates where the new resource lives. The Location header can point to a resource on the same server, or on a completely different server.

```
serverapp.get('/api/posts', function(req, res) {
  res.redirect(301, '/api/v2/posts');
});
```

```
serverapp.get('/api/v2/posts', function(req, res) {
  res.json(POSTS);
});
```

This code sets the HTTP status to 301 (because you want to permanently redirect users), and sets the Location header to your new resource at /api/v2/posts. In addition to this code, any `xhr.setRequestHeader` code in client.html should be deleted. This prevents the client from initiating a preflight request (you'll see why this is important in a moment).

If you restart the server and visit client.html, you'll see two HTTP requests in your Network tab, as shown in figure 6.16. The first request hits /api/posts. This first request is then redirected to /api/v2/posts.

There are a couple of other caveats when handling a redirect with CORS. First, if the client is redirected to a resource on a different server, the Origin header will be set to `null`. So far we've only encountered `null` Origin values when working with local files, but this is an example of a null origin in a different context. The next listing shows what would happen if instead of redirecting to your own server, you redirected requests from /api/posts to www.HTML5Rocks.com/en/.

Listing 6.13 Redirecting a CORS request to a server at a different origin.

First request:
```
GET /api/posts HTTP/1.1
Host: 127.0.0.1:9999
Origin: http://localhost:1111
Accept: */*
Accept-Encoding: gzip,deflate,sdch
Accept-Language: en-US,en;q=0.8
Cache-Control: no-cache
Connection: keep-alive
Referer: http://localhost:1111/client.html
```

> CORS request is sent to
> http://127.0.0.1:9999/api/posts with
> Origin set to http://localhost:1111.

```
HTTP/1.1 301 Moved Permanently
Location: http://www.html5rocks.com/en/
Access-Control-Allow-Credentials: true
Access-Control-Allow-Origin: http://localhost:1111
Access-Control-Expose-Headers: X-Powered-By
Connection: keep-alive
Content-Length: 63
Content-Type: text/plain
Date: Sat, 05 Apr 2014 18:35:31 GMT
Vary: Origin
X-Powered-By: Express
```

> /api/posts redirects to
> www.HTML5Rocks.com/en/.

> Redirect also includes
> valid CORS headers.

Redirected request:
```
GET /en HTTP 1.1
Accept: */*
Accept-Encoding: gzip,deflate,sdch
Accept-Language: en-US,en;q=0.8
Connection: keep-alive
Host: www.html5rocks.com
```

```
Origin: null
Referer: http://localhost:1111/client.html

HTTP 1.1 200 OK
Access-Control-Allow-Origin: *
Cache-Control: no-cache
Content-Encoding: gzip
Content-Length: 4291
Content-Type: text/html; charset=utf-8
Date: Sat, 05 Apr 2014 18:35:32 GMT
```

Second request is made to www.HTML5Rocks.com/en/, with the Origin set to null.

HTML5Rocks.com responds with valid CORS headers.

The Origin header is set to `null` because the browser doesn't want to leak the origin value to the new server. Remember that redirects are followed automatically, so the client has no way to intervene before following the redirect. This could lead to a case where the client is redirected to a site that they didn't expect or want. In this case, hiding the Origin header value by setting it to `null` is a safety precaution.

The other caveat is that CORS preflight requests will never follow redirects. If you're making a CORS request that has a preflight, and the server tries to redirect you,

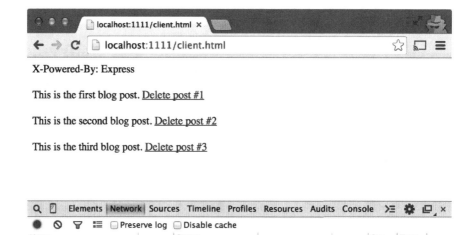

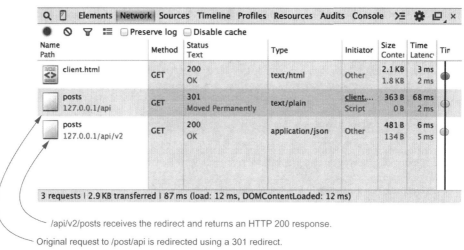

/api/v2/posts receives the redirect and returns an HTTP 200 response.

Original request to /post/api is redirected using a 301 redirect.

Figure 6.16 Viewing the HTTP redirect in Chrome's Network tab

Figure 6.17   Error when redirecting a request with a preflight

the request will fail. Figure 6.17 shows the error message you'll see in Chrome if you try to redirect a request that requires a preflight.

In this case, you'll need to manually inspect the response's Location header to figure out where the server is trying to redirect you, then send your request directly to that URL.

Here is a recap of how CORS works with redirects:

- Simple CORS requests will follow redirects.
- Preflight requests will not follow redirects.
- If the redirect is to the same server as the original request, the Origin header will stay the same. Otherwise, the Origin header will be set to `null`.

You probably won't run into redirects often, but it's still useful to understand how they work so you can build your API appropriately.

6.9   Summary

This chapter opened with questions you should ask yourself about your own CORS needs. After answering those questions, you should have a better idea of how you want to configure your server. The chapter then took a closer look at how to configure the various CORS-specific headers for your own needs. Here is a recap of each header:

- Access-Control-Allow-Origin:
  - Use the * value to allow requests from all origins.
  - Use a whitelist to allow only certain origins.
- Access-Control-Allow-Credentials:
  - Setting the value to `true` allows cookies on requests.
  - Enable cookies only if you're sure you need them.
  - If your server does support cookies, be sure to also validate the origin and implement CSRF protection.

- Access-Control-Allow-Methods:
  - This header only needs to be present on preflight responses.
  - It indicates which HTTP methods are allowed on a URL.
  - Common values include HEAD, OPTIONS, GET, POST, PUT, PATCH, and DELETE.
- Access-Control-Allow-Headers:
  - This header only needs to be present on preflight responses.
  - It indicates which HTTP headers are allowed on a URL.
  - Echo the Access-Control-Request-Headers value to get full header support.
- Access-Control-Max-Age:
  - This header only needs to be present on preflight responses.
  - It indicates how many seconds to cache preflight requests for.
  - Browsers may have their own maxAge caps.
- Access-Control-Expose-Headers:
  - This header indicates which response headers to expose to clients.
  - It's an optional header that isn't required for a successful CORS request.

The chapter also took a look at the security of CORS. It's important to remember that CORS in and of itself doesn't also serve as a mechanism for securing a server. If you need to serve protected content, consider some other authorization mechanism, such as cookies or OAuth2. If your CORS implementation allows cookies, it's also important to have CSRF protection in place.

Finally, this chapter examined how to minimize preflight requests by reducing the circumstances that lead to preflights. Reducing preflight requests is desirable because it eliminates an extra HTTP request, which can be expensive on resource-constrained devices such as mobile phones.

Part 3

Debugging CORS requests

The previous two parts of this book focused on how CORS works from both the client's and the server's perspective. Because there is both a client- and server-side component to CORS, there are many places where things can go wrong, and debugging these issues can be difficult.

Chapter 7 provides details on how to debug CORS requests. It starts by introducing you to the browser's developer tools. These developer tools provide a lot of insightful information about CORS requests, including any CORS-related errors, and a view into the request and response headers. If the developer tools aren't sufficient, the chapter looks at Wireshark, which is a tool that analyzes network traffic. Wireshark can help shed some light on why CORS requests are failing.

Next, the chapter looks at other tools that can be useful for debugging CORS requests, such as curl and test-cors.org. Then the chapter moves on to tips for debugging requests from mobile devices. Finally, the chapter covers where to go to get help on CORS-related issues.

Debugging CORS requests

7

This chapter covers

- Using network sniffers like Wireshark to view network traffic
- Using curl to make an HTTP request
- Debugging requests from mobile devices
- Getting more help on CORS-related questions

Suppose that, using the guidance from the previous chapters, you now have a working CORS server with a web page that makes CORS requests. You fire up your server, visit your web page...and nothing happens. Now what?

Up until this point, we've focused on how to build a working CORS server implementation. But what happens when things go wrong? Over the course of developing any application, things inevitably go wrong and need to be debugged. You may be building a CORS server, and find that requests aren't going through. Or you may be coding a client that talks to a CORS server, and find that the request is failing. Either way, you need to know how to figure out what is going wrong.

This chapter introduces tools that can be used to debug CORS requests. It starts by introducing features of the Chrome Debugger Tool. Next it looks at how to monitor request and response headers using Wireshark. Then it turns to using curl

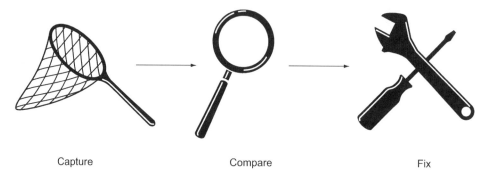

Capture   Compare   Fix

Figure 7.1   Three steps to fixing CORS errors

and test-cors.org to make CORS requests. It ends with resources where you can find answers to your CORS questions.

7.1   Solving CORS errors

With all the platforms, libraries, and frameworks out there, it can be daunting to know where to start debugging CORS requests. But regardless of whether you're using ASP.NET running on Mono or Tomcat running on Linux, debugging CORS comes down to one thing: isolating and analyzing the HTTP headers. The server and client communicate using HTTP headers, and most CORS errors indicate a mismatch between the client request headers and the server response headers.

Regardless of what tools you use to solve the issue, the steps to solving CORS errors are the same (see figure 7.1):

1 Capture a snapshot of the request and response headers
2 Compare the headers to see if and where there is a mismatch
3 Fix the issue by either
  a Updating the client to send the correct headers
  b Updating the server to allow the client headers

The rest of this chapter will explore tools you can use to capture and view the HTTP headers. But first, let's create a request you can test against. To understand how to debug broken requests, you need to break a request. The code from chapter 6 introduced configuration options that can be used to configure how a CORS-enabled server behaves. The following listing modifies the configuration options in a way that breaks the client.

Listing 7.1   Configuring the CORS server to only allow the Timezone-Offset header

```
var originWhitelist = [
  'null',
  'http://localhost:1111'
];
```

```
var corsOptions = {
  allowOrigin: createWhitelistValidator(originWhitelist),
  allowCredentials: true,
  shortCircuit: true,
  allowMethods: ['GET', 'DELETE'],
  allowHeaders: ['Timezone-Offset'],
  maxAge: 120,
  exposeHeaders: ['X-Powered-By']
};
```

Allows Timezone-Offset request header, but not Sample-Source header ◁┘

```
...
serverapp.get('/api/posts', function(req, res) {
  res.json(POSTS);
});
```

Removes redirect from chapter 6 ◁┘

These configuration options are essentially the same as those from the previous chapter, but with one critical difference. This code only allows the Timezone-Offset request header, even though the client is configured to send both the Timezone-Offset and the Sample-Source request headers. This means that the preflight request will fail, because the Access-Control-Allow-Headers response header won't match the Access-Control-Request-Headers request header (figure 7.2).

Access-Control-Request-Headers: Timezone-Offset, Sample-Source

Access-Control-Allow-Headers: Timezone-Offset

Figure 7.2   The CORS request fails because the Access-Control-Request-Headers doesn't match the Access-Control-Allow-Headers header.

The fix to this error is as easy as adding the Sample-Source header to the `allowHeaders` array. But even though you know how to fix this, set this knowledge aside and forget about it for a while. The rest of this chapter will approach this sample as if you were debugging an unknown error, and will walk through the tools that can be used to debug the request.

7.2   Using the browser's developer tools

If you restart the sample server and visit the client page, you'll be greeted with the error page rather than the blog posts. To figure out what went wrong, let's start by inspecting the error using your browser's developer tools.

All modern browsers have a suite of developer tools, which are in-browser panels that can help a web developer catch and diagnose issues with a site. The following sidebar explains how to find the developer tools in various browsers.

Finding your browser's developer tools

All modern browsers contain a suite of developer tools. While all developer tools perform the same functions, they can be found in different places depending on which browser you use. Here is a breakdown of how to find the developer tools in each browser.

- *Chrome*—Choose the Chrome menu at the top-right of your browser window, then choose Tools > Developer Tools. Or press F12 or Ctrl + Shift + I (or Cmd + Opt + I on a Mac). For more information, see https://developers.google.com/chrome-developer-tools/.
- *Firefox*—Choose the Tools menu, then choose Web Developer > Toggle Tools. Or press F12 or Ctrl + Shift + I (or Cmd + Opt + I on a Mac). For more information, see https://developer.mozilla.org/en-US/docs/Tools.
- *Internet Explorer*—Internet Explorer's developer suite is called F12 because you can launch the developer tools by pressing F12. For more information, see http://msdn.microsoft.com/library/ie/bg182326(v=vs.85).
- *Opera*—Opera's developer suite is called Dragonfly and it can be found by choosing the Tools menu, then Advanced > Opera Dragonfly. Or press Ctrl + Shift + I (Cmd + Opt + I on a Mac). For more information, see http://www.opera.com/dragonfly/.
- *Safari*—To use Safari's developer tools, you must first enable the feature by clicking Show Develop Menu in the Menu Bar found in Safari's preferences under the Advanced pane. This will show a Develop menu in the toolbar. Next, choose Develop > Show Web Inspector. Or press Cmd + Opt + I after enabling the Develop menu. For more information, see https://developer.apple.com/safari/tools/.

The developer tools contain many different features, including:

- *Console*—Logs errors and other useful messages, and enables developers to interactively execute JavaScript on a page.
- *JavaScript debugger*—Allows the developer to set breakpoints and trace through JavaScript code.
- *Network monitor*—Logs the request and responses for all network traffic. Can be filtered by resource type.
- *DOM inspector*—Enables the developer to view the DOM associated with elements on the page.
- *Profiler*—Tracks the performance of actions on the site, and enables the developer to uncover performance bottlenecks.

When debugging CORS requests, we'll focus on two features in particular: the console and the network monitor. The examples from the rest of this chapter will use Chrome, but the developer tools from any browser can perform the same functions. Let's see how you can use these tools to debug CORS requests.

Figure 7.3   Error message from the missing request header

7.2.1   Using the console

The console can be found in the developer tools and under the Console tab (if it isn't already selected). The console serves two purposes:

- It logs any messages or errors that occur while a site loads and runs.
- It allows you to enter JavaScript commands that can be run against the page.

The console is the first place to check when something on the page goes wrong. With that in mind, if you reload the sample client, the error from figure 7.3 should appear.

The text of the error message may differ from browser to browser. Chrome and Safari happen to give very detailed error messages for CORS errors. In the message from figure 7.3, you can see exactly what is wrong: "Request header field Sample-Source isn't allowed by Access-Control-Allow-Headers."

The console also lets you run JavaScript commands from the page. If you made changes to the server, you could reissue the CORS request without reloading the page by calling the `getBlogPosts` function directly. To do this, type `getBlogPosts()` in the console window and press Enter. Because the request will still fail, you'll see the same error message as in figure 7.3.

So, the console tells you what the error is, but not much more. To debug this request further, you need to look at the HTTP request itself. This can be done from the Network tab.

7.2.2   Using the Network tab

The Network tab shows the HTTP requests and responses from a page, as shown in figure 7.4. This includes requests for CSS style sheets, JavaScript files, images, fonts, Web-Sockets, and any HTTP requests triggered from `XMLHttpRequests`.

The Network tab for the sample shows two requests:

- The client.html page itself
- The CORS request to load the blog posts

The request to load the blog posts, shown in the bottom row, is a failing request.

The Network tab also provides additional information about the request, also shown in figure 7.4. This includes information such as the HTTP method, the HTTP status, the content type of the request, the location on the page that initiated the request, the size of the response, and the time it takes to load the response.

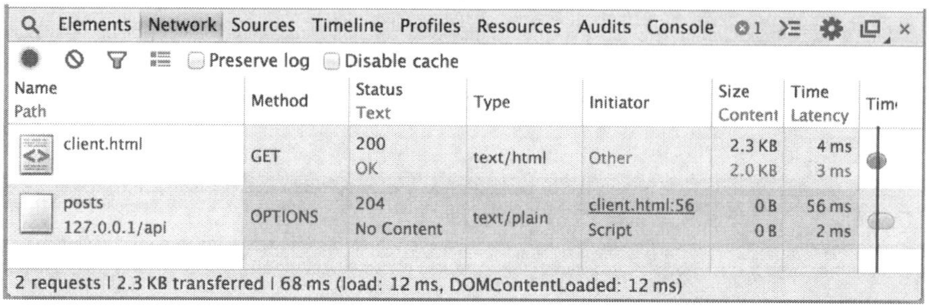

Figure 7.4   The Network tab in Chrome's developer tools

Right clicking a column can configure the view to show and hide additional bits of information. There are two additional columns that are hidden by default, but can be useful when debugging CORS requests. The Remote Address column indicates the server the request is going to, and can be useful for identifying cross-origin requests; the Vary column indicates the value of the Vary header (as you learned in chapter 6, the Vary header indicates which header values should be taken into account when calculating caching resources).

Clicking the request reveals even more detailed information, such as the request and response headers, as shown in figure 7.5. When debugging CORS requests, it's important to pay special attention to any CORS-specific headers, such as the Origin header and any header prefixed with Access-Control.

The Network tab provides more insight into why the request is failing. The HTTP method is OPTIONS, which means that the preflight request is failing. Because the preflight request fails, the actual request is never issued. This is verified by the fact that you don't see a second GET request to load the blog posts. By inspecting the HTTP headers, you can see that although the request has an Access-Control-Request-Headers: timezone-offset, sample-source header, the server responds with Access-Control-Allow-Headers: Timezone-Offset, and is missing the Sample-Source header.

Now that we've diagnosed the root cause of this issue, there are a few ways to proceed. If the request header is expected and valid, the server configuration can be updated to allow the request header. But this only works if you have control over the server configuration (as you do in this sample). If you're making requests against a server you don't have control over (for example, if you're querying a third-party API built by a different company), your options are more limited. You can remove the Sample-Source header from the client. That is easy in this particular case, because the Sample-Source header doesn't do anything. But if the request header is important to the request, you may need to reach out to the server owner and ask them to allow your particular header. Table 7.1 explores ways to fix this issue.

The console log message coupled with inspecting and comparing the HTTP request and response headers is usually sufficient to diagnose most CORS issues. But there are times when the developer tools don't tell the whole story. If you issue a simple

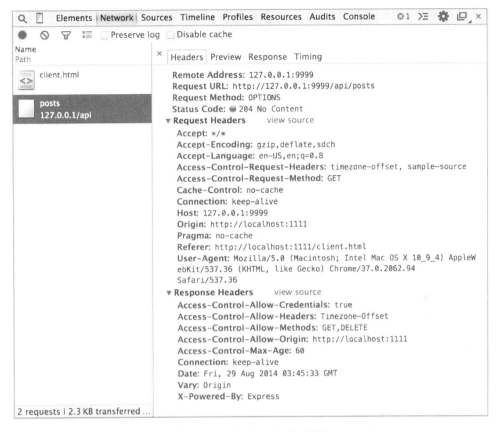

Figure 7.5 Viewing the request and response headers for the failing request

Table 7.1 CORS issue can either be fixed in the client code or the server code

In the client code	In the server code
| ```
xhr.setRequestHeader(
  'Timezone-Offset',
  new Date().getTimezoneOffset());
xhr.setRequestHeader(
  'Sample-Source',
  'CORS in Action');
``` | ```
var corsOptions = {
  ...
  allowHeaders: [
    'Timezone-Offset',
    'Sample-Source']
};
``` |
| Remove the disallowed header from the request | Add the failing header to the `allowHeaders` whitelist (only works if you can change the server code) |

cross-origin `GET` request that fails, Chrome's developer tools will hide the response headers. The response headers are hidden because of the browser's policy of hiding any information that the server hasn't opted in to. This also makes it hard to debug cross-origin requests. The next section looks at how to use a network sniffer like Wireshark to view the HTTP request and response headers.

7.3   *Monitoring network traffic*

Sometimes Chrome developer tools won't show all the HTTP header information. To see this in action, let's once again break the sample code, but in a different way. The following code snippet removes the Timezone-Offset and Sample-Source custom request headers from the client.html file:

```
var xhr = createXhr('GET', 'http://127.0.0.1:9999/api/posts');
xhr.onload = function() {
  var data = JSON.parse(xhr.responseText);
...
```

> Removes Timezone-Offset and Sample-Source request headers from client.html

Next, the app.js server code is updated to remove the client http://localhost:1111 from the whitelist:

```
var originWhitelist = [
  'null'
];
```

> Removes http://localhost:1111 from whitelist in app.js

This essentially means that the client won't be able to make requests, because there won't be an Access-Control-Allow-Origin header in the response. If you restart the sample and reload the page, you'll once again see an error, but there will be some slight differences.

Figure 7.6 shows the Console and Network tabs for the request to /api/posts. The request still fails, but this time the failure is on the actual GET request, because there is no preflight request. (Remember there is no preflight request because you removed the custom request headers from the request.) The HTTP status is labeled as (canceled). Clicking the request itself shows that while you can see the request headers, the response headers are missing and there is an error that says "CAUTION: Provisional headers are shown." This error means that the response headers are unavailable. In this particular case, because the CORS request fails, the browser follows the conservative route and hides any response information, even though an HTTP response was sent to the server.

Even though Chrome won't display the response headers, there are other options available. You could always try a different browser. Browsers such as Internet Explorer and Firefox will display the response headers (although it's possible that they could change this behavior in the future).

Another option is to use a packet analyzer, such as Wireshark or Fiddler. Packet analyzers show all the network traffic flowing through your system, including the cross-origin request from the browser. The rest of this section explores how to use Wireshark or Fiddler to capture and view network traffic.

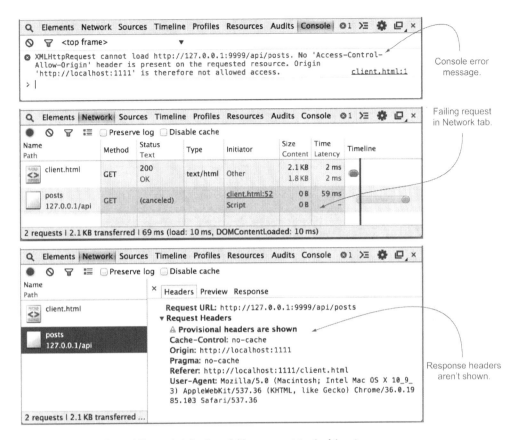

Figure 7.6   Console and Network tabs for a failing request to /api/posts

7.3.1   Using Wireshark

Wireshark is a tool that monitors and logs all network traffic passing through your computer. The network traffic isn't limited to HTTP requests, but it includes all network traffic, including TCP and UDP traffic. Wireshark fits under the general category of tools called *packet analyzers*. But what makes it appealing is that it's an open source tool that runs on most platforms (including Windows, Mac, and Linux). Wireshark can be downloaded from http://wireshark.org. Appendix B goes into more details on how to download and install Wireshark.

> **NOTE**   While this section focuses on Wireshark, you don't need to use it to obtain network data. Any packet analyzer will do. Other popular tools with network monitoring support include Fiddler and Charles.

Wireshark is a rich app with many features, so we'll focus on the features you can use to debug CORS requests. When you first fire up Wireshark, you're greeted with a starting page similar to figure 7.7.

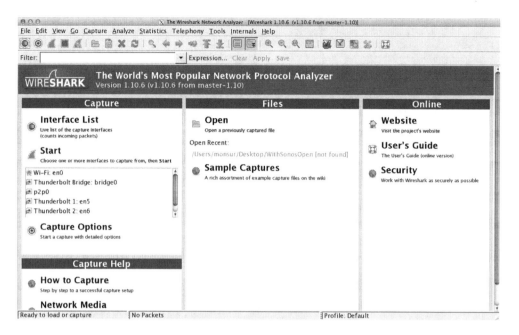

Figure 7.7   Wireshark startup screen

TIP   It might be a good idea to close all open tabs and any other sources of network traffic while Wireshark is running. This will make it easier to find your CORS requests among all the other network chatter.

This screen offers a lot of choices, but we're going to focus on starting a network capture. To initiate a network capture, choose your network interface and click Start. The network interface is the interface through which network requests are made. Choosing the right network interface can be tricky. If you're making requests to the outside world, you should choose the interface you're connected with, such as Wi-Fi. But if you're following along with the sample code, you should select the "loopback" interface, because the sample is making a request from your computer to your computer.

NOTE   Windows users may have issues with this step. If you're on Windows, you can skip ahead to the next section, which covers Fiddler, a packet analyzer for Windows.

Once the network capture has started, Wireshark switches to the view in figure 7.8. Wireshark is now monitoring and logging all the network traffic passing through your computer. Each line in the log is a network request or response. Don't worry about making sense of this output at the moment; you'll learn how to filter the data to find what you're looking for.

Now that the network capture has started, you need to trigger a CORS request so that it can be logged. You can do this by reloading the page at http://localhost:1111/client.html.

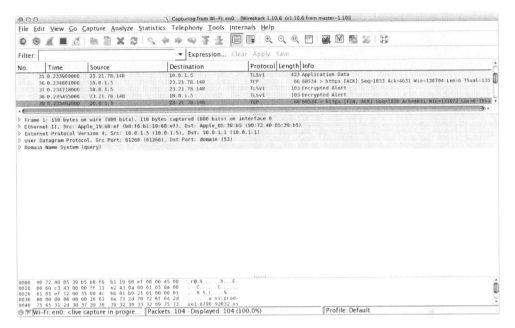

Figure 7.8 Wireshark capturing network traffic

Reloading the page will trigger an HTTP request to your server. Once the page has reloaded, you can stop the capture in Wireshark by clicking Stop.

The CORS request is logged somewhere in the network capture log, but finding it can be like spotting a needle in a haystack. Luckily Wireshark provides a rich filtering language to help narrow down the entries in the log. A simple way to find the CORS request is to filter the network log by HTTP requests. This is as simple as typing `http` in the filter box. Figure 7.9 shows the results of filtering by HTTP requests. You can clearly see both the request and response for the client.html page and the /api/posts pages.

Notice that unlike in Chrome's developer tools, you can see the response to the /api/posts request. Clicking each log item will show more details about the request, including the headers. If you click the response to the /api/posts requests, you can see that although the request has an Origin header, the response doesn't have an Access-Control-Allow-Origin header, and therefore the request fails. Figure 7.10 shows the discrepancy in the headers.

Wireshark is useful for digging into HTTP requests when the browser doesn't provide the information you need. This is often the case when making simple GET or POST requests that don't have a preflight request.

7.3.2 *Using Fiddler*

Fiddler is another packet analyzer. It is easier to use than Wireshark, but it's available only on Windows. In addition to network analysis, Fiddler supports a lot of other features, such as web debugging, web session manipulation, performance testing, and

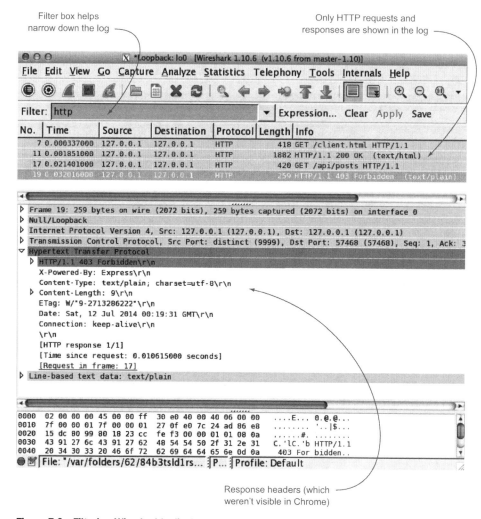

Figure 7.9   **Filtering Wireshark's display to only show HTTP requests and responses**

security testing. But for the purposes of debugging CORS requests, we'll focus on the network analysis.

Fiddler is a free tool, and it can be downloaded from www.telerik.com/fiddler. If you'd like to follow along with this example, install and run Fiddler (see appendix B for installation details).

NOTE When opening Fiddler, Windows 8 users may see a popup referring to `AppContainer`. It's safe to ignore this message. Go ahead and click either No or Cancel.

From the moment you open Fiddler it starts recording network traffic. If you go back to your browser and navigate to http://localhost:1111/client.html, you'll see the requests appear in Fiddler, as shown in figure 7.11.

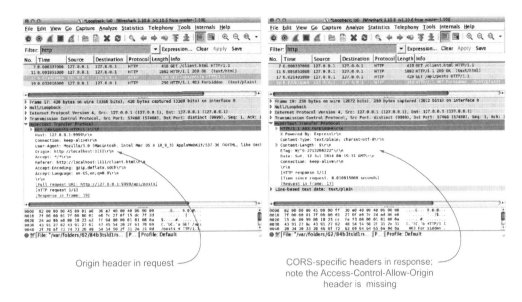

Origin header in request ⟶

CORS-specific headers in response;
note the Access-Control-Allow-Origin
header is missing

Figure 7.10 CORS request and response to /api/posts

Network requests ⟶

Request details,
including HTTP headers ⟶

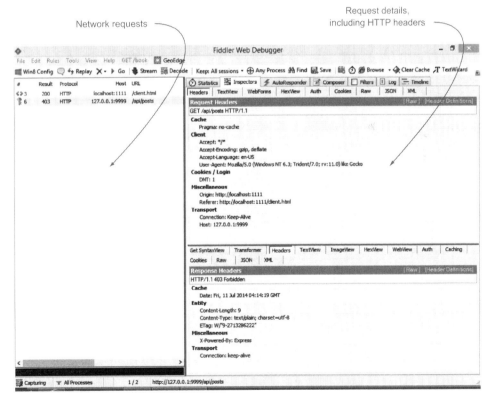

Figure 7.11 Viewing network traffic in Fiddler

The left pane records each request, and includes such details as the protocol, response status, host, and URL. You should see the requests to both client.html and /api/posts in the left pane. Selecting the /api/posts request opens up more details in the right pane, such as the request headers, response headers, response body, and cookie details. Selecting the Inspector tab, followed by the Headers tabs (there should be two Headers tabs, one for requests and one for responses), will show you the request and response headers. In figure 7.11, you can see that while the request has an Origin header, the response doesn't have the corresponding Access-Control-Allow-Origin header.

If you have other browser windows open, you may notice the left pane fills up with requests pretty quickly. Fiddler allows you to filter requests so you can only focus on those requests that matter to you. Figure 7.12 shows how to use the Filter tab to limit requests to only those from localhost or 127.0.0.1. As you can see from the figure, there are myriad other ways to filter requests.

This section only scratches the surface of what Fiddler can do. If you're using Windows, Fiddler is a simple, yet powerful tool for analyzing network traffic. This section covered tools for monitoring network traffic. But when testing CORS requests, it can also be useful to trigger various types of requests. Next, let's look at how to initiate CORS requests using curl.

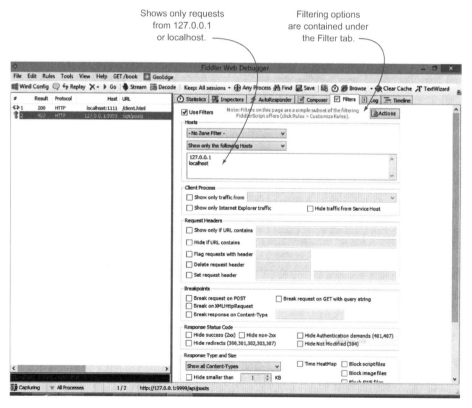

Figure 7.12 Filtering requests in Fiddler

7.4   *Using curl to simulate CORS requests*

When building a new CORS implementation, it's often useful to craft HTTP requests to the server and observe the results. One way to do this is to create a web page with an XMLHttpRequest that performs exactly the request you need. While this works, it can grow tedious to edit an HTML page, refresh it in the browser, then check the results in the developer tools. Curl is a command-line tool that lets you craft HTTP requests to the server and view the results. Let's look at how you can use curl to make requests to the sample server.

7.4.1   *Making CORS requests using curl*

Curl comes preinstalled on most Linux and Mac systems, but you'll have to download it for Windows (appendix B goes into detail on how to install curl). You can see if you have curl installed on your computer by typing curl --version. If this returns an error, you'll need to install curl from http://curl.haxx.se/.

> **NOTE**   Some versions of Window's Powershell already have an alias to curl that points to the Invoke-Webrequest cmdlet. If typing curl --version returns an error about "Bad Gateway," you're using the wrong curl. You can work around this issue by installing and using the curl tool from http://curl.haxx.se/.

Curl can be used to send HTTP requests to servers. Let's start with a simple example. The following command can be used to send an HTTP request to Google:

```
curl http://www.google.com
```

If you type in this command, it will return the HTML response from Google.com. Next, let's turn this curl request on the sample server. The following command hits the sample blogging API:

```
curl http://127.0.0.1:9999/api/posts
```

If you run this command, you'll receive the response Forbidden. While the request was sent to the server, this message doesn't shed any insight into what is wrong, especially because there aren't HTTP headers in the response. Curl's --verbose option can be used to display the request and response headers. To view the HTTP headers, add the --verbose option to the curl request:

```
curl --verbose http://127.0.0.1:9999/api/posts
```

This command will not only print Forbidden, but also the request and response headers, as shown in figure 7.13.

The request headers are prefixed with >, while the response headers are prefixed with <. Looking at the response headers, you can clearly see that the Access-Control-Allow-Origin header is missing.

If you look closely at the request headers, you can also see that the Origin header is missing. The browser automatically adds the Origin header. When using curl, you need to manually add the Origin header. You can set headers on curl requests by

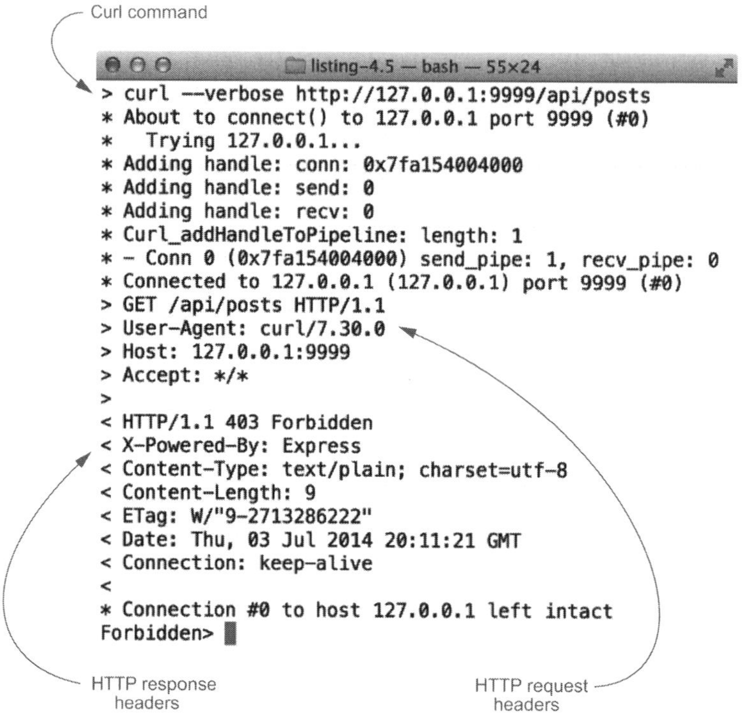

Curl command

```
> curl --verbose http://127.0.0.1:9999/api/posts
* About to connect() to 127.0.0.1 port 9999 (#0)
*   Trying 127.0.0.1...
* Adding handle: conn: 0x7fa154004000
* Adding handle: send: 0
* Adding handle: recv: 0
* Curl_addHandleToPipeline: length: 1
* - Conn 0 (0x7fa154004000) send_pipe: 1, recv_pipe: 0
* Connected to 127.0.0.1 (127.0.0.1) port 9999 (#0)
> GET /api/posts HTTP/1.1
> User-Agent: curl/7.30.0
> Host: 127.0.0.1:9999
> Accept: */*
>
< HTTP/1.1 403 Forbidden
< X-Powered-By: Express
< Content-Type: text/plain; charset=utf-8
< Content-Length: 9
< ETag: W/"9-2713286222"
< Date: Thu, 03 Jul 2014 20:11:21 GMT
< Connection: keep-alive
<
* Connection #0 to host 127.0.0.1 left intact
Forbidden> █
```

HTTP response   HTTP request
headers   headers

Figure 7.13 Request and response headers from the curl command

using the -H flag, as shown in the following code snippet. If you wanted to mimic a request from the sample client, you could set the Origin as follows:

```
curl --verbose -H "Origin: http://localhost:1111" http://127.0.0.1:9999/api/
    posts
```

Setting the Origin header is useful when you want to test an Origin but don't want to host a page on that origin. For example, the preceding command tested a request from http://localhost:1111 without having to upload and run code on the actual http://localhost:1111 site. The following command changes the Origin to a null value to mimic a request from a file:

```
curl --verbose -H "Origin: null" http://127.0.0.1:9999/api/posts
```

If you run this command, you'll see an Access-Control-Allow-Origin header in the response. This is because the null value is in the origin whitelist. The -H command can be used to add any request header. If you want to mimic a request from Firefox, you could add Firefox's User-Agent header to the request.

Debugging CORS requests is all about comparing the request headers to the response headers. The actual body of the response isn't too important, and it can get in the way of the header information (especially when a response has a ton of text that pushes the headers off the screen). The response body can be hidden by redirecting it to a different location. The command to do this on Windows is

```
curl --verbose -H "Origin: null" http://127.0.0.1:9999/api/posts > NUL
```

The same command on Mac/Linux looks like this:

```
curl --verbose -H "Origin: null" http://127.0.0.1:9999/api/posts > /dev/null
```

Using this syntax makes the output easier to read. Now that you have a basic understanding of how curl works, let's take a look at how to use curl to mimic a preflight request.

7.4.2 *Making preflight requests using curl*

Curl can also be used to send preflight requests. Figure 7.14 (introduced in chapter 4 as figure 4.9) highlights the characteristics of a preflight request.

A preflight request will have an OPTIONS HTTP method ❶, an Origin header ❷, and an Access-Control-Request-Method header ❸. To mimic a preflight request using curl, you need to mimic these three characteristics.

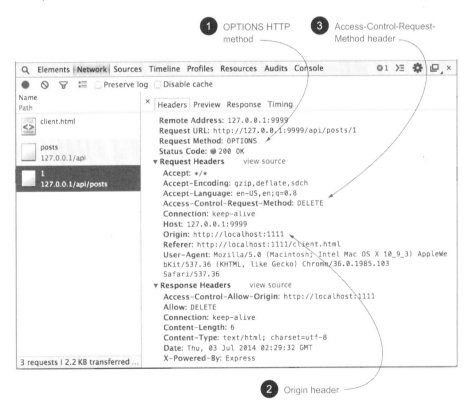

Figure 7.14   The pieces of a preflight request

The previous section showed you how to add an Origin header to the curl request. The -H flag can also be used to add an Access-Control-Request-Method header to the request. Finally, the -X flag can be used to set the HTTP method. The final curl request looks like this:

```
curl --verbose -H "Origin: null" -H "Access-Control-Request-Method: GET"
   -X OPTIONS http://127.0.0.1:9999/api/posts
```

After running this command, the server will reply with the preflight response.

7.4.3   Why use curl?

There are reasons why using curl can be advantageous over making requests from a web page, including:

- Developer velocity
- Request flexibility
- Ease-of-use
- Isolation

Let's delve further into what each of these items mean.

DEVELOPER VELOCITY

Developer velocity is the speed at which you can iterate and develop your app. Tools with high developer velocity enable you to work faster.

The traditional development process for CORS is to edit code, reload the web page, and view the headers in either the developer tools or Wireshark. Curl can speed up this process because making a curl request and viewing the headers can all be done in the same window.

If you have a complicated web app, there may be additional pieces of the page that need to load, or you may need to click a button to trigger the CORS request. Another way in which curl speeds development is that it focuses solely on the HTTP request, and doesn't need to load any of those extraneous pieces.

REQUEST FLEXIBILITY

Curl is flexible enough to craft any type of HTTP request you can imagine. You can do things with curl that you can't do from a web page.

Suppose you want to test your server's behavior with requests from different origins. To do this from a browser, you'd need to upload your client code to each site that you want to test, which is cumbersome. With curl, you have the flexibility to set the Origin header (and any other header) to any value you need.

EASE-OF-USE

Curl's ease-of-use was demonstrated earlier when you learned how to trigger a preflight request from CORS. Triggering the same preflight request from JavaScript code can be a little more difficult, because you have to build the actual request, then rely on the browser to send the correct preflight. In curl, you don't need to jump through hoops to trigger a preflight.

NOTE Chrome and Firefox's Network tab include a Copy as cURL option when you right-click a request. This allows you to copy a request from the browser as a curl command you can run from the command line. This makes curl even easier to use.

ISOLATION

Perhaps most importantly, curl provides isolation. When you make a request from JavaScript code, there are places where things can go wrong. The developer's JavaScript code may have a bug in it, or your assumptions of which headers the browser is adding may be different from what the browser is doing.

With curl, what you see on the command line is exactly what is sent to the server. If you have an error in your code, but the curl request works just fine, you know there is something wrong in your code. If you have an error in your code and the curl request fails, you know the issue is somewhere on your server.

7.5 *Sending requests using test-cors.org*

Full disclosure: I am the creator and maintainer of test-cors.org. I built the site because I found it difficult to find information on how CORS requests behave in actual browsers. The test-cors.org site offers four features for testing CORS requests:

- A curl-like interface to send CORS requests to a remote server. This can be useful for testing actual CORS requests from a browser against your server.
- A mechanism for configuring a server's response, then testing a request against this response. This can be useful if you want to learn how server and client settings interact.
- A mechanism to view events in an XMLHttpRequest's lifecycle.
- A mechanism to get the JavaScript code for the request you're testing. These last two features are useful for client-side CORS users as well.

When you first visit test-cors.org, you're greeted with the page in figure 7.15.

The page is divided into three parts: the client panel, the server panel, and the results panel. Let's dig deeper into how these panels interact by exploring the various features of test-cors.org.

7.5.1 *Sending requests to a remote server*

The first way to use test-cors.org is to send cross-origin requests to a remote server. This is similar to how curl works, but it makes its request from the browser using an XMLHttpRequest object, rather than the command line. This can be helpful because it makes an HTTP request the same way you'd expect a client. For example, curl will let you add a Host header to the request. But the Host header can't be set from test-cors.org, because the browser controls this header.

To use test-cors.org to send a request to your sample server, begin by recreating the request to /api/posts in the client panel. This is a GET request that includes cookies and has the Timezone-Offset and Sample-Source headers set. Next, choose the Remote

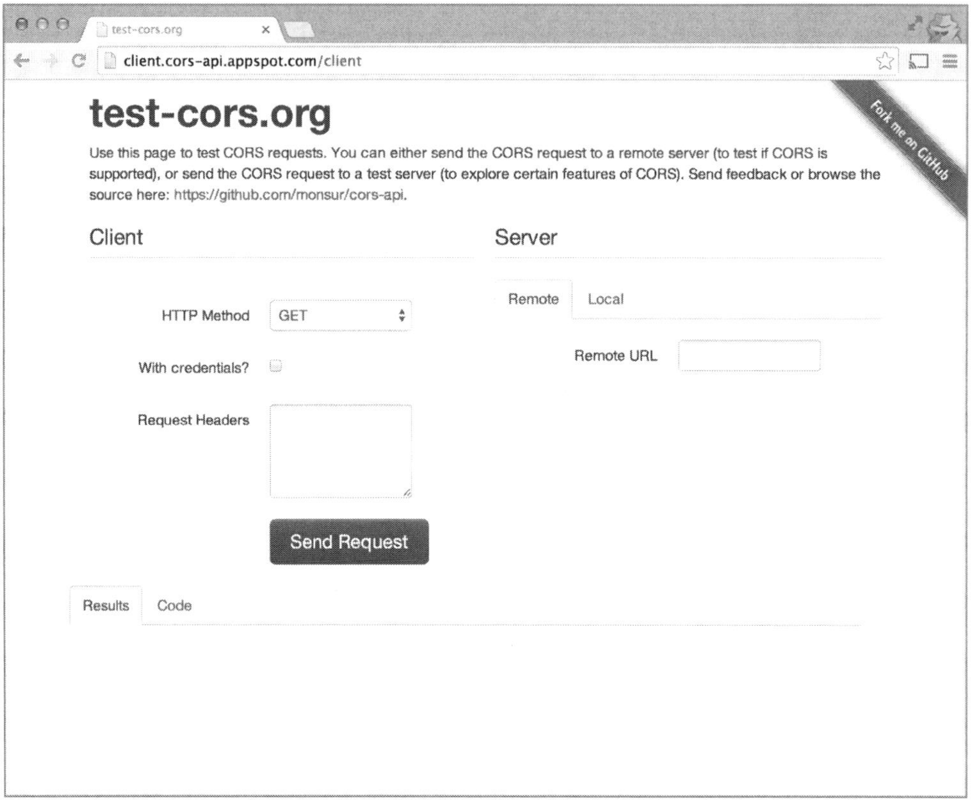

Figure 7.15   The test-cors.org landing page

tab in the response panel (if it's not already selected) and enter http://127.0.0.1:9999/api/posts in the Remote URL textbox.

> **NOTE**   You'll also need to whitelist the origin http://client.cors-api.appspot.com in your server app.

If you click the Send Request button, it will send the request to your test server. Figure 7.16 shows an example of what the page should look like.

It may seem odd that the test-cors.org website, which lives on a different server, can access your local server at 127.0.0.1:9999. But remember that test-cors.org makes requests from the browser, so the test-cors.org server itself isn't involved in the request. Since the JavaScript code is running on your computer, it can make requests to localhost.

Another convenient feature of test-cors.org is that you don't need a working CORS implementation to use it. The site also allows requests to be made to its own local server. The next section takes a look at how to do this, and why it's useful.

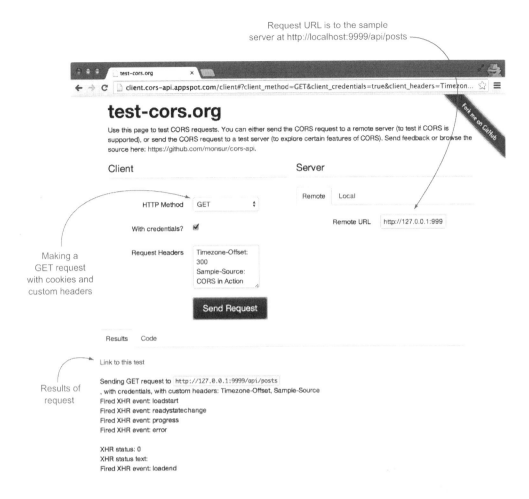

Figure 7.16 Making a request to the sample server

7.5.2 *Sending requests to the local server*

In addition to sending cross-origin requests, test-cors.org can send requests to its own local server. This local server can be configured using the parameters in the response panel, which control how the server responds to CORS requests.

Let's configure the local server to respond to the same GET request configured in the previous section. Choose the Local tab in the response panel. This shows the options that can be configured in the local server. If you click Send Request, you'll see that the error event handler will fire. This code throws an error because you haven't configured the local server to support cookies and custom headers.

Each box under the Local tab corresponds to a particular CORS header. You can add support for cookies and custom headers by first clicking the Allow Credentials checkbox, then typing `Timezone-Offset`, `Sample-Source` in the Allow Headers check-box. After making these changes and clicking Send Request, the request should succeed, as shown in figure 7.17.

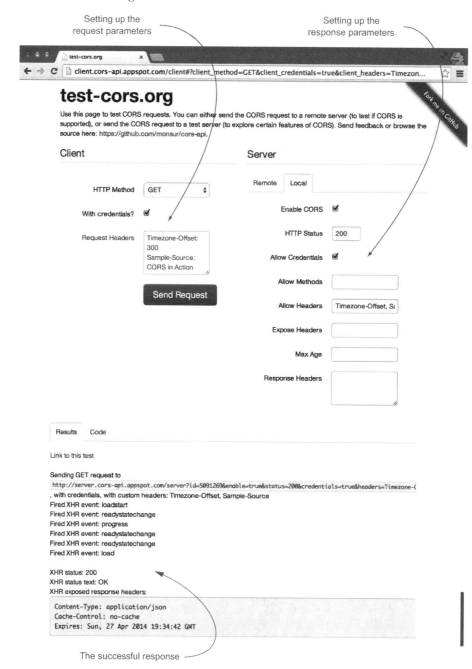

Figure 7.17   Recreating the request to /api/posts on the test-cors.org server

This particular feature was intended as a playground for exploring how CORS works. CORS can be a difficult feature to learn because it requires both a server and a client. This feature gives you both a server and a client that you can customize and play around with. Hopefully it can be a useful tool for answering your CORS questions.

7.5.3 Understanding how the client works

Test-cors.org can also be used to get a better handle on how the client behaves when making cross-origin requests. The log panel displays the following bits of information (see figure 7.18):

- All the client-side event handlers that fire during the course of the request. This can be useful to view things like when and in what order the events fire.
- The status code and status text associated with the response.
- Any response headers visible to the client. This can help verify which headers are exposed through the Access-Control-Expose-Headers header.

In addition, the site gives you the JavaScript code associated with the request. Choosing the Code tab will show the JavaScript code used to send the request, as shown in figure 7.19.

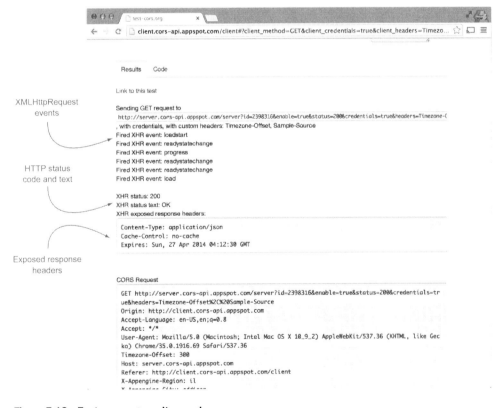

Figure 7.18 Test-cors.org results panel

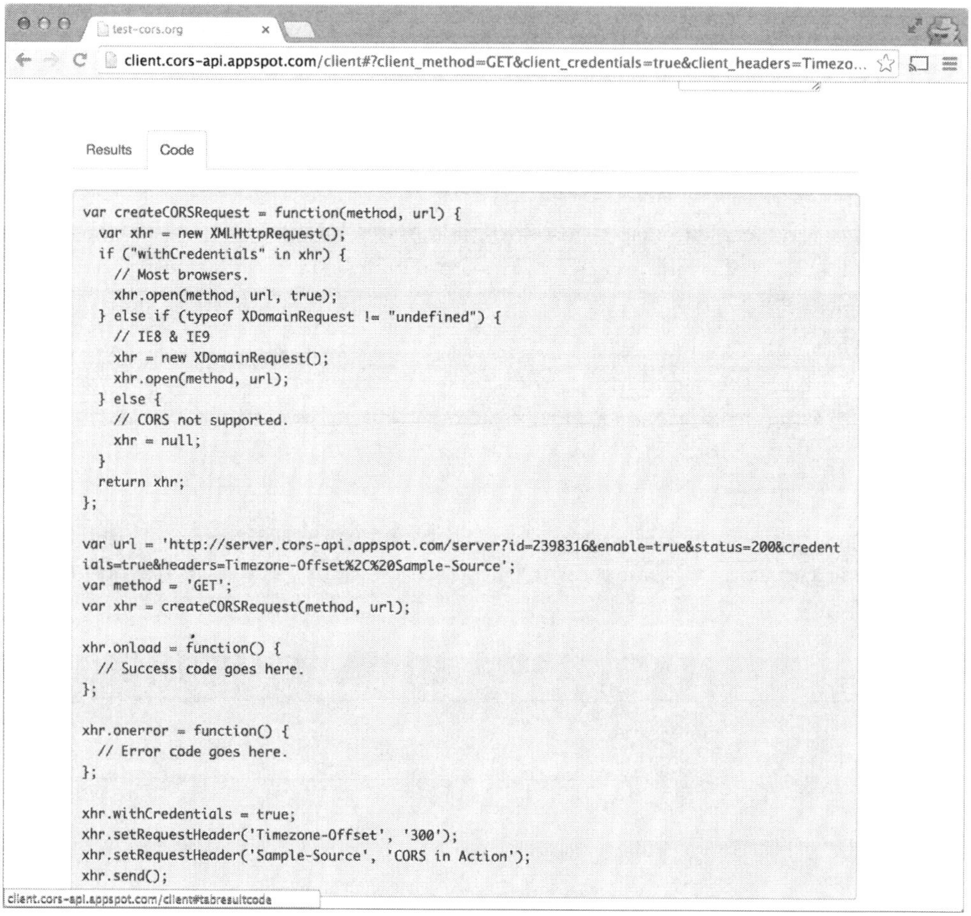

Figure 7.19   JavaScript code used to make the HTTP request

The code in figure 7.19 creates an XMLHttpRequest that uses the GET method, sets with-Credentials to true, and sets the Timezone-Offset and Sample-Source request headers. You can copy and paste this code into your own page to recreate the same request.

The tools and techniques described here work great for debugging from a computer. It can be a bit harder to debug requests from mobile devices. For example, there is no way to run Wireshark on your iPhone. The next section looks at tips for debugging requests from mobile devices.

7.6   *Tips for mobile debugging*

Debugging requests from mobile phones can be a challenge because the tools described in this chapter aren't available on a mobile phone. But if you're debugging requests from a mobile phone, there are still techniques you can use to capture the HTTP headers.

7.6.1   Log requests on the server

If you're in charge of the server that receives the request, you could configure it to log HTTP headers. The following code will log the request headers to a Node.js server's output:

```
console.log(req.headers);
```

The headers can be logged to the output, to the server logs, or to anywhere that is convenient for you. The exact configuration of where to log the headers depends on your server and logging framework.

7.6.2   Use test-cors.org

We covered test-cors.org in the previous section. Because test-cors.org is a web tool, it can be accessed from any browser, including mobile browsers. If you visit test-cors.org from your mobile phone, you can send a series of test requests to your own server or to the test-cors.org server and view the response.

7.6.3   Use remote debugging tools

There are remote debugging tools available for mobile phones and they all work in the same way. You connect your phone to your computer, and the computer logs request and response information from the phone. Here are a few remote debugging options:

- Chrome has built-in remote debugging options for Android phones. More details can be found at https://developer.chrome.com/devtools/docs/remote-debugging.
- Safari supports remote debugging for iPhones and iOS devices, but only from a Mac. More details can be found at http://webdesign.tutsplus.com/articles/quick-tip-using-web-inspector-to-debug-mobile-safari–webdesign-8787.
- Fiddler is a tool that allows you to proxy mobile requests through your computer, and logs the request and response details. Fiddler can be used with both iOS and Android, but it only runs on Windows. You can learn more about Fiddler at www.telerik.com/fiddler.

7.6.4   Use a mobile simulator

Google, Apple, and Microsoft all provide mobile simulators to test their respective mobile platforms. These simulators are programs that run in your computer, but mimic a mobile phone interface. Figure 7.20 shows an example of Apple's iOS simulator running on a Mac.

Using a simulator will give you a good idea of how a request will behave on a mobile device. It's also handy when you want to test a device you may not have access to (for example, if you own an Android phone, but want to test an iPhone).

So far I've covered techniques for testing and debugging CORS requests. But what if you've tried all these techniques and you're still stuck? The next section looks into some options for getting help with CORS questions.

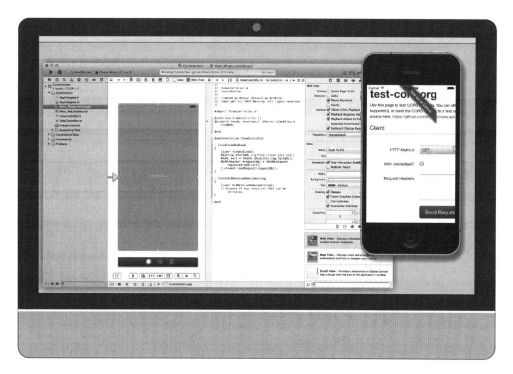

Figure 7.20   Apple's iOS simulator

7.7   *Getting help*

If you're stuck on some CORS issues, here are a few resources you can consult to get some help. The first is the site enable-cors.org (full disclosure: I maintain this site as well). The site seeks to catalog how to enable CORS in all the programming languages and platforms. The examples in this book are built around Node.js, but if you're using a different platform, such as Tomcat, you can turn to enable-cors.org to learn more about configuring CORS in Tomcat.

Enable-cors.org catalogs over 10 different platforms. It also contains pointers to learning more about CORS, as well as links to other CORS-enabled APIs. The site is also open source and hosted at GitHub at https://github.com/monsur/enable-cors.org, so you can contribute your own edits or content.

Stack Overflow (http://stackoverflow.com) is a good place to ask CORS-related questions. It is a popular, community-driven, question-and-answer site for programming-related issues. Each question can be categorized with a set of tags, and you can find CORS questions tagged with a "cors." If you post a question here, including the request and response headers from your code (using either Chrome developer tools or Wireshark, as described previously) can go a long way toward helping others to answer your question.

7.8   *Summary*

This chapter presented tools you can use to debug issues with CORS requests. When faced with a broken CORS request, the steps to solve it are always the same:

1. Grab a snapshot of the request and response headers.
2. Compare the headers to see if and where there is a mismatch.
3. Fix the issue by either
   a. Updating the client to send the correct headers.
   b. Updating the server to allow the client headers.

This chapter also covered the following tools and resources, which can aid in debugging CORS requests:

- *Developer tools*—Can be used to show errors, network traffic, and request/ response headers
- *Wireshark*—Can be used to monitor network traffic
- *Curl*—Can be used to send HTTP requests
- *Test-cors.org*—Can be used to test cross-origin requests in the browser
- *Enable-cors.org*—Can show how to configure CORS in your own platform
- *Stackoverflow.com*—Where you can ask CORS-related questions

While CORS can be a powerful tool for enabling open APIs, it can sometimes prove challenging to work with. I hope this chapter and this book help you to successfully implement CORS on your own servers, and tackle any CORS-related issues that come your way. The web has always been driven forward by a vision of simplicity and openness. By supporting and using CORS, you're doing your part to help promote this vision.

appendix A
CORS reference

Clients and servers using CORS "talk" to each other through request and response headers. This appendix documents headers and other terms used when making CORS requests. It's based on the latest version of the CORS spec at the time of writing (W3C Recommendation, January 16, 2014, which can be found at www.w3.org/TR/2014/REC-cors-20140116/).

A.1 *HTTP headers*

This section documents HTTP headers used by CORS. Headers can be categorized in different ways: they can either be present on the request from the browser, or on the response from the server; or they can be present on the preflight request, the actual request, or both (although it doesn't hurt if preflight request headers are also on the actual request).

Request headers

The browser is responsible for setting the CORS request headers, and these headers can't be overridden by the client code. Table A.1 documents the headers that may be present on CORS requests.

Response headers

The server is responsible for setting the CORS response headers. Using these response headers, the server can control how cross-origin requests behave. Table A.2 documents the headers that may be present on all CORS responses (preflight and actual responses).

Table A.1   Request headers on all CORS requests

Header	Included on preflight request, actual request, or both?	Details
Origin	Both	The client's origin. For example, for a request from http://www.example.com/sample/path, the Origin header value would be http://www.example.com. Required on all CORS requests (preflight and actual). Some browsers may add the Origin header on same-origin `PUT`, `POST`, and `DELETE` requests. The origin is defined in RFC6454 "The Web Origin Concept" (http://tools.ietf.org/html/rfc6454). This spec is separate from the CORS spec.
Access-Control-Request-Headers	Preflight	A comma-separated list of headers the client would like to send on the actual request. Used during a preflight request to ask the server's permission to send certain request headers. Simple headers (defined in A.2.2) may not be included in this header.
Access-Control-Request-Method	Preflight	The HTTP method the client would like to use for the actual request. This header is required on all preflight requests, even if the value is a simple method (defined in A.2.1).

Table A.1   Response headers on all CORS responses

Header	Included on preflight response, actual response, or both?	Details
Access-Control-Allow-Credentials	Both	The header has only one valid value: `true`. This header is optional. Its presence with `true` value indicates that the server allows user credentials such as cookies on cross-origin requests. If the client would like to include user credentials on cross-origin requests, they must also set the `XMLHttpRequest`'s `withCredentials` property to `true`. If the server doesn't allow user credentials on cross-origin requests, this header should be omitted.
Access-Control-Allow-Headers	Preflight	A comma-separated list of headers that the server allows on cross-origin requests. If a value is a simple header (defined in A.2.2), it doesn't need to be included in this header. Adding headers in the list causes no harm.
Access-Control-Allow-Methods	Preflight	A comma-separated list of HTTP methods that the server allows on cross-origin requests. If the value is a simple method (defined in A.2.1), it doesn't need to be included in this header.

Table A.1   Response headers on all CORS responses *(continued)*

Header	Included on preflight response, actual response, or both?	Details
Access-Control-Allow-Origin	Both	Gives permission to make a cross-origin request. Valid values include: *, null, or the client's actual origin value (for example, http://www.example.com). Required on all CORS responses.
Access-Control-Expose-Headers	Actual	A comma-separated list of HTTP headers. Indicates which response headers a client can read from the server's response. If a header is a simple response header (defined in A.2.3), it doesn't need to be included in this list.
Access-Control-Max-Age	Preflight	The number of seconds the preflight request cache should store the preflight response. Browsers may cap this value. Chrome won't cache preflight responses for more than 5 minutes, while Firefox won't cache preflight responses for more than 24 hours.

A.2   *Other terms used in CORS*

In addition to the headers just noted, there are a few other important terms used by CORS.

Simple method

A *simple method* is an HTTP method that won't trigger a preflight request. The simple methods are defined as:

- GET
- HEAD
- POST

Note that requests with a simple method may still trigger a preflight request if they contain nonsimple headers. The next section covers simple headers.

Simple header

A *simple header* is an HTTP request header that won't trigger a preflight request. The client doesn't need the server's permission (via a preflight) to make requests with only these headers. The simple headers are defined as:

- Accept
- Accept-Language
- Content-Language
- Content-Type, but only if the value is one of the following:
  - application/x-form-urlencoded
  - multipart/form-data
  - text/plain

Simple response header

During a same-origin request, the client JavaScript code can access the HTTP response headers using the `getResponseHeader` or `getAllResponseHeaders` methods on the `XMLHttpRequest` object. But cross-origin requests are limited in which response headers are visible to the client. Simple response headers are those that are visible to the client by default. All other headers need permission from the server to be viewed on the client; the server gives permission by using the Access-Control-Expose-Headers header. The simple response headers are defined as:

- Cache-Control
- Content-Language
- Content-Type
- Expires
- Last-Modified
- Pragma

appendix B
Configuring your environment

This appendix shows you how to install and configure tools used throughout this book. Some of these tools make extensive use of the command line. For a crash course on how to use the command line, visit http://learnpythonthehardway.org/book/appendixa.html.

B.1 Setting up for the sample application

Chapter 3 introduced a sample application that's used throughout the book. The prerequisites for running the sample are

- Node.js
- NPM
- Express

The rest of this section explains what these prerequisites are and how to set them up. Note that these instructions may change in the future. If you're having trouble installing these tools, you can always visit their respective websites to get the latest installation instructions.

B.1.1 Node.js and NPM

The sample runs in Node.js, a development platform for writing server apps. Node.js apps can be written in JavaScript, which is convenient because the client code is also written in JavaScript. Node.js can be downloaded and installed from http://nodejs.org. This page has a giant Install button right on the front that you can click to download the Node.js installer, as shown in figure B.1.

The following subsections look at installing Node.js on different operating systems. In addition to installing Node.js, the installer will install the Node Package

Figure B.1   Node.js homepage with an Install button.

Manager (NPM), which is a helper app used to download and install Node.js libraries. You'll use NPM later on to download and install Express and other modules.

INSTALLING NODE.JS ON WINDOWS

Windows will download a MSI installer file. Double-click this file to begin the installation process. Feel free to accept the default values for the options presented during the installation.

There are a few things to note when installing Node.js on Windows. First, you may be presented with a security dialog during the installation process, as shown in figure B.2

Figure B.2   Security warning when installing Node.js on Windows. Click Yes to continue.

Figure B.3   Finding and running the Node.js command prompt

(in fact, you may see this security dialog for all apps you install on Windows). It's safe to click Yes to continue.

Second, Node.js comes with its own command prompt which is preconfigured with all the proper variables for running Node.js. You can find this command prompt by searching for "Node.js command prompt" in the Start menu, as shown in figure B.3.

Throughout the rest of the samples in this book, when the instructions ask you to use a terminal window, use the Node.js command prompt.

INSTALLING NODE.JS ON MAC OS X

The Mac installer comes as a PKG file. Double-click this file to begin the installation process. As you walk through the installation, use the default values for all the options.

The final step of the installation process asks you to "Make sure /usr/local/bin is in your $PATH", as shown in figure B.4.

You can easily verify this by opening a terminal window and typing `echo $PATH`. This command will print output similar to figure B.5; you should see /usr/local/bin somewhere in that path.

If for some reason that path doesn't have that value, you can manually add it with the following command:

```
export PATH=$PATH:/usr/local/bin
```

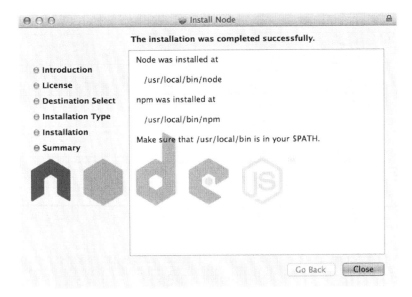

Figure B.4   Installation message about $PATH

Figure B.5   Displaying the $PATH environment variable

INSTALLING NODE.JS ON LINUX

The Node.js website has a .tar.gz file with compiled binaries for Linux. If you have the .tar.gz file, you can install Node.js with the following commands:

```
> tar xzf node-v0.10.29-linux-x64.tar.gz
> ./configure
> make
> sudo make install
```

> **NOTE**   The .tar.gz filename may differ slightly depending on which version of Node.js you downloaded.

An easier way to install Node.js on Linux is to use the package manager. Most Linux distributions have a package manager for installing tools. This can make it a little easier to install Node.js, but the downside is that the version of Node.js is sometimes a little behind the latest version. But the samples in this book should work, even for slightly older versions of Node.js.

Type the following commands into a command prompt to install Node.js from the command line (if you are not using a Debian-based distro the commands may be a little bit different):

```
> sudo apt-get update
> sudo apt-get install nodejs npm
```

After typing these commands and following the prompts, Node.js will be installed.

VERIFYING THE INSTALLATION

You can verify that Node.js and NPM are installed correctly by typing the following two commands:

```
> node --version
> npm --version
```

You should see a version number for each tool. The samples in this book were run using Node.js version 0.10.29 and NPM version 1.4.14.

> **NOTE** Some Linux versions have a program called node. If you type node --version and nothing happens, you're probably running into this conflict. In this case, Node.js should be mapped to nodejs. Try typing nodejs --version instead.

If there is an issue with your install, visit the support at the Node.js homepage at http://nodejs.org. You can also learn more about installing Node.js on various platforms at https://github.com/joyent/node/wiki/Installing-Node.js-via-package-manager.

B.1.2 Express

The sample server is implemented using a web application framework called Express. Express simplifies the process of building web servers on Node.js by providing middleware that handles common web server operations. *Middleware* is a term used to describe functions inserted into the web server–processing pipeline that can act on the HTTP request or HTTP response. These functions are termed middleware because they sit in the middle of the incoming request and the actual code that processes the request. For example, Express has middleware pieces to handle common web server functionality such as authentication, compression, and cookie sessions. Figure B.6 shows how a request passes through pieces of middleware in Express.

You certainly don't have to use Express (or any web application framework for that matter), but it makes things easier by taking care of the grunt work of setting up a web server. This allows you to focus on the details of adding CORS support to the server. You can learn more about Express at http://expressjs.com.

You can use NPM (which was installed previously) to install Express. The installation instructions are the same for all OSes. To install Express, open up a terminal window in the location you wish to install to and type npm install express. That should be all you have to do! You can verify that Node.js and Express are installed

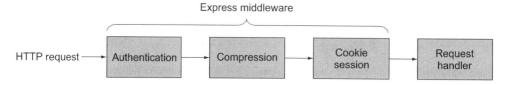

Figure B.6 An Express server with three middleware components

Figure B.7 Working installation of Node.js and Express

properly by opening up a terminal window and typing `node`, followed by pressing the Return key. This brings you into the Node.js development environment, where you can type in JavaScript code and have it immediately interpreted by Node.js. For example, type `var e = require('express');` and press the Return key. If Node.js and Express are installed properly, you shouldn't see any errors (though you may see the word `undefined`; that's okay). Figure B.7 shows what the result of these two commands looks like.

The samples in this book were built using Express version 4.6.1, but any version greater than 4 should work. Note that Express 4 introduced breaking changes, so if you're using Express 3 or earlier, the sample code won't work. Now that you've installed all the tools, you can return to chapter 3 and continue with the sample code.

B.2 Debugging tools

Chapter 7 introduced tools to help debug CORS requests. This section covers how to install these tools.

B.2.1 Wireshark

Wireshark (www.wireshark.org) is a packet analyzer that can help view CORS request and response headers. You can download the tool from www.wireshark.org/download.html. When you visit the Wireshark download page, the correct installer for your system will be highlighted. Download and run the installer to begin the process.

INSTALLING WIRESHARK ON WINDOWS

As mentioned in chapter 7, Wireshark has issues with debugging the sample on Windows because Windows has trouble capturing traffic over localhost (learn more about this issue at http://wiki.wireshark.org/CaptureSetup/Loopback). Windows users should use Fiddler to debug the sample app. Installing Fiddler is covered in the next section.

But Wireshark can still be installed on Windows to debug traffic to servers outside your local computer. To install Wireshark, just run the Wireshark installer and follow the instructions. During the installation process, you'll be asked to install WinPcap (if you don't have WinPcap installed already). WinPcap offers an API for capturing network traffic for Windows. After the WinPcap installer runs and finishes, you'll be taken back to the Wireshark installation process. Learn more about WinPcap at www.winpcap.org/.

INSTALLING WIRESHARK ON MAC OS X

Installing Wireshark on OS X requires that you first install XQuartz, a version of X server, which is a windowing system common in Unix systems. Think of X server (commonly called X11) as the thing that displays the Wireshark UI.

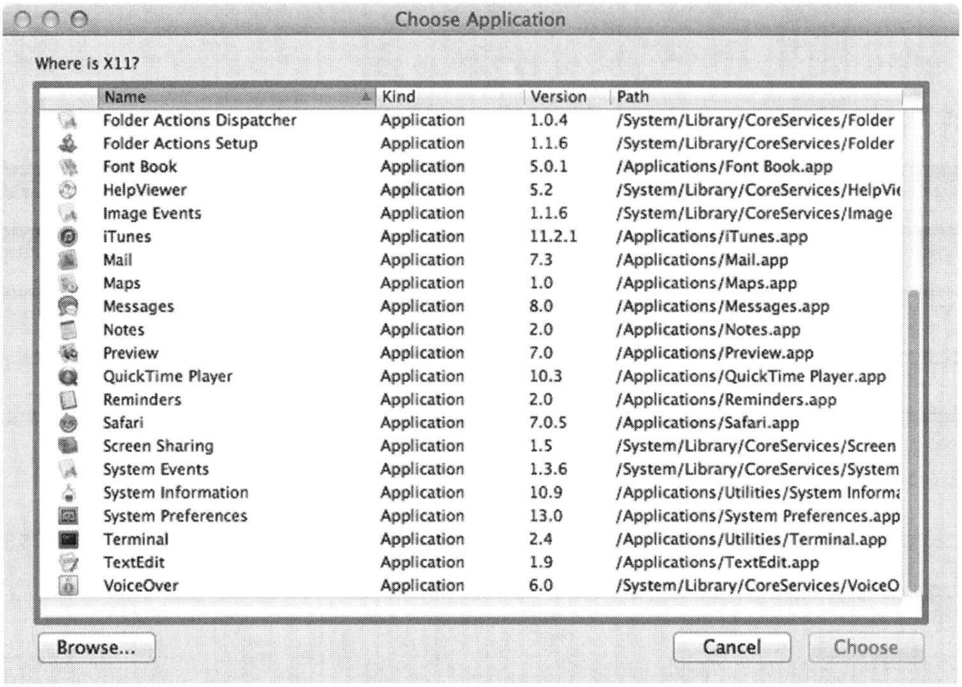

Figure B.8   Wireshark asks where XQuartz is installed the first time it runs.

The XQuartz installer can be downloaded from http://xquartz.macosforge.org/. Download and run the installer. After XQuartz is installed, it's a good idea to reboot your system. (I was unable to get Wireshark to work without a reboot.)

Once XQuartz is installed, you can download and run the Wireshark installer. When you first run Wireshark, you may be greeted with the dialog box shown in figure B.8.

This dialog is asking for the location of XQuartz. You can find XQuartz by selecting Browse..., navigating to the Application > Utilities > XQuartz app, and then clicking Choose. Wireshark should ask you this only the first time it runs; after that, Wireshark should start right up. Note that the first time Wireshark runs, it may take a long time to appear while it refreshes its fonts.

INSTALLING WIRESHARK ON LINUX

Wireshark can be installed on Debian-based Linux simply by running

```
> sudo apt-get install wireshark
```

Once this finishes running, Wireshark will be installed. To be able to run Wireshark without it requiring root permissions, you need to run the following commands:

```
> sudo dpkg-reconfigure wireshark-common
> sudo adduser $USER wireshark
```

These commands will give your user account the proper permissions for running Wireshark. Once that is done, you'll need to restart your system. After the restart, you can run Wireshark simply by typing `wireshark`.

B.2.2 *Fiddler*

Fiddler is a Windows-only app with a ton of networking-related features, including capturing network traffic. Fiddler can be downloaded from www.telerik.com/fiddler. The download page allows you to choose between Fiddler4 and Fiddler2. If you know you have .NET 4 installed or have Windows 8+, choose Fiddler4, otherwise choose Fiddler2.

Installing Fiddler is as simple as running the installer and following the instructions.

> **NOTE** There is also a relatively new port of Fiddler for Mac OS X and Linux. You can find it at http://fiddler.wikidot.com/mono.

B.2.3 *Curl*

The curl website is at http://curl.haxx.se/. To help you download the correct version of curl for your OS, there is also a handy download wizard at http://curl.haxx.se/dlwiz/?type=bin.

INSTALLING CURL ON WINDOWS

Some versions of PowerShell already have a tool called "curl". But this tool is not the curl you're looking for. You can check which curl you have by running `curl --version`. If you receive an error like that shown in figure B.9, you don't have the correct curl tool.

You can use the curl download wizard to download the curl installer for Windows. I recommend using an MSI file, which can be downloaded at www.confusedbycode.com/curl/#downloads. Run the installer to install curl. The installer installs curl to the C:\Program Files\cURL\bin directory.

You can verify that curl is installed properly simply by typing `curl --version`. If curl still doesn't work, it could be that Windows doesn't know where to find the tool.

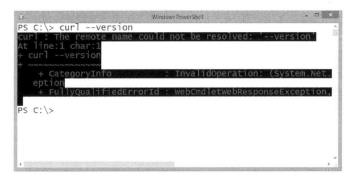

Figure B.9 PowerShell's curl tool

This can be fixed by adding the curl directory to your $PATH variable. You can do that with the following steps:

1 Right-click your computer and choose Properties to enter the System Properties dialog. (If you don't see a window with tabs, click Advanced System Settings.)
2 Choose the Advanced tab.
3 Choose the Environment Variables button.
4 In the User Variables window, select the PATH variable and click the Edit button. If there's no such variable, add it using the New… button.
5 Add the value "C:\Program Files\cURL\bin" (including the quotes) to the path. If there is already a value in this box, you can add a new one by adding a semicolon followed by the path.

After doing this, curl should work from the command line (although you may have to reopen your command prompt for the changes to take effect).

INSTALLING CURL ON MAC OS X
Curl comes preinstalled on OS X, so you shouldn't need to install it. If curl isn't available on your system, you can download and install it from the curl download wizard.

INSTALLING CURL ON LINUX
Curl may be preinstalled on some Linux systems; you can check by typing curl --version. If curl is not installed, you can install it by typing sudo apt-get install curl.

B.3   Resources

This appendix introduces a lot of tools. If you'd like to learn more about any of these tools, here are pointers to their websites:

- Node.js/NPM, http://nodejs.org
- Express, http://expressjs.com
- Wireshark, http://wireshark.org
- Fiddler, www.telerik.com/fiddler
- Curl, http://curl.haxx.se/

In addition, here are a couple books that dive into more details about Node.js and Express:

- *Node.js in Action* (Cantelon et al., Manning, 2013)
- *Express.js in Action* by Evan Hahn, to be published by Manning (http://manning.com/hahn/).

appendix C
What is CSRF?

Chapter 6 introduced the concept of cross-site request forgery (CSRF). This appendix takes a closer look at CSRF.

C.1 What is CSRF?

Let's step out of the CORS mindset for a bit and talk about regular, old same-origin requests. Cookies are always included on same-origin requests, regardless of how that request was initiated. If you're logged in to www.twitter.com, any time your browser navigates to a www.twitter.com site, the cookies will be included in the request. It doesn't matter where the request originates: you can visit www.twitter.com directly or click a link to go to www.twitter.com. Even if a page merely links to an image hosted on www.twitter.com, the request for that image will include your cookies. You have no control over this behavior. If your browser has cookies associated with a site, they're always included on the request.

Suppose a hacker creates a page that adds a new tweet to Twitter. Whenever someone visits this site, it sends a request to Twitter to create a tweet that says, "I have hacked your site!" (see figure C.1). If the hacker can somehow trick you into visiting his page, the tweet will be added to your own Twitter feed!

This is at the heart of CSRF: an unauthorized site makes a request on your behalf using your cookies.

> **NOTE** We often think of hacking in terms of a hacker gaining access to your data. But in the case of CSRF, the hacker can do damage without ever reading your data. Actions with side effects such as adding a tweet or changing a password can have devastating consequences, without ever compromising your data.

Of course, Twitter has taken steps to guard against this issue. Figure C.2 shows an actual request to Twitter to create a new tweet.

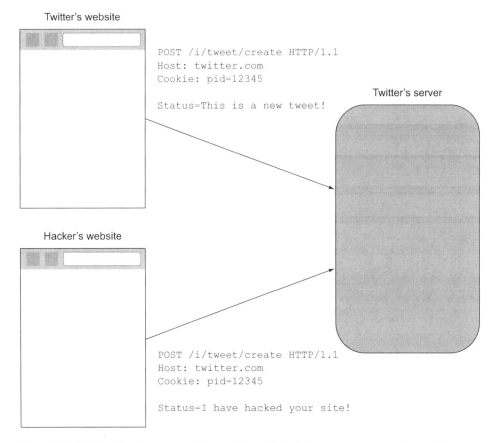

Twitter's website

```
POST /i/tweet/create HTTP/1.1
Host: twitter.com
Cookie: pid=12345

Status=This is a new tweet!
```

Twitter's server

Hacker's website

```
POST /i/tweet/create HTTP/1.1
Host: twitter.com
Cookie: pid=12345

Status=I have hacked your site!
```

Figure C.1   CSRF exists because cookies are always included on requests, regardless of where the request comes from Luckily Twitter protects itself from CSRF with an authenticity_token..

Along with things like the text of the tweet, the request includes an `authenticity_token`. This token is an encrypted string that Twitter uses to verify that the request is coming from Twitter's own servers, and not from someone else. If Twitter receives a request without this `authenticity_token` (or with an invalid token), the request will fail.

Twitter's `authenticity_token` is an example of a CSRF token. A CSRF token is a server-generated, cryptographically secure token that's included on requests to verify that the request comes from a trusted server. It's similar to the origin header in that it helps validate where the request originates from, but because the CSRF token is cryptographically secure, it can't be generated by anyone but Twitter. This ensures that a request to create a new tweet comes only from Twitter's own web page.

Figure C.3 shows the lifecycle of Twitter's `authenticity_token`. When you first make a request to Twitter, its server generates a unique `authenticity_token` and includes it as a hidden form field in the HTML response. Next, when you compose a new tweet and click the Tweet button, the text of the new tweet and the authen-

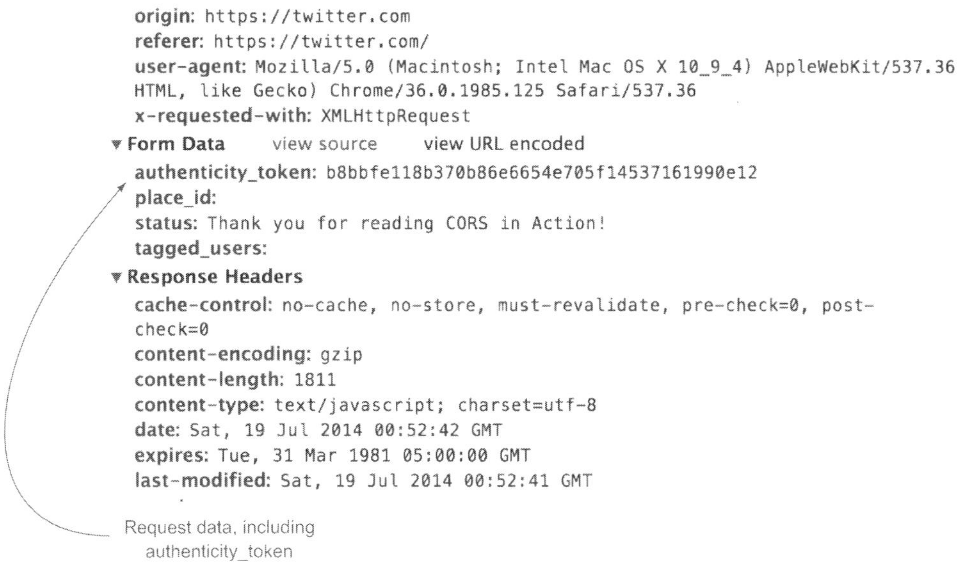

origin: https://twitter.com
referer: https://twitter.com/
user-agent: Mozilla/5.0 (Macintosh; Intel Mac OS X 10_9_4) AppleWebKit/537.36
HTML, like Gecko) Chrome/36.0.1985.125 Safari/537.36
x-requested-with: XMLHttpRequest
▼ Form Data view source view URL encoded
authenticity_token: b8bbfe118b370b86e6654e705f14537161990e12
place_id:
status: Thank you for reading CORS in Action!
tagged_users:
▼ Response Headers
cache-control: no-cache, no-store, must-revalidate, pre-check=0, post-check=0
content-encoding: gzip
content-length: 1811
content-type: text/javascript; charset=utf-8
date: Sat, 19 Jul 2014 00:52:42 GMT
expires: Tue, 31 Mar 1981 05:00:00 GMT
last-modified: Sat, 19 Jul 2014 00:52:41 GMT
Request data, including authenticity_token

Figure C.2 Sending a new tweet request to Twitter. The `authenticity_token` guards against CSRF.

ticity_token are sent to Twitter's servers. Finally, Twitter's servers compare the authenticity_token against the expected value. If they match, the new tweet is created; otherwise, the request is rejected.

CSRF protection works because it introduces an "active" form of protection (the CSRF token) to a "passive" form of protection (the cookie). By passive, I mean that

Twitter's server
Twitter's servers set authenticity_token value in HTML as a hidden form field.
<html><body>
<form>
<input type="hidden" name="authenticity_token" value="abcde" />
<input type="text" name="status" />
</form>
</body></html>
POST /i/tweet/create HTTP/1.1
Host: twitter.com
Origin: http://twitter.com
status=new tweet!&
authenticity_token=abcde
authenticity_token is included in POST request to create a new tweet.

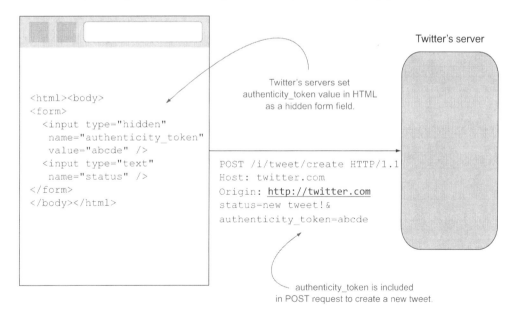

Figure C.3 How Twitter uses the `authenticity_token` field to guard against CSRF

the browser will always include the cookie on requests, without looking at where the request comes from. The CSRF token fills this hole by serving as a marker that indicates where the request is coming from. It's active because the client making the request must manually add the token to the request. There is no way for the browser to automatically add the CSRF token to the request, or to even know what the value of the CSRF token is.

What is in a CSRF token?

We've talked about validating the CSRF token in abstract terms, but what exactly is inside the CSRF token that needs to be validated? Different servers implement CSRF tokens differently. The CSRF token in Express (from the CSURF package from https://github.com/expressjs/csurf) looks like this:

CSRF token = salt + crypto(salt + secret)

Here is what each of those pieces means:

- *Secret*—The secret is a per-server secret value. This can be set by the user in the session (which is important for coordinating secrets across servers, as you'll see later on), otherwise it will be randomly generated.
- *Salt*—The salt is another random value. But unlike the secret, the user cannot choose its value. The salt also has a fixed number of characters; at the time of this writing, Express's salt has 10 characters (the number of characters in the salt comes into play when validating the token).
- *Crypto*—The crypto function hashes the salt plus the secret using SHA1, and then base64 encodes the result. Hashing is a one-way operation that can't be reversed or decrypted.

Finally, the unencrypted salt value is prepended to the encrypted token value, and the sum is the CSRF token.

Let's look at an example of how to calculate the CSRF token. Suppose the server's secret is `SECRET`, and the salt is `0123456789`. The first step is to hash the value `0123456789SECRET` (the secret plus the salt). Suppose the result of this hash is `ABCDEF` (the hash value will look completely different from the secret and the salt). Finally, the salt is added to the hashed value, which is `0123456789ABCEDF`. This is the CSRF token.

When validating the token, the server doesn't decrypt the token and look at each part. (In fact, it can't decrypt the token, because hashing the token is a one-way operation that can't be reversed.) Instead, it looks at the incoming request CSRF token and grabs the first 10 characters. This is the salt value for this token. It then combines the salt value with the server secret to generate another token (using the same equation just noted). If the newly generated token matches the request CSRF token, the request is valid.

Turning again to the example, when the server receives the CSRF token `0123456789ABCEDF`, it first strips off the first 10 characters to get the salt, which is `0123456789`. Next, it runs the salt through the same equation. If this new value matches the CSRF token from the request, the request is valid.

Based on this explanation, the CSRF token may sound very similar to the Origin header. After all, they both describe where a request originates. However, there are some key differences, as summarized in table C.1. These differences make it a good idea to use a CSRF token even if an Origin header is available. CSRF protection is especially important for simple requests, where there is no preflight to protect the server from invalid requests.

Table C.1 Differences between the Origin header and CSRF token

Origin header	CSRF token
Set by the browser	Set by the server
Value is in plain text	Value is encrypted
Can be guessed (and spoofed using tools like curl)	Cannot be guessed or spoofed
Only present on cross-origin requests (although some browsers, such as Chrome and Safari, include Origin headers on some same-origin requests)	Present on cross-origin and same-origin requests

The next section looks at how to implement CSRF protection for same-origin requests. The techniques here don't apply to CORS, but they're useful for getting an understanding of how CSRF protection works.

C.2 *Implementing CSRF protection for same-origin requests*

It may be easier to understand CSRF tokens by looking at a new example that isolates the core concepts of CSRF. Listing C.1 shows a simple web server that implements a CSRF token. Note that this is new server code, so you should put this in a new app.js file (but running it is the same as before—just run `node app.js`). The Express framework has middleware support for CSRF tokens. You can install this middleware (and its dependencies) by running the following command:

```
npm install express body-parser cookie-parser express-session csurf
```

Listing C.1 Example of implementing CSRF protection

```
var express = require('express');
var bodyParser = require('body-parser');
var cookieParser = require('cookie-parser');
var session = require('express-session');
var csrf = require('csurf');

var app = express();
app.use(bodyParser.urlencoded({
  extended: true
}));
app.use(cookieParser());
app.use(session({
  secret: 'CORSInAction',
  saveUninitialized: true,
  resave: true}));
app.use(csrf());
```

Creates new server and adds middleware components

Adds functions to process CSRF token

```
app.get('/csrftest', function(req, res) {
    var form = '<html><body><form action="/csrftest" method="post">\r\n';
    form += '<input type="text" name="_csrf" \r\n';
    form += '\tvalue="' + req.csrfToken() + '" />\r\n';
    form += '<input type="submit" value="Submit" />\r\n';
    form += '</form></body></html>';
    res.send(form);
});
app.post('/csrftest', function(req, res) {
    res.send('Successfully received CSRF token!');
});

app.use(function(err, req, res, next) {
    res.status(403).send('ERROR parsing CSRF token!');
});

app.listen(2468);
```

Adds function to handle an invalid CSRF token

Once the code is set up and running, you can visit the page at http://localhost:2468/csrftest. This page displays an input box containing the CSRF token itself, along with a Submit button, as shown in figure C.4.

The HTML source of this page is shown in figure C.5. The page is a simple web form with a text box and submit box. The text box is named _csrf, and contains the value of the CSRF token.

Clicking the Submit button will send a POST request to the server with the CSRF token in the POST

Figure C.4   CSRF token test page

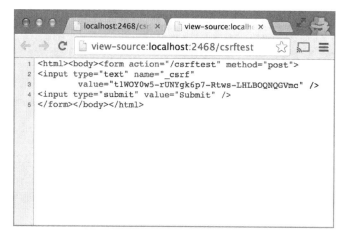

Figure C.5   HTML source for the CSRF sample

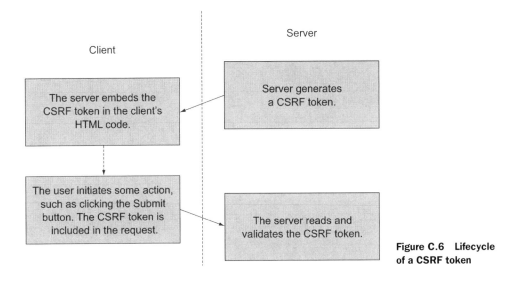

Figure C.6 Lifecycle of a CSRF token

body. In this sample, the CSRF token is included as part of the POST body, but it can be included anywhere in the request, including in the request URL or as a request header. The server reads the value of the CRSF token from the _csrf field, and checks that it's a valid value. If the token is valid, the server responds with a successful message.

Figure C.6 shows the lifecycle of the CSRF token. First, the server generates the CSRF token which is embedded somewhere in the client's HTML. When the user performs an action, such as clicking the Submit button, the request includes the CSRF token. Finally, the server reads the CSRF token and checks whether or not it's valid.

The sample also lets you change the value of the CSRF token by typing in the text box. If you navigate back to the form, edit the CSRF token to something new, and click

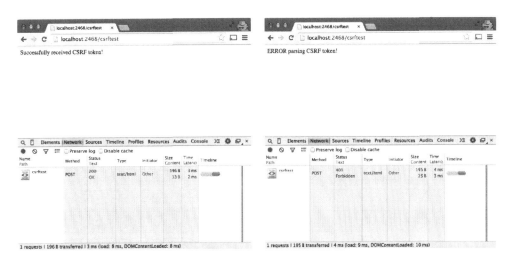

Figure C.7 Sample app with valid (left) and invalid (right) CSRF tokens

the Submit button again, you should see an error message with an HTTP status 403. Figure C.7 shows both the success and error messages.

As you can see from this example, the Express middleware takes care of the details of implementing the CSRF token.

appendix D
Other cross-origin techniques

This appendix covers alternatives to CORS. Before CORS, the techniques described here could be used to make cross-origin requests. While CORS is the standard for modern web applications, these alternative techniques are useful for making cross-origin requests from older browsers.

Each technique follows a similar pattern, as illustrated in figure D.1. The client wants to make a request to a server that lives at a different origin. In between there is a proxy mechanism that processes the request from the client and sends it to the server.

Figure D.1 will reappear in each section that follows to help highlight how each technique operates.

D.1   JSONP

JSONP, which stands for JSON with padding, uses the browser's own script tag to send cross-origin requests, as shown in figure D.2.

Client initiates request to a server on a different origin

Proxy receives request from client and forwards it to server

Server receives request and sends response back to proxy, which sends it to client

Figure D.1   All cross-origin techniques follow a similar pattern.

Figure D.2   JSONP uses a `<script>` tag to send cross-origin requests.

The following listing shows how to use JSONP to recreate the Flickr example from chapter 1.

Listing D.1   Using JSONP to access Flickr

```
<!DOCTYPE html>
<html>
<body>
<div id="photos"></div>
<script>
function loadPhotos(data) {
  if (data.stat == 'ok') {
    var photos = data.photos.photo;
    for (var i = 0; i < photos.length; i++) {
      var img = document.createElement('img');
      img.src = photos[i].url_q;
      document.getElementById('photos').appendChild(img);
    }
  } else {
    alert(data.message);
  }
};
</script>
<script src="https://api.flickr.com/services/rest/
    ?method=flickr.people.getPublicPhotos&user_id=32951986%40N05&extras=url_
    q&format=json&jsoncallback=loadPhotos&api_key=<YOUR API KEY HERE>"></
    script>
</body>
</html>
```

Callback function that handles response.

Request is made via a `<script>` tag.

In this listing, the `XMLHttpRequest` is replaced with a `<script>` tag that initiates a request to the Flickr API server. The `<script>` tag can be created either by embedding a `<script>` tag in the HTML, or by dynamically creating it with JavaScript (by using `document.createElement('script')`). A `<script>` tag traditionally points to a file that contains JavaScript code. But in this case, the Flickr API server responds with code that wraps the API response in a JavaScript function. When the browser receives the response, it executes the JavaScript code, which in turn executes the callback function. Figure D.3 shows what a typical JSONP flow looks like.

The key to a successful JSONP request is the callback function. When initiating a JSONP request, the `<script>` tag has a parameter set to the name of the callback function. In figure D.3, the callback function is named `loadPhotos`. When sending a response back to the client, the server first pads the response with the name of the

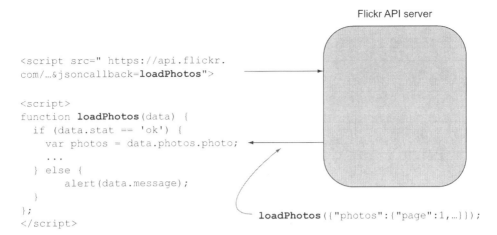

Figure D.3 Making a cross-origin request using JSONP

callback function (this is where the word padding in JSON with padding comes from). For example, if the API response looks like this:

```
{ "photos": { "page": 1, "photo": [...] } }
```

JSONP would wrap the response in a callback, like this:

```
loadPhotos({ "photos": { "page": 1, "photo": [...] } });
```

Finally, when the browser receives the server's response, it actually calls the callback function with the data provided by the server. In this example, the loadPhotos function defined by the client gets called with the API response data.

JSONP is one of the oldest cross-origin techniques out there, and it enjoys wide browser support. But because it uses a <script> tag, JSONP can only support GET requests. There is no way to make a POST, PUT, or DELETE request using JSONP. If the browser has any cookies from the server, those cookies will be included on the request. This can open up the API to cross-site forgery requests.

JSONP is ideal for sharing publicly available data. The preceding Flickr example is a perfect use case for JSONP: the images are publicly available, and the sample is only displaying the images on the page. Due to the cross-site forgery concerns, JSONP shouldn't be used to make updates to data, or to share sensitive user data. Finally, because the server is essentially executing arbitrary JavaScript in the user's browser, it's important that the client fully trust the response from the server.

D.2 *Flash*

Adobe's Flash is a software platform that brings rich, interactive applications to the browser. Flash applications are written in a language called ActionScript, which can make cross-origin requests to a remote server, as shown in figure D.4.

Similar to CORS, Flash requires the server to grant permission to clients making cross-origin requests. Except instead of HTTP headers, Flash uses an XML file that lives

Figure D.4   Flash applications have native support for cross-origin requests.

on the server. This XML file is named crossdomain.xml, and it specifies rules such as which origins are allowed to make cross-origin requests, and which headers are allowed. The following code shows an example of the crossdomain.xml file from the Flickr API server.

```
<cross-domain-policy>
<allow-access-from domain="*" secure="false"/>
<allow-http-request-headers-from domain="*" headers="Authorization"/>
<site-control permitted-cross-domain-policies="master-only"/>
</cross-domain-policy>
```

The file in the preceding code indicates that any origin can make cross-origin requests (domain="*"), regardless of whether or not the origin supports SSL (secure="false"). The Authorization request header is allowed (headers="Authorization") from all origins (domain="*"). A full specification of crossdomain.xml is available at www.adobe.com/devnet/articles/crossdomain_policy_file_spec.html.

Figure D.5 shows the flow of a cross-origin request from Flash. Before issuing a cross-origin request, Flash first reads the crossdomain.xml file ❶. If the policy maps to the client issuing the request, Flash sends the request to the server ❷.

Flash works best in cases where you need rich HTTP support, but you also need deep browser support. Like JSONP, Flash has been around for a long time, and it enjoys wide support across desktop browsers. It's more powerful than JSONP because

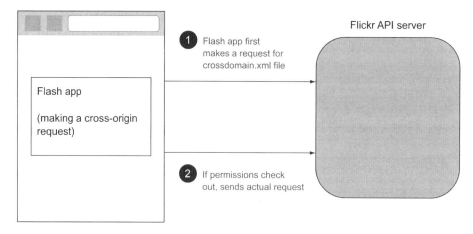

Figure D.5   Making a cross-origin request using Flash

Figure D.6 `postMessage` **allows two** `<iframe>` **tags from different origins to communicate.**

it allows different HTTP methods. And like CORS, Flash puts the servers in charge of how cross-origin requests behave by using the crossdomain.xml file.

Using Flash requires that developers learn and use ActionScript. And while Flash enjoys strong desktop support, it has limited support on mobile devices (while some Android phones support Flash, all iPhones and iPads do not).

D.3 *postMessage and easyXDM*

HTML5's Web Messaging API defines the `postMessage` method, which allows documents from different origins to communicate with each other, as shown in figure D.6. Using `postMessage`, a page can send an HTTP request to an `<iframe>` HTML tag embedded on the page, and the `<iframe>` tag can make an `XMLHttpRequest` to its own server.

Because the `<iframe>` code and the server are from the same origin, the `XMLHttpRequest` is a same-origin request. Figure D.7 shows the request flow when using `postMessage`.

The `postMessage` spec was implemented before the CORS spec, so for a brief time period there were browsers that supported `postMessage` but didn't support CORS. Internet Explorer 8, Internet Explorer 9, Firefox 3.0, and Opera versions less than 12

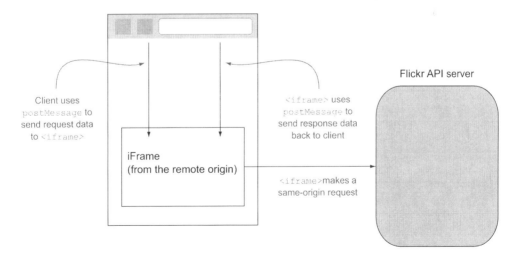

Figure D.7 Making a cross-origin request using `postMessage`

don't fully support CORS but do support <iframe>-to-<iframe> communication via postMessage. As you saw in chapter 2, Internet Explorer 8 and Internet Explorer 9 have limited support for CORS, so if those browsers are important to you, the post-Message technique may be a good alternative.

An alternative option is the easyXDM library, which can be found at http://easyxdm.net/. The easyXDM library provides a consistent interface for making cross-origin requests across all browsers. The library uses the postMessage technique for browsers that support postMessage, and falls back on other techniques (such as Flash) for browsers that don't support postMessage. The easyXDM library handles the complex details of making a cross-origin request so you don't have to.

D.4   *Server-side request*

Unlike JavaScript code running in a browser, code running on a server isn't constrained by the same-origin policy. If none of the other techniques work for your cross-origin needs, you can always write server-side code to make a cross-origin request, as shown in figure D.8.

Server code can make a request to any web page, regardless of whether that web page has CORS headers or not. Figure D.9 shows what a request flow looks like when using a server to make cross-origin requests:

1 The client initiates the request by making an XMLHttpRequest to the client's own web server. This is different from CORS, where the XMLHttpRequest was made directly to the remote server ❶.
2 The client's server makes a request to the API server and receives the response ❷.
3 The client's server forwards the response back down to the client's JavaScript code. Because the request from the client's JavaScript code to the client's server all takes place on the same origin, there is no need for CORS headers on the response ❸.

Making server-side requests can enable almost any type of cross-origin request. Because this is such a powerful technique, remote servers may not look too kindly on this technique, and may even take steps to block clients from making these types of requests. If you make cross-origin requests from the server, be sure to get the remote server's permission to do so. The one thing server-side requests can't do is include cookies from the remote origin. If the remote origin saved any cookies in the user's browser, there is no way for the client JavaScript code to read those cookies and include them on the request.

Figure D.8   Server-side code isn't constrained by the browser's same-origin policy.

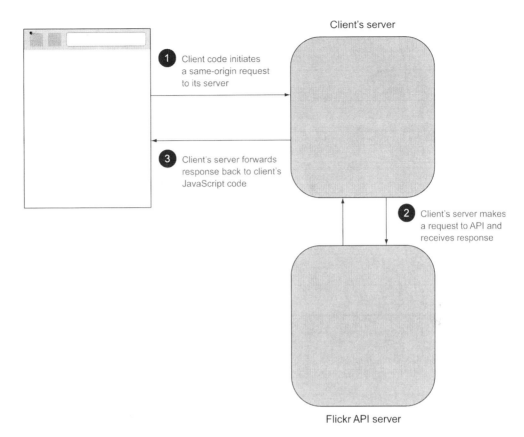

Figure D.9 Making a cross-origin request using a server-side proxy

index

A

abort method 20
Accept header 180
Accept-Charset header 18
Accept-Encoding header 18
Accept-Language header 180
Access-Control-Allow-Credentials header 100,
    102–104, 179
Access-Control-Allow-Headers header 78–82, 179
Access-Control-Allow-Methods header 76–78,
    179
Access-Control-Allow-Origin header 7, 180
  allowing access for everyone 115
  cookies and 106
  firewalls and 115–116
  null origin 123–124
  Origin header and 124–126
  with origin value 59
  overview 55
  proxy servers and 121–123
  specifying origins allowed access
    overview 116–117
    using regular expression 119–121
    using whitelist 117–119
  valid values for 114–115
  with wildcard (*) value 56
Access-Control-Expose-Headers header 108, 110,
    142, 180–181
Access-Control-Max-Age header 92–93, 139, 180
Access-Control-Request-Headers header 18, 179
Access-Control-Request-Method header 18, 74,
    179
ActionScript 201
Adobe Flash 201

Ajax (asynchronous JavaScript and XML) 137
ajax method 34
alternatives to CORS
  easyXDM library 204
  Flash 201–203
  JSONP 199–201
  overview 199–204
  postMessage method 203–204
  server-side request 204
Android 175
application/json Content-Type 141
application/x-www-form-urlencoded Content-
    Type 71
asynchronous JavaScript and XML. *See* Ajax
asynchronous requests 21, 31
ATM analogy 47, 64
audience, obtaining wider 9
authenticity_token 192
authorization
  cookies and 95
  OAuth2 132–134
Authorization header 137

B

Basic authentication 95
blacklisting origins 120
browsers
  cross-origin request support 14–15
  developer tools
    console 155
    Network tab 155–158
    overview 153–155
  monitoring network traffic 158–159
  requests and 49

C

cache
  reducing preflight requests 139–141
  response caching 90–93
Cache-Control header 181
canvas 32–34
Charles 159
Chrome 14–15
  Copy as cURL option 169
  developer tools 154
  JavaScript Console 44
  Origin header 124
  preflight cache in 93
  remote debugging for Android phones 175
clients
  cookie support 100–101
  cross-origin cookies and 104
  requests and 48
  sample code setup 42
  user vs. 48
command line 182
Connection header 18
console 154–155
Content-Language header 180–181
Content-Length header 18, 143
Content-Type header 31, 71, 137, 180–181
Cookie header 18
Cookie2 header 18
cookieParser() middleware 97
cookies
  Access-Control-Allow-Credentials header and 102–104
  Access-Control-Allow-Origin header and 106
  cross-origin cookies and client 104
  including in requests 100–101
  including on request 128–129
  preflight request and 104–106
  purpose of 95
  reading 97–98
  setting 95–97
  setting from CORS 107
  using XMLHttpRequest object 27–28
  withCredentials property and 102–104
  XDomainRequest object and 31
CORS (Cross-Origin Resource Sharing)
  advantages of
    easy for developers 10
    flexibility 10
    reduced maintenance overhead 10–11
    security 9–10
    wider audience 9
  alternatives to
    easyXDM library 204
    Flash 201–203

JSONP 199–201
    overview 199–204
    postMessage method 203–204
    server-side request 204
  defined 4–5
  example using Flickr
    overview 5–7
    processing response 7–9
    sending request 7
    setting up request 7
  planning for support of 114
  redirects and 144–148
  security and 126–128
crossOrigin attribute 33
Cross-Origin Resource Sharing. See CORS
crypto function 194
CSRF (cross-site request forgery) 106, 129
  overview 191–195
  protecting against 195–198
CSURF package 194
curl
  advantages of using 168–169
  installing 189–190
  making CORS requests 165–167
  making preflight requests 167–168
custom headers 81

D

database queries to validate origins 120
dataType property 35
Date header 18, 143
debugging
  additional help 176–177
  browser developer tools
    console 155
    Network tab 155–158
    overview 153–155
  curl 189–190
  Fiddler 189
  mobile 175
  monitoring network traffic
    in browser 158–159
    using Fiddler 161–164
    using Wireshark 159–161
  process overview 152–153
  sending requests using test-cors.org
    client data in 173–174
    to local server 171–173
    to remote server 169–170
  simulating requests using curl
    advantages of using curl 168–169
    making CORS requests 165–167
    making preflight requests 167–168

debugging *(continued)*
    Wireshark
        installing on Linux 188–189
        installing on Mac OS X 187–188
        installing on Windows 187
DELETE method 67, 74, 76
developer tools, browser
    console 155
    Network tab 155–158
    overview 153–155
DNT header 18
document.cookie property 104
DOM inspector 154
Dropbox 132

E

easyXDM library 204
enable-cors.org 176
environment
    curl 189–190
    Express framework 186–187
    Fiddler 189
    Node.js
        installing on Linux 185–186
        installing on Mac OS X 184
        installing on Windows 183–184
        overview 182–183
        verifying installation 186
    resources 190
    Wireshark
        installing on Linux 188–189
        installing on Mac OS X 187–188
        installing on Windows 187
error response 24–26
ETag header 143
ETags 137
event handlers
    using XDomainRequest object 32
    using XMLHttpRequest object 26–27
Expect header 18
Expires header 143, 181
Express framework 41, 126, 186–187, 195
Express.js in Action 190

F

Facebook 95, 132
Fiddler 161–164, 189
Firefox 14–15
    Copy as cURL option 169
    developer tools 154
    Origin header 124
    preflight cache in 93
firewalls 115–116

Flash 201–203
Flickr API example
    overview 5–7
    processing response 7–9
    sending request 7
    setting up request 7

G

GET method 31, 71, 180
getAllResponseHeaders method 24, 108, 181
getImageData method 32
getResponseHeader method 24, 108–109, 181
GitHub 132
Google 132
Google Calendar API 132
Google Chrome. *See* Chrome
Google Drive API 114

H

handleCors function 56
HEAD method 180
headers, HTTP
    CORS and 4
    request 178–179
        allowing all 137–139
        reducing preflight requests 141–142
        whitelisting 136–137
    response 178–180
        adding support for 108–111
        overview 107–108
        reading 108
    simple 180
    simple response 110, 181
    using XMLHttpRequest object 18–19
help 176–177
Host header 18
HTML5 (Hypertext Markup Language 5)
    203–204
HTML5Rocks.com website 58, 115, 145
HTTP methods
    reducing preflight requests 142
    whitelisting 136
HTTP OPTIONS method 73–74
httplib2 library 9
Hypertext Markup Language 5. *See* HTML5

I

If-Match header 137
If-Modified-Since header 137
If-None-Match header 137
iframe element 203
If-Unmodifed-Since header 137

images, canvas 32–34
<img> tags 71
installing
   curl 189–190
   Node.js
      on Linux 185–186
      on Mac OS X 184
      on Windows 183–184
      verifying installation 186
   Wireshark
      on Linux 188–189
      on Mac OS X 187–188
      on Windows 187
Internet Explorer 15
   developer tools 154
   Origin header 124
   planning for version support 114
   preflight cache and 93
   version 8/9 36
Invoke-Webrequest cmdlet 165
iOS 175

J

JavaScript Console 44
jQuery 34–36
JSON (JavaScript Object Notation) 9
JSONP (JSON with padding) 199–201

K

Keep-Alive header 18

L

Last-Modified header 143, 181
lifecycle
   of preflight requests 64
   of requests 49
Linux
   installing curl 190
   installing Node.js 185–186
   installing Wireshark 188–189
logging requests 175

M

Mac OS X
   installing curl 190
   installing Node.js 184
   installing Wireshark 187–188
middleware 186
mobile debugging 175
multipart/form-data Content-Type 71

N

Network tab, Chrome 155–158
network traffic
   in browser 158–159
   using Fiddler 161–164
   using Wireshark 159–161
Node Package Manager. *See* NPM
Node.js
   installing on Linux 185–186
   installing on Mac OS X 184
   installing on Windows 183–184
   overview 182–183
   verifying installation 186
Node.js in Action 190
node-oauth project 134
NPM (Node Package Manager) 183
null origin 123–124, 145–146

O

OAuth2 132–134
onabort event 21, 26
onerror event 8, 21, 24–26, 32
onload event 8, 20–24, 32, 43
onloadend event 21, 26
onloadstart event 21, 26
onprogress event 21, 27, 32
onreadystatechange event 21, 27
ontimeout event 21, 27, 32
Opera 15
   developer tools 154
   Origin header 124
   preflight cache in 93
OPTIONS method, HTTP 73–74
Origin header 179
   defining origin 52
   preflight requests and 72–73
   same-origin requests and 124–126
   same-origin vs. cross-origin requests 54
   setRequestHeader method and 18
   setting 55
   viewing 51
origins
   including cookies on requests 129
   specifying allowed
      overview 116–117
      using regular expression 119–121
      using whitelist 117–119

P

packet analyzers 159
POST method 31, 180
postMessage method 203–204

Powershell 165
Pragma header 181
preflight requests
    Access-Control-Request-Method header 74
    ATM analogy 64
    caching responses 90–93
    client code and 87–88
    cookies and 104–106
    HTTP OPTIONS method 73–74
    identifying at server 75
    lifecycle of 64
    Origin header 72–73
    overview 72, 85–87
    purpose of 64–67
    reducing
        overview 139
        reducing custom headers 141–142
        reducing HTTP methods 142
        using cache 139–141
    request headers
        allowing all 137–139
        whitelisting 136–137
    responding to
        Access-Control-Allow-Headers header 78–82
        Access-Control-Allow-Methods header
            76–78
        rejecting preflight request 83–85
        sending actual request 83
    simulating using curl 167–168
    stateless requests 88–89
    successful preflight and actual request
        success 87
    for upload events 89–90
    when to use 71–72
    whitelisting HTTP methods 136
Profiler 154
protocol property 126
proxy servers 121–123

R

Range header 137
readyState property 21, 27
redirects 144–148
reducing preflight requests
    overview 139
    reducing custom headers 141–142
    reducing HTTP methods 142
    using cache 139–141
Referer header 18
regular expressions 119–121
rejecting preflight request 83–85
rejecting requests 59
remote debugging tools 175
req.protocol property 125

requests
    anatomy of 47
    browser support 14–15
    canvas and 32–34
    cross-origin explained 13–14
    headers in
        allowing all 137–139
        reducing preflight requests 141–142
        reference table of 178–179
        whitelisting 136–137
    including cookies 128–129
    involvement with
        browser 49
        client 48
        server 49
    from jQuery 34–36
    lifecycle of 49
    making 45
    Origin header
        defining origin 52
        same-origin vs. cross-origin requests 54
        setting 55
        viewing 51
    responding to
        Access-Control-Allow-Origin header 55
        Access-Control-Allow-Origin header with ori-
            gin value 59
        Access-Control-Allow-Origin header with wild-
            card (*) value 56
        rejecting requests 59
    sample code setup
        API 40
        client 42
        running app 44
    sending 7
    sending using test-cors.org
        client data in 173–174
        sending requests to local server 171–173
        sending requests to remote server 169–170
    setting up 7
    simulating using curl 165–167
    spoofing 127
XDomainRequest object
    asynchronous requests only 31
    Content-Type text/plain only 31
    cookies and 31
    custom request headers and 31
    event handlers 32
    GET and POST requests only 31
    limited scheme support 31
    overview 28–30
    response from 32
XMLHttpRequest object
    error response 24–26
    event handlers 26–27

requests *(continued)*
    HTTP headers 18–19
    including cookies 27–28
    overview 15–17
    sending request 19–20
    setting up request 17–18
    successful response 20–24
response property 23
responses
    Access-Control-Allow-Origin header
        overview 55
        with origin value 59
        with wildcard (*) value 56–58
    caching 90–93
    headers in
        adding support for 108–111
        exposing to client 142–143
        overview 107–108
        reading 108
        reference table of 178–180
        simple response 181
    to preflight requests
        Access-Control-Allow-Headers header
            78–82
        Access-Control-Allow-Methods header
            76–78
        rejecting preflight request 83–85
        sending actual request 83
    processing 7–9
    rejecting requests 59–62
    using XDomainRequest object 32
    using XMLHttpRequest object
        error 24–26
        success 20–24
responseText property 23
responseXML property 23

S

Safari 14–15
    developer tools 154
    Origin header 124
    preflight cache in 93
    remote debugging for iOS devices 175
salt 194
same-origin policy 4, 9
same-origin requests
    cross-origin requests vs. 54–55
    Origin header and 124–126
sample code setup
    API 40–42
    client 42–44
    running app 44–45
<script> tags 71

Secure Sockets Layer. *See* SSL
security
    advantages of CORS 9–10
    authorizing requests using OAuth2
        132–134
    cookies included on request 128–129
    CORS and 126–128
send() method 7, 87
sending requests 19–20
servers
    configuring flexibility in 113
    cookies support 100
    CORS and 9
    logging requests 175
    requests and 49
server-side requests 204
setRequestHeader method 18
simple headers 72, 180
simple methods 72, 180
simple response headers 110, 181
simulating requests using curl
    advantages of using curl 168–169
    making CORS requests 165–167
    making preflight requests 167–168
spoofing CORS requests 127
SSL (Secure Sockets Layer) 27, 95
Stack Overflow 176
stateless requests 88–89
status property 23, 25
statusText property 23, 25
successful response 20–24
support 176–177

T

TE header 18
terminology 180–181
test-cors.org
    mobile debugging 175
    sending requests using
        client data in 173–174
        sending requests to local server
            171–173
        sending requests to remote server
            169–170
text/plain Content-Type 71
timeout property 20
toBlob method 32
toDataURL method 32
token, CSRF 192, 194
Tomcat 176
Trailer header 18
Transfer-Encoding header 18
Trusted Sites 47

U

Upgrade header 18
upload events 89–90
URLs (Uniform Resource Locators) 52
user credentials 94–95
user vs. client 48
User-Agent header 18

V

Via header 18
VPN (virtual private network) 115

W

whitelisting
    HTTP methods 136
    request headers 136–137
    specifying allowed origins 117–119
wildcard (*) value 56–58
Windows
    installing curl 189–190
    installing Node.js 183–184
    installing Wireshark 187
Windows Powershell 165
WinPcap 187
Wireshark 159–161
    installing on Linux 188–189
    installing on Mac OS X 187–188
    installing on Windows 187
withCredentials property 7, 18, 27, 100,
    102–104

X

XDomainRequest object
    asynchronous requests only 31
    Content-Type text/plain only 31
    cookies and 31
    custom request headers and 31
    event handlers 32
    GET and POST requests only 31
    limited scheme support 31
    overview 28–30
    response from 32
    XMLHttpRequest object vs. 30–31
XMLHttpRequest object 7, 10
    client involvement 48
    error response 24–26
    event handlers 26–27
    HTTP headers 18–19
    including cookies 27–28
    overview 15–17
    reading response headers 108
    sending request 19–20
    setting up request 17–18
    successful response 20–24
    upload events and 72
    XDomainRequest object vs. 30–32
X-Powered-By header 108, 142
XQuartz 187
X-Requested-With header 137

Y

YouTube API 114

Printed in the United States
by Baker & Taylor Publisher Services